SYDNEY

SYDNEY

✈ AT COST TRAVEL

LITTLE HILLS PRESS

ACKNOWLEDGEMENTS

Thanks to Geoff Hogan, City Rail and Cary Budd, State Transit for their help. Our thanks to our friends in Ruby Street, Mosman for permission to use their property from which to take the cover picture. Thanks also to Anthony, Matt and Marion for their help with the Wollongong section and Jeff for his help with the Central Coast section.

© Text: Little Hills Press, 1993 - Editorial Board - Director Fay Smith, assisted by Louise Burfitt, Charles Burfitt.
© Photographs - Little Hills Press, 1992

Cover by IIC Productions
Printed in Australia
ISBN 1 86315 031 5

Little Hills Press
Regent House
37-43 Alexander Street
Crows Nest NSW 2065
Australia

Moorland Publishing Company
Moor Farm Road, Airfield Estate, Ashbourne
Derbyshire DE6 1HD England

(UK only) ISBN 0 86190 474 5

DISCLAIMER

Whilst all care has been taken by the publisher and author to ensure that the information is accurate and up to date, the publisher does not take responsibility for the information published herein. The recommendations are those of the author, and as things get better or worse, places close and others open, some elements in the book may be inaccurate when you get there. Please write and tell us about it so we can update in subsequent editions.

Little Hills ™ and 🔺 are registered trademarks of Little Hills Press Pty Ltd.

Cover Picture: A view of the City of Sydney from Mosman on the North Shore.

CONTENTS

INTRODUCTION

Sydney is the capital city of the State of New South Wales, the birthplace of the Nation of Australia, and the largest city in the country.

It is located on the south-east coast of Australia, latitude 33 53' south, longitude 151 13' east, on the shores of Sydney Harbour, arguably the most beautiful harbour in the world.

Life in this cosmopolitan city is geared to outdoor activities, taking advantage of the long hours of sunshine and the moderate climate.

HISTORY

Although many Europeans visited the vast continent of Australia during the 17th and 18th centuries, the honour of discovery goes to Captain James Cook, who sailed into Botany Bay on April 29, 1770. He landed and raised the flag at a spot now known as Kurnell, taking possession of the whole eastern coast in the name of King George III, and calling it New South Wales.

The powers that be in England did nothing about their new possession until 1786, when they were trying to decide where to relocate the growing number of convicts they could no longer send to independent America. The botanist from the Cook expedition, Joseph Banks, had been suggesting for years that they be sent to New South Wales, and finally Captain Arthur Phillip, RN, was ordered to establish a penal colony at Botany Bay.

The First Fleet set sail on May 13, 1787, and comprised HMS *Sirius*, the armed tender *Supply*, three storeships and six transports, with food, clothing and other supplies for two years. The ships also carried 1044 people, comprising 568 male and 191 female convicts with 13 children, 206 marines with 27 wives and 19 children, and 20 officials. The fleet anchored in Botany Bay, but could not find a source of fresh water, so they continued their journey and sailed into Port Jackson (Sydney Harbour) on January 26, 1788. Fresh water was discovered, and work on the new settlement began the next day, when the convicts from the *Scarborough* began clearing trees.

The local Aborigines called the area Warrane, but this name didn't suit the British, who had thought of calling the new settlement Albion. Phillip, however, had other ideas, and named the inlet in honour of his patron, Baron Sydney of Chiselhurst. The original name was actually Sydney Cove, but general usage tended to drop the word 'Cove' and everyone simply called it 'Sydney'. Sydney Cove still exists as a location on maps and charts, although its outline has changed drastically from the original, and Sydneysiders now refer to it as 'The Quay'.

The freshwater stream, called 'Tank Stream', is still in existence, but it now flows beneath a modern city. Bridge Street, which runs roughly parallel to Alfred Street (Circular Quay), gets its name because it was the track that crossed Tank Stream.

The infant colony was not without its problems. The soil, except for a small area in what is now the Botanical Gardens, was found to be of inferior quality. The majority of convicts were city people, with no experience of farming. And the government in Britain was very good at giving orders as to what was to be done, but not very good at understanding the colony's problems, or in giving assistance. They simply kept sending more convicts, thereby putting more strain on supplies.

Nevertheless the settlement survived and grew. Intrepid explorers discovered vast areas of fertile land and small satellite settlements were formed, the first at Parramatta, 24km west of Sydney.

CLIMATE

Sydney has a temperate climate, and the average temperatures are: January max 26C (79F) - min 19C (66F); July max 17C (63F) - min 8C (46F). The Seasons are:

    Summer - December through February
    Autumn - March through May
    Winter - June through August

Spring - September through November.

The average annual rainfall is 1216mm (48 ins), with the heaviest falls in the period from February to July. Sydney does not experience snow or sleet, and quite often the temperature on a winter's day is higher than that of London or San Francisco in the middle of their summers.

POPULATION

The population of Sydney is around 3,700,000, more than half that of the entire State of New South Wales, and it would be hard to think of an ethnic group that is not represented in that number.

LANGUAGE

Australians speak English, and apart from a few differently pronounced words, the accent is the same in Sydney as in any other city in the country.

RELIGION

Because of the multinational population, all religions and sects are present in Sydney. There are parish churches in all the suburbs, but following is a list of churches in the inner city area.

Anglican
St Andrew's Cathedral, George Street (next to the Town Hall), ph 265 1661.
St James' Church, 173 King Street, ph 232 3022.
St Philip's Church Hill, 3 York Street, ph 247 1071.
Christ Church St Laurence, George Street South, ph 211 0560.
The Garrison Church, Argyle & Lower Fort Streets, The Rocks, ph 247 2664.

Baptist
Central Baptist Church, 619 George Street, ph 211 1833.

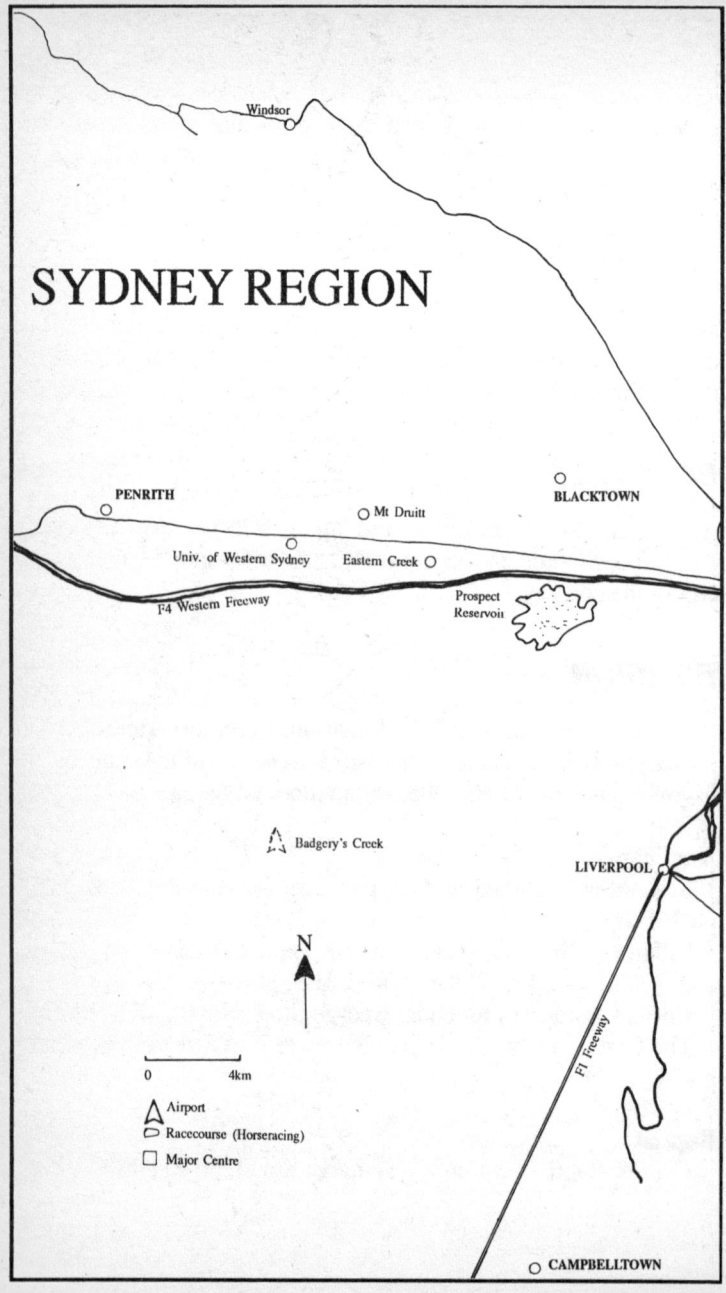

SYDNEY REGION

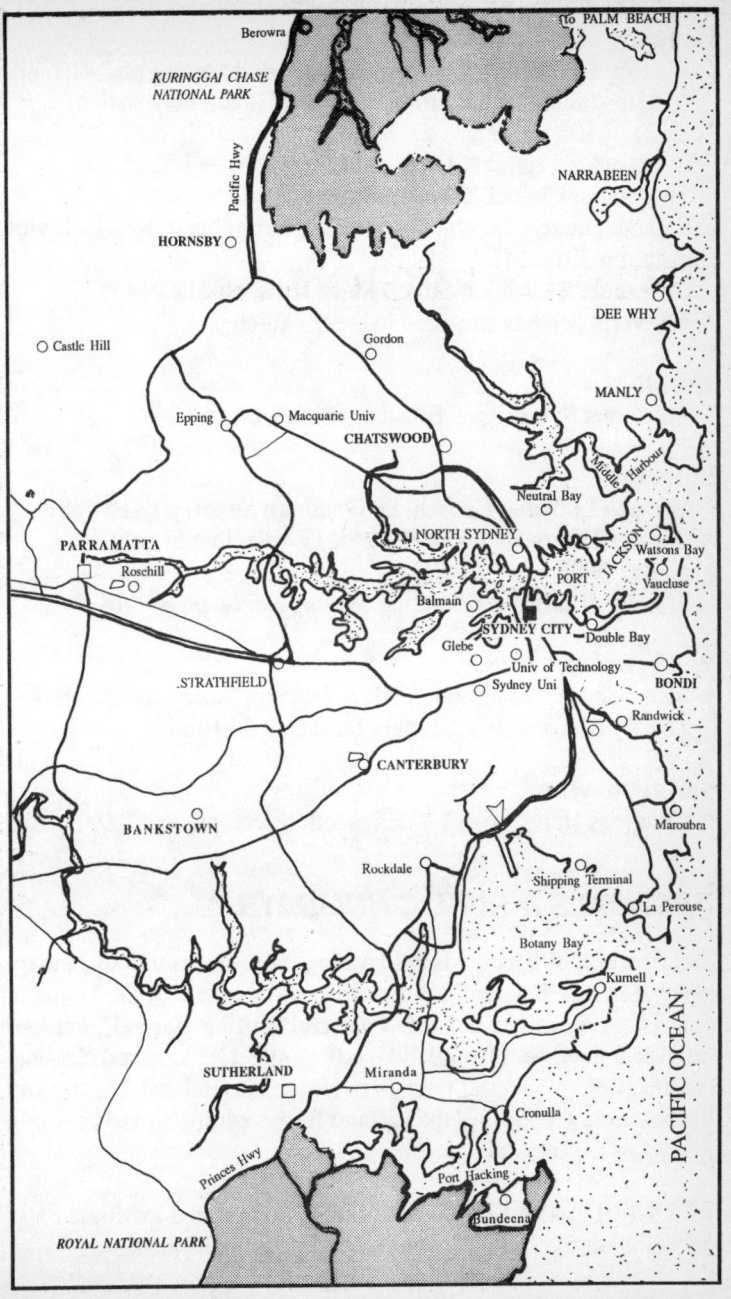

Catholic

St Mary's Cathedral*, College & Cathedral Streets, ph 232 3788.
St Peter Julian's Church*, 641 George Street, Haymarket,
ph 211 4100.
St Patrick's Church*, Grosvenor Street, ph 247 3525.
The Marist Chapel, 5 Young Street, ph 247 9292.
Sacred Heart Church, Oxford & Darlinghurst Road, Taylor
Square, ph 331 2147.
St Francis, 80 Albion Street, Surry Hills, ph 212 2145.
* Several Masses each day in these churches.

Jewish

The Great Synagogue, Elizabeth Street, ph 267 2477, 358 3726.

Lutheran

German Lutheran Church, 90 Goulburn Street, ph 416 4881.
Central Trinity Lutheran Church, 17 Valentine Street,
ph 211 5983.
St Paul's Lutheran Church, 3 Stanley Street, ph 331 1822.

Presbyterian

Scots Church, Margaret, York & Jamison Streets, ph 29 1804.
The Welsh Church, Chalmers Street, ph 569 4607.

Salvation Army

Congress Hall Corps, 140 Elizabeth Street, ph 267 7093.

FESTIVALS & PUBLIC HOLIDAYS

The **Festival of Sydney** is held during the entire month of January
each year, and has twilight and open-air concerts in the Domain,
contemporary music at Hyde Park and Darling Harbour, outdoor
movies at the Opera House, bike rallies, street theatre, and classical
theatre performances at the Opera House, the Belvoir Theatre and
the Seymour Centre. All the harbour ferries compete in a Ferrython
as part of the festival.

The Royal Easter Show is held at the Showground in Moore Park.
It begins on the Friday before Good Friday and finishes on Easter

Tuesday. Advertised as "when the country comes to town", there's something for everyone, with displays of horticulture, livestock, crafts, hi-tech machinery. For kids, there are rides and sideshows and sample bags, and for all ages there is non-stop entertainment in the show ring with livestock judging, trotting races, equestrian events, the Grand Parade, bands, sky divers, clowns, rodeos, and fireworks displays. Over the twelve days of the show, around 850,000 people go through the turnstiles, with attendances on the public holidays being between 80,000 and 100,000.

Dates for future Shows are:
    1993 - 2 April to 13 April
    1994 - 25 March to 5 April
    1995 - 7 April to 18 April
    1996 - 29 March to 9 April
    1997 - 21 March to 1 April
    1998 - 3 April to 14 April
    1999 - 26 March to 6 April
    2000 - 14 April to 25 April

The **National Folkloric Festival** is an annual multicultural event featuring dancers and musicians from many ethnic backgrounds. It is held in June, and begins with a Sunday parade that terminates at the Opera House, the scene for the many events of the following weekend.

The **Biennale of Sydney** is an international exhibition of contemporary art held every two years. Since its inception in 1973, the Biennale has brought the world's leading artists to Sydney, and more than 800 artists from over 45 countries have been exhibited. Future Biennales will be held to coincide with the Festival of Sydney. The Biennale is not only confined to Sydney as visiting artists travel giving lectures, workshops and artist-in-residency programs, and special lectures and displays are organised.

The **Sydney to Hobart Yacht Race** can hardly be classed as a festival, but it does generate a lot of excitement. Every Boxing Day thousands of people line the vantage spots around the harbour to watch the mini and maxi yachts set off on their adventure, and there are so many boats of all sorts on the Harbour, farewelling the entrants, that it is a wonder they ever get through the Heads. The race is closely monitored by news crews in light aircraft, and hourly reports are given on TV and radio as to who is in the lead, and by how much. Meanwhile, the people in Hobart get ready for the big welcoming party.

The City to Surf Fun Run is another annual event. Held every year in August, thousands of people of all ages assemble for the start of the run to Bondi Beach, and as the starting gun goes off, Park Street becomes a sea of people. Of course, the race is always won by a professional marathon runner, but winning is not really what the spectacle is all about. Everyone who finishes receives a certificate, and their names are listed in the newspapers. Even those who don't finish are congratulated for entering, and there is a real spirit of comradeship as you watch people helping each other along the way.

Public Holidays
Christmas, Boxing Day, New Year and Easter are obviously celebrated at the same time as everywhere else in the world.
 Holidays that are purely Australian are:
Australia Day - January 26.
Anzac Day - April 25.
Queen's Birthday - the second Monday in June.
Labour Day - the first Monday in October.

Another day is *Bank Holiday*, which is held on the first Monday in August, but only banks, government offices, insurance companies and the like are closed.

ENTRY REGULATIONS

All travellers to Australia need a valid passport, and visitors of all nationalities except New Zealand, must obtain a visa before arrival. These are available at Australian Embassies, High Commissions and Consular offices listed in local telephone directories. No vaccinations are required.
 Each incoming traveller over the age of 18 is allowed duty free

goods to the value of $400 plus one litre of liquor and 200 cigarettes.

EXIT REGULATIONS

There is a departure tax of $20 for everyone over the age of 12 years who is leaving the country by air.

CONSULATES

Over seventy countries have diplomatic representation in Canberra, the Capital City of Australia, but Consuls can be found in the State capitals. The addresses for those in Sydney are:

Canada: 50 Bridge Street, Sydney, ph 231 6522.
Great Britain: 1 Macquarie Street, Sydney, ph 247 7521.
Japan: 52 Martin Place, Sydney, ph 231 3455.
New Zealand: 25th floor, 52 Martin Place, Sydney, ph 233 8388.
United Kingdom: 1 Macquarie Street, Sydney, ph 247 7521.
United States: cnr Park & Castlereagh Streets, Sydney, ph 261 9200.
Singapore: There is no representation in Sydney. Refer to the Singapore High Commission, Forster Street, Yarralumla, ph (06) 273 3944.

MONEY

Australia uses a decimal currency system with 100 cents equalling one dollar. The notes are in denominations of $100, $50, $20, $10, $5, and coins are $2, $1, 50 cents, 20 cents, 10 cents and 5 cents. The notes come in different sizes and colours, according to denomination, which makes them very easy to distinguish. Visitors from the United States, though, disparagingly refer to Australian currency as 'Monolopy money'.

Opening Times
Most banks change travellers cheques and foreign currencies, and bank trading hours are Mon-Thurs 9.30am-4pm, Fri 9.30am-5pm, but the major banks in the city area are open Mon-Fri 8.15am-6pm.

Also, in the large suburban shopping centres some banks are open until 8pm on Thursdays, and 9.30am-noon on Saturdays.

Outside Banking Hours

Outside banking hours, travellers cheques and foreign currencies can be exchanged at the following Thomas Cook's Currency Exchange Centres:

Sydney, 175 Pitt Street, ph 229 6677 - open Mon-Fri 8.45am-5.15pm, Sat 8.45am-noon.

The Queen Victoria Building, Shop 22, ph 264 1133 - open Mon-Fri 9am-5.30pm (Thurs till 8pm), Sat 9am-4pm, Sun & public holidays (except Christmas and Easter) 11am-4pm.

Kings Cross, Hyatt Kingsgate Hotel (top of William Street), ph 356 2211 - open Mon-Fri 8.45am-5.30pm, Sat-Sun 8.45am-1pm, public holidays 8.45am-noon. This centre is open 365 days a year.

Bondi Beach, Bondi Pavilion, Queen Elizabeth Drive, ph 365 0727 - open Mon-Fri 8am-3pm, Sat 8am-noon.

| Tip |

Department stores will only accept travellers cheques that are in Australian currency, as will some small stores in the tourist areas.

Credit Cards

American Express, Diners, Visa and Mastercard are widely accepted. Shops and restaurants have the logos of the cards they accept near the front door, or at the check out.

Phone numbers to ring in the event of loss or theft of cards are:

American Express - Cards, 886 0666
                Travellers Cheques, 886 0689
                (after business hours, 886 0688)

Diners Club - 008 331 199

Mastercard - ANZ Bank - 008 033 844
           Citibank - 008 037 067
           Commonwealth Bank - 685 1122
           National Bank - 008 033 103
           State Bank (National) - 13 1818

Westpac Bank - 201 8030
Bank of Qld - 008 077 024
R & I Bank of WA - 008 999 273
Overseas cards - 229 6611

Visa - Australian cards - 643 1131
Japanese cards - 008 800 828
International cards - 008 801 256

COMMUNICATIONS

Mail
The General Post Office is in Martin Place, between Pitt and George Streets, and is open Mon-Fri 8.15am-5.30pm, Sat 8.15am-noon, ph 230 7122 or 230 7593.

Suburban post offices are open Mon-Fri 9am-5.30pm.

The postage for mailing a postcard by Air Mail is:
To New Zealand - 70c
    Singapore - 80c
    Hong Kong and Japan - 90c
    United States and Canada - 95c
    United Kingdom - $1.00.

Telephone
Public telephones are found in hotels, shops and cafes, and on street corners, and a local call costs 30c, irrespective of the length of the call.

Calls to places out of the Sydney 02 Area Code are time-charged, and the fee varies with the distance involved, and the time of day the call is placed.

| Tip |

The cheapest time to ring is from 6pm Sat to 8am Mon, or every day from 10pm to 8am, when savings are up to 60% of the day time rate.

The area codes for places outside the Sydney area are found in the back of the A-K White Pages of the Sydney Telephone Book.

Overseas calls can be dialled direct, and the International Access Code is 0011.

The International Direct Dial country and area codes are also found in the back of the A-K White Pages of the Sydney Telephone Book. *The Country Code for Australia is 61.*

Country Direct is a service which enables travellers in Australia to gain direct access to telephone operators in their home country so as to make telephone credit card or reverse charge (collect) calls. *It may be necessary to insert the local call fee to make a Country Direct call.* The telephone numbers are found in the Calling Information section in the front of the A-K White Pages of the Sydney Telephone Book, and include:

New Zealand - 0014 881 640
Singapore - 0014 881 650
Hong Kong - 0014 881 852
Japan - 0014 881 810
Canada - 0014 881 150
USA Direct (AT & T) - 0014 881 011
USA (MCI) - 0014 881 100
USA (SPRINT) - 0014 881 877
UK (BTI) - 0014 881 440.

Time Zones
Australian Eastern Standard Time is Greenwich Mean Time + 10 hours. If Daylight Saving is not involved, when it is Noon in Sydney, the following times are applicable:

Auckland - 2.00pm
London - 2.00am
Los Angeles - 6.00pm (previous day)
New York - 9.00pm (previous day)
Ottawa - 9.00pm (previous day)
Singapore - 10.00am
Hong Kong - 10.00am
Tokyo - 11.00am
Vancouver - 6.00pm (previous day)

Sydney, and indeed all of New South Wales, has **Daylight Saving,** and clocks are put forward one hour at 2.00am on the last Sunday in October every year. Australian Eastern Summer Time continues until 2.00am on the first Sunday in March, when clocks are put back one hour.

If you decide to ring home to the Northern Hemisphere when Sydney is not in Daylight Saving, chances are that your country is on Summer Time, so appropriate adjustment must be made to the times mentioned above. It does not make people conducive to accepting the charges for an overseas call if you wake them up at some ungodly hour.

Useful Telephone Numbers

Emergencies - Fire, Police, Ambulance - 000

Directory Assistance - Local - 013
Country & Interstate - 0175
Overseas - 0103

Call enquiries and costs - calls within Australia - 012
Overseas calls - 0102

Newspapers

Sydney has three daily newspapers **Mon-Sat:**
the national paper, *The Australian* - 60c (the Saturday edition is called *The Weekend Australian* - $1);
The Sydney Morning Herald (60c);
The Telegraph-Mirror (60c).

On Sunday, the choice is between *The Sun-Herald* (80c) and *The Sunday Telegraph* (90c).

The Thursday edition of the *Telegraph-Mirror* has a section called "The Gig Guide" which tells what's on and where, but it is not as comprehensive as the "Metro" liftout in Friday's edition of the *Sydney Morning Herald*.

| Tip |

"Metro" has information on all exhibitions, gallery showings and

alternative entertainment as well as classical and rock music programs and venues, movies, theatre, ballet - in short, everything for everybody.

Every suburb has at least one local paper that is delivered free to every household, and has news of local interest and happenings.

MISCELLANEOUS

Clothing
Lightweight clothing is necessary for the summer months, and medium to heavy for the winter months. A raincoat, or at least an umbrella, should be included in your suitcase whatever the season.

The dress code is mostly smart casual. Although the 'typical' Aussie man is thought to spend his life attired in shorts, singlet top and thongs, he would not be allowed in any of the licensed clubs unless he changed to a shirt with a collar, and long pants, or at least dress shorts and long socks. Restaurants consider long pants a necessity, and a few demand the addition of a tie. For women, it is the same as the rest of the world - the more upmarket the venue, the more upmarket the gear you wear.

Tipping
Tipping is not a way of life Down Under. Of course, if you are particularly impressed by the service you have been given, it is OK to tip. If you decide not to, however, you will not be harassed as you would be in some other countries. It is entirely up to you.

Some restaurants add a small percentage to their bills for weekend trading, and some set a minimum account level. The latter is usually to make sure that customers purchase food as well as beverages, and the limit is usually set at the price of the lowest priced meal.

Alcohol
The legal age for purchasing alcohol is 18 years.

Children are permitted into lounge bars where food is served as long as they are accompanied by an adult. Many hotels have outside 'beer gardens' and children are allowed entry to these.

The licensed clubs have their restaurants situated in such a way that children can enter them without passing through any of the gambling areas.

The legal limit of blood alcohol while driving is 0.05 per cent.

Smoking

Sydney is fast becoming a 'Smoke Free Zone' and it will soon be possible to smoke only in the confines of one's own home.

Most theatres and cinema complexes do not allow smoking on their premises; the great majority of restaurants have a 'no smoking' section, and some have banned smoking completely; all Government buildings and banks are smoke free; the larger hotels have 'no smoking' floors, the smaller have smoke free rooms; the Domestic and the International Airports are cluttered with 'No Smoking' signs; and smoking is forbidden on all intra and interstate flights. The list goes on. The government is doing its bit to help by regularly increasing the tax on tobacco to the point where the price of cigarettes is becoming prohibitive in itself.

If you are one of the dwindling band of nicotine addicts, grab a carton in the duty free shop on arrival, and see if you can make it stretch out for the length of your stay.

Electricity

Domestic electricity supply throughout Australia is 230-250 volts, AC 50 cycles. Three-pin plugs are fitted to domestic appliances, so 110 appliances, such as hairdryers and contact lens sterilisers, cannot be used without a transformer.

Many of the hotels and motels have adaptor plugs.

City Bus Connection

TRAVEL INFORMATION

HOW TO GET THERE

By Air (from Overseas)

Sydney is the major gateway to Australia from overseas, and all the overseas airlines servicing Australia fly into Kingsford-Smith International Airport at Mascot.

Qantas, the national flag carrier, has flights to Sydney from:
Amsterdam - daily
Auckland - daily
Bangkok - daily
Chicago - daily
Christchurch - daily
Frankfurt - Wed & Fri
Hong Kong - daily
Honolulu - daily
London - daily
Los Angeles - daily
New York - daily, via Los Angeles
Singapore - daily
Tokyo - daily
Toronto - Wed, Fri & Sun, via Honolulu
Vancouver - daily except Fri
Washington - daily, via Los Angeles
Wellington - daily.
Reservations and flight confirmations - ph 957 0111.

Air New Zealand has flights to Sydney from:
Auckland - daily
Chicago - daily, via Auckland
Christchurch - daily
Frankfurt - Wed and Sat

London - Thurs, Fri & Sunday, via Los Angeles
Los Angeles - daily
New York - daily, via Los Angeles
San Francisco - daily, via Los Angeles
Toronto - daily, via Los Angeles, Wed & Fri , via Auckland
Vancouver - daily, via Los Angeles, Tues-Fri, via Auckland
Wellington - daily.
Reservations and flight confirmations - ph 965 4111.

Canadian Airlines have daily flights from Vancouver to Sydney.
Reservations and flight confirmations - ph 299 7843.

British Airways have daily flights from London to Sydney, via
Singapore.
Reservations and flight confirmations - ph 258 3300.

Cathay Pacific has daily flights to Sydney from Hong Kong, and
flights via Hong Kong, from:
Amsterdam - Thurs & Sat
Frankfurt - daily
London - daily
Tokyo - daily
Vancouver - daily.
Reservations and flight confirmations - ph 931 5555.

Continental Airlines have daily flights to Sydney from:
San Francisco
Los Angeles (change planes in Auckland)
Auckland
Reservations and flight confirmations - ph 249 0111.

Northwest Airlines have flights to Sydney from:
New York - Mon, Wed & Fri, via Osaka
Los Angeles - daily, except Wed, via Honolulu
Reservations and flight confirmations - ph 290 4455.

Singapore Airlines has daily flights to Sydney from Singapore, and
flights via Singapore, from:
Frankfurt - daily, except Sun

London - daily
Los Angeles - Wed, Sat & Sun
San Francisco - daily
Tokyo - daily.
Reservations and flight confirmations - ph 236 0111.

United Airlines have flights to Sydney from:
Los Angeles - daily (non-stop)
Chicago - daily, via San Francisco, Honolulu and Auckland
New York - daily, via either Chicago or LA.
Reservations and flight confirmations - ph 237 8888.

By Air (within Australia)

Australian Airlines (now a part of Qantas), *Ansett* and *East-West* are the major internal Australian airlines, and they have regular flights from major Australian cities to Sydney.

Air NSW, *Eastern Airlines*, *Hazelton*, *Sky West* have flights from country towns to Sydney.

Airports

Kingsford-Smith International Airport is situated in the suburb of Mascot, 10km from the city centre. The Domestic Terminals are 3km to the east of the Overseas, and are connected by taxis and express buses. The buses run every 20 minutes, 7 days a week, and the **one-way fares are $2.50 adults, $1.50 children.**

The State Transit Airport Express has a service every 10 minutes from the Airport to Central Railway Station.
Bus Route 300 travels between the Airport and Circular Quay, stopping at specially-identified places along George Street and in Eddy Avenue near Central Station.

Route 350 travels between the Airport and Elizabeth Bay, passing through Kings Cross.

The services run 7 days a week, and the fares are **one-way adults $5, children $3, return ticket is $8** and the return journey can be taken up to 60 days after the initial trip.

Kingsford-Smith Airport Services (KSA) operate a bus service between the Airport, City, Kings Cross and Glebe. **Buses meet all incoming international and major domestic flights.** Passengers may alight en route at hotels on request, and transfer time is around 40 minutes.

To arrange a KSA transfer to the Airport, phone one hour in advance.

Services run daily every half-hour, 6am-8pm, ph 667 3221 and 667 0663, and **the fares are $4.50 adults, $3 children** under 12 years old.

By Bus

Coach companies that have services to Sydney from interstate and country areas include: Batterhams, Bus Australia, Casino 99, Firefly, Fearnes, Greyhound, Kirklands, Leslies, Lindsays, Mc-Caffertys, Murrays, Mylons, Pioneer, Stateliner and Trans City.
Reservations can be made through the companies themselves, or through a booking agent.

Two such agencies in Sydney are:
Dial-A-Coach, ph 231 3699, and
Bus Booking Centre, ph 264 3691.

By Rail

State Rail has XPT services between Sydney and Albury, Dubbo, Tamworth and Murwillumbah (with bus connections to the Gold Coast and Brisbane). The XPTs are fast, smooth and comfortable with air-conditioning, aircraft-style seats and big panoramic windows.

There is an overnight interstate service from/to Melbourne, and an overnight service from/to Brisbane.

The *Alice* runs between Sydney and Alice Springs, and the *Indian Pacific* crosses the continent from/to Perth in 65 hours.

By Road

From Melbourne: via the Hume Highway (877km); via the Princes Highway (959km); or via the Olympic Way and Hume Highway.

From Brisbane: via the Pacific Highway (1011km); via the New

England and Cunningham Highways (1033km).

From Adelaide: via the Mid Western Highway (1418km); via the Sturt Highway (1427km); or via the Barrier Highway (1668km).
From Darwin: via Dubbo, Bourke. Charleville and Mount Isa (4167km).

From Perth: 4000km, involving a hot, boring drive across the Nullabor Plain.

TOURIST INFORMATION

The **Travellers Information Service** at the Airport can make accommodation bookings, and also has a telephone information service that operates 7 days a week between 5am and 11pm, ph 669 5111.

| Tip |

First stop in Sydney for all visitors should be the **Travel Centre of New South Wales**, MLC Building, 19 Castlereagh Street (near the corner of Martin Place), ph 231 444. The office is open Mon-Fri 9am-5pm, and has numerous brochures, maps, etc. and a large and very helpful staff. Pick up copies of all the current city information guides and you will have plenty of reading material, and good tips on what to see and where to go.

The **Sydney Tower Visitors Information and Booking Service** is located at the top of the tower, ph 229 7430. It is open 7 days, 9.30am-9.30pm (Sat till 11.30pm), and is a minefield of information for those people brave enough to take the lift to the top of the tower.

The **Sydney Convention and Visitors Bureau** has an information kiosk in Martin Place which is open Mon-Fri 9am-5pm, ph 235 2424.

The Rocks Visitor Information Centre, 104 George Street, The Rocks, is open 7 days, 9am-5pm, ph 247 4972, or Rocks Hotline 11 606.

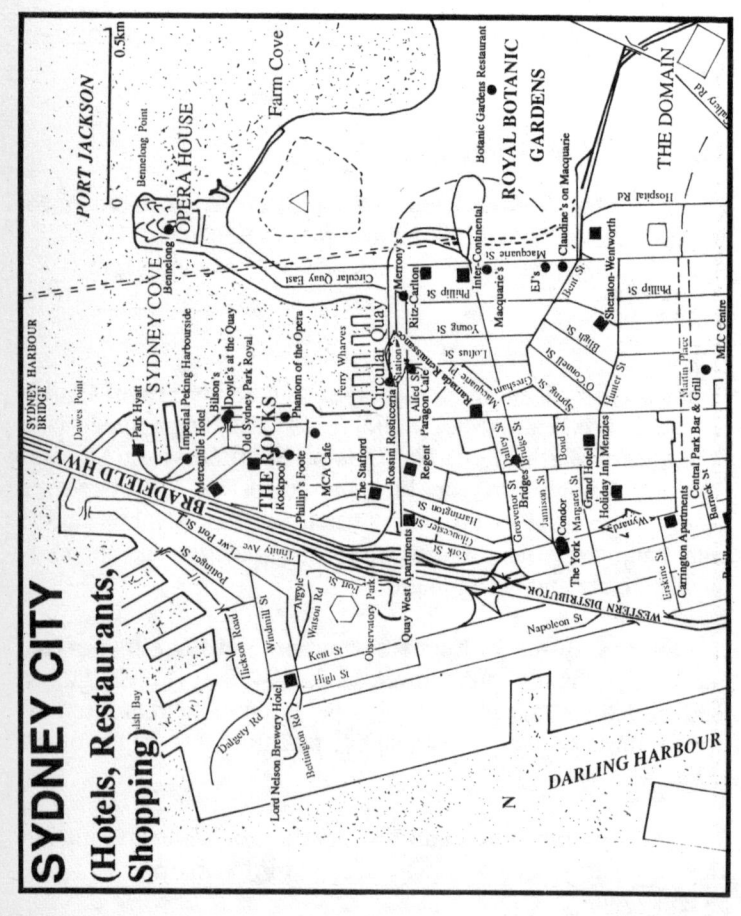

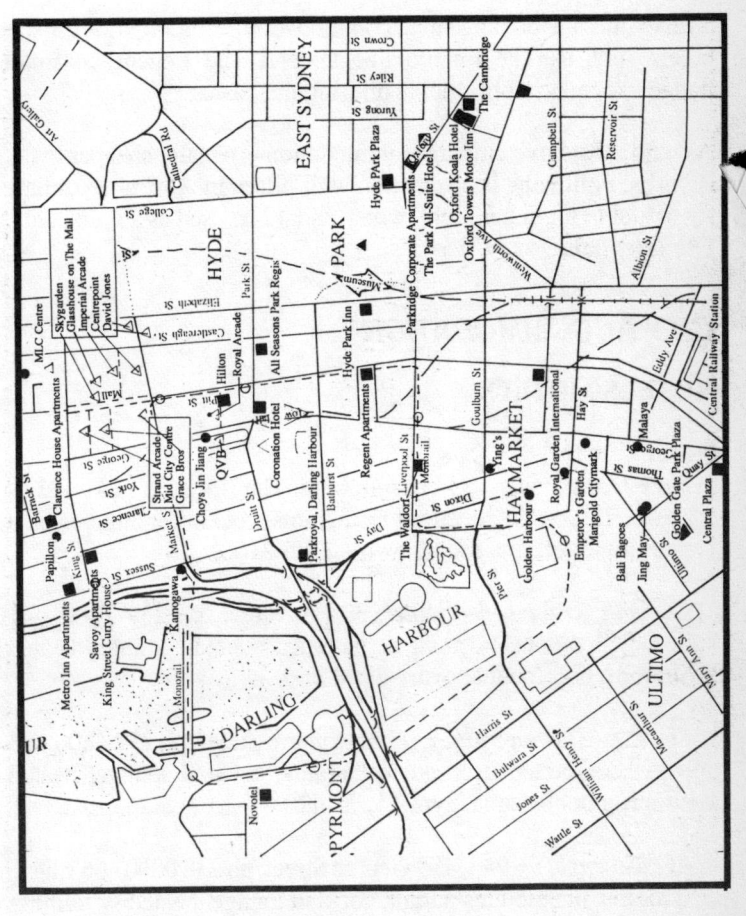

ACCOMMODATION

Sydney has a wide range of accommodation, from luxurious 5-star hotels such as The Intercontinental and The Regent, to small budget-priced establishments offering the basics.

As with most large cities, accommodation is usually cheaper in the suburbs. Following is a selection with prices in Australian dollars for a double room per night, which should be used as a guide only. *The Telephone Area Code is 02*.

CITY ACCOMMODATION

HOTELS/MOTELS

5-Star
  Park Hyatt Sydney, 7 Hickson Road, The Rocks, ph 241 1234 - 4 suites, 159 rooms, licensed restaurants, cocktail lounge, heated swimming pool, spa, sauna, gym - $395-2100.

  Ramada Renaissance Hotel, 30 Pitt Street, ph 259 7000 - 41 suites, 558 rooms, licensed restaurants, cocktail lounge, heated swimming pool, sauna, gym - $290-360.

  The Ritz-Carlton Sydney, 93 Macquarie Street, ph 252 4600 - 13 suites, 106 rooms, licensed restaurants, cocktail lounge, heated swimming pool, sauna, gym - $275-420.

  The Regent of Sydney, 199 George Street, ph 238 0000 - 66 suites, 530 rooms, licensed restaurant, cocktail lounge, heated swimming pool - $270-400.

Hotel Inter-Continental Sydney, 117 Macquarie Street, ph 230 0200 - 42 suites, 502 rooms, licensed restaurants, cocktail lounges, heated swimming pool, sauna, gym - $285-350.

Hilton International Sydney, 259 Pitt Street, ph 266 0610 - 28 suites, 585 rooms, licensed restaurants, cocktail bars, heated swimming pool, spa, sauna, gym - $260-355.

Sheraton Wentworth Sydney, 61 Phillip Street, ph 230 0700 - 42 suites, 423 rooms, licensed restaurants, cocktail lounges, gym - $260-295.

Golden Gate Park Plaza International, 169 Thomas Street, ph 281 6888 - 5 suites, 251 rooms, licensed restaurant, swimming pool, spa - $165-285.

Holiday Inn Menzies Sydney, 14 Carrington Street, ph 299 1000 - 15 suites, 438 rooms, licensed restaurants, cocktail bars, heated indoor pool, spa, sauna, gym - $203-250.

4-Star

Old Sydney Parkroyal, 55 George Street, The Rocks, ph 252 0524 - 174 rooms, licensed restaurant, cocktail lounge, swimming pool, spa, sauna - $260.

Parkroyal at Darling Harbour, 150 Day Street, ph 261 4444 - 22 suites, 295 units, licensed restaurant, cocktail lounge - $150-230.

Hyde Park Plaza Hotel, 38 College Street, ph 331 6933 - 47 suites, 135 units, licensed restaurant, cocktail lounge, heated swimming pool, spa, sauna - $175-220 (includes continental breakfast).

Novotel Sydney on Darling Harbour, 100 Murray Street, Pyrmont, ph 934 0000 - 24 suites, 530 units, licensed restaurant, cocktail lounge, swimming pool, sauna, gym, tennis - $180-210.

The Cambridge, 212 Riley Street, ph 212 1111 - 40 suites, 136 units, licensed restaurant, heated indoor pool, sauna - $170-185.

Central Plaza Hotel, cnr George & Quay Streets, ph 212 2544 - 116 rooms, licensed restaurant, swimming pool, sauna - $167-255.

Hyde Park Inn, 271 Elizabeth Street, ph 264 6001 - 6 suites, 86 units, licensed restaurant (closed Sun), cocktail lounge - $135.

3-Star
Royal Garden International, 431 Pitt Street, ph 281 6999 - 10 suites, 220 rooms, licensed restaurant, pool, spa - $145-150.

All Seasons Park Regis, cnr Castlereagh & Park Streets, ph 267 6511 - 120 units, swimming pool - $121.

All Seasons Harbour Rocks, 34 Harrington Street, The Rocks, ph 251 8944 - 54 rooms, licensed restaurant, cocktail bar - $116-182.

Oxford Koala Hotel, cnr Oxford & Pelican Streets, ph 269 0645 - 12 suites, 343 units, licensed restaurant, swimming pool - $90.

Oxford Towers Motor Inn, 13 Waine Street, Darlinghurst, ph 267 8066 - 122 units, licensed restaurant, swimming pool - $75.

2-Star
Mercantile Hotel, 25 George Street, ph 247 3570 - 24 rooms (15 with private facilities nearby), licensed restaurant - B&B 85-150.

Grand Hotel, 30 Hunter Street, ph 232 3755 - 18 rooms (no private facilities) - B&B $80.

Coronation Hotel, 7 Park Street, ph 267 8362 - 21 rooms (no private facilities) - $59-69.

1-Star
The Lord Nelson Brewery Hotel, cnr Kent & Argyle Streets, The Rocks, ph 251 4044 - 6 rooms (no private facilities), licensed restaurant - B&LtB $60-100.

SERVICED APARTMENTS

5-Star

Quay West Apartments, 98 Gloucester Street, ph 240 6000 - 144 suites, licensed restaurant, heated indoor pool, spa, sauna, gym - $255-425.

The York, 5 York Street, ph 210 5000 - 35 units, 95 suites - licensed restaurant, heated swimming pool, spa, sauna - $193-233.

4-Star

The Park All-Suite Hotel, 16 Oxford Street, ph 331 7728 - 135 units, licensed restaurant, heated swimming pool, spa, sauna - $215-260.

The Waldorf, 57 Liverpool Street, ph 261 5355 - 91 suites, licensed restaurant, swimming pool, spa, sauna - $215-260.

Clarence House Apartments, 114 Clarence Street, ph 290 1166 - 15 units - $130-180.

Parkridge Corporate Apartments, 6 Oxford Street, ph 361 8600 - 40 suites, licensed restaurant, heated swimming pool, spa, sauna - $128-160.

The Savoy Apartments, cnr King & Kent Streets, ph 267 9211 - 63 units - $125-170.

Darlington, 253 Goulburn Street, ph 281 6429 - 20 units, swimming pool, spa, sauna - $130-200.

Carrington Apartments, 57 York Street, ph 290 1166 - 35 units - $140-180.

3-Star

The Stafford, 75 Harrington Street, The Rocks, ph 251 6711 - 40 units, swimming pool, spa, sauna, gym - $170.

Metro Inn Apartments Darling Harbour, 132 Sussex Street, ph 290 9200 - 37 units - $150.

The Regent Apartments, 359 Pitt Street, ph 290 1166 - 40 units - $95-120.

SUBURBAN ACCOMMODATION

The suburbs listed here are within a 10km radius of the city centre.

HOTELS/MOTELS/SERVICED APARTMENTS

Artarmon (10km north of the city)

4-Star
The Shore Inn, 450 Pacific Highway, ph 427 7000 - 4 suites, 158 units, licensed restaurant, heated swimming pool, spa, sauna, half-court tennis - $105-158.

3-Star
Artarmon Inn, 472 Pacific Highway, ph 412 1644 - 64 units, licensed restaurant, swimming pool, sauna - $95-125.

Twin Towers Motor Inn, 260 Pacific Highway, ph 439 1388 - 3 suites, 41 units, licensed restaurant, swimming pool, spa - $95-105.

2-Star
Linwood Lodge, 312 Pacific Highway, ph 439 6333 - 10 units - $55-70.

Ashfield (10km west of the city)

4-Star
Palm Court Motel, 17 Parramatta Road, ph 797 6111 - 2 suites, 32 units, licensed restaurant - $105.

Ashfield's Philip Lodge, 156 Parramatta Road, ph 797 9411 - 2 suites, 48 units, licensed restaurant, swimming pool - $88-98.

Metro Motor Inn (Parramatta Road), 171 Parramatta Road, ph 798 7666 - 1 suite, 44 units, licensed restaurant, swimming pool, sauna - $79-89.

3-Star

Metro Motor Inn (Liverpool Road), 63 Liverpool Road, ph 798 0333 - 38 units - $79.

2-Star

Charlotte Motor Inn, 62 Charlotte Street, ph 798 8918 - 12 units - B&B $80.

Bondi Beach (8km east of the city)

4-Star

Ramada Hotel Bondi Beach, cnr Campbell Parade & Beach Road, ph 365 5666 - 203 suites, licensed restaurant, heated swimming pool, spa, sauna, gym - $210-380.

City Beach Motor Inn, 99 Curlewis Street, ph 365 3100 - 25 units, swimming pool - $95-140.

3-Star

Bondi Beachside Inn, 152 Campbell Parade, ph 305 311 - 70 units, licensed restaurant - $66-85.

Alice Motel, 30 Fletcher Street, ph 305 231 - 31 units, licensed restaurant, swimming pool - $59-69.

2-Star

Bondi Hotel, 178 Campbell Parade, ph 303 271 - 3 suites, 49 rooms, licensed restaurants - $35-45.

Bondi Junction (5km east of the city)

3-Star

The Waverley Motel, 79 Oxford Street, ph 389 9466 - 81 units, unlicensed restaurant - $90.

2-Star
Bayline Motor Inn, 3 Waverley Crescent, ph 387 5388 - 27 units - $60-67.

Camperdown (5km south of the city)

4-Star
Camperdown Travelodge, 9 Missenden Road, ph 516 1522 - 138 units, licensed restaurant, swimming pool, sauna, gym - $121-145.

3-Star
Camperdown Towers, 144 Mallett Street, ph 519 5211 - unlicensed restaurant, swimming pool - $90.

Coogee (8km east of the city)

5-Star
Edgecumbe Executive Apartments, 2 Edgecumbe Avenue, ph 664 2888 - 33 units, swimming pool, spa - $150-175.

4-Star
Holiday Inn Coogee Beach, 242 Arden Street, ph 315 7600 - 207 rooms, licensed restaurant, heated swimming pool, gym, tennis - $150-180.

Coogee Sands Motor Inn, 161 Dolphin Street, ph 665 8588 - 50 units, licensed restaurant, swimming pool - $99-120.

3-Star
Corban International Motel, 183 Coogee Bay Road, ph 665 2244 - 38 units, licensed restaurant, swimming pool - $95.

Coogee Bay Hotel, 253 Coogee Bay Road, ph 665 0000 - 4 suites, 41 rooms, licensed restaurant, **Selinas Night Club** (could be noisy Thurs-Sun) - $80.

Cremorne (6km north of city)

4-Star
Metropole Hotel, 287 Military Road, ph 909 8888 - 4 suites, 84

rooms, licensed restaurant, lounge, **Steps Night Club** (could be noisy Thurs-Sun) - $145-175.

Darlinghurst (2km east of the city)

4-Star
Morgans of Sydney Serviced Apartments, 304 Victoria Street, ph 360 7955 - 26 units, licensed restaurant - B&LtB $135-150.

3-Star
Camelot Inn, 358A Victoria Street, ph 331 7555 - 37 units - $70.

Double Bay (4km east of the city)

5-Star
The Ritz-Carlton, 33 Cross Street, ph 362 4455 - 15 suites, 140 rooms, licensed restaurant, swimming pool, gym - $215-305.

4-Star
Savoy Double Bay Hotel, 41 Knox Street, ph 326 1411 - 2 suites, 33 units - B&LtB $125-140.

Elizabeth Bay (3km east of the city)

5-Star
Sebel Town House, 23 Elizabeth Bay Road, ph 358 3244 - 25 suites, 143 rooms, licensed restaurant, cocktail lounge, heated swimming pool, sauna, gym - $280-335.

Gazebo Hotel, 2 Elizabeth Bay Road, ph 358 1999 - 8 suites, 391 units, licensed restaurant, cocktail lounge, heated swimming pool, sauna - $160-180.

4-Star
Seventeen Elizabeth Bay Serviced Apartments, 17 Elizabeth Bay Road, ph 358 8999 - 49 units - B&LtB $160-220

3-Star
Madisons Ward Avenue, 6 Ward Avenue, ph 357 1155 - 8 suites, 33 units - B&LtB $109.

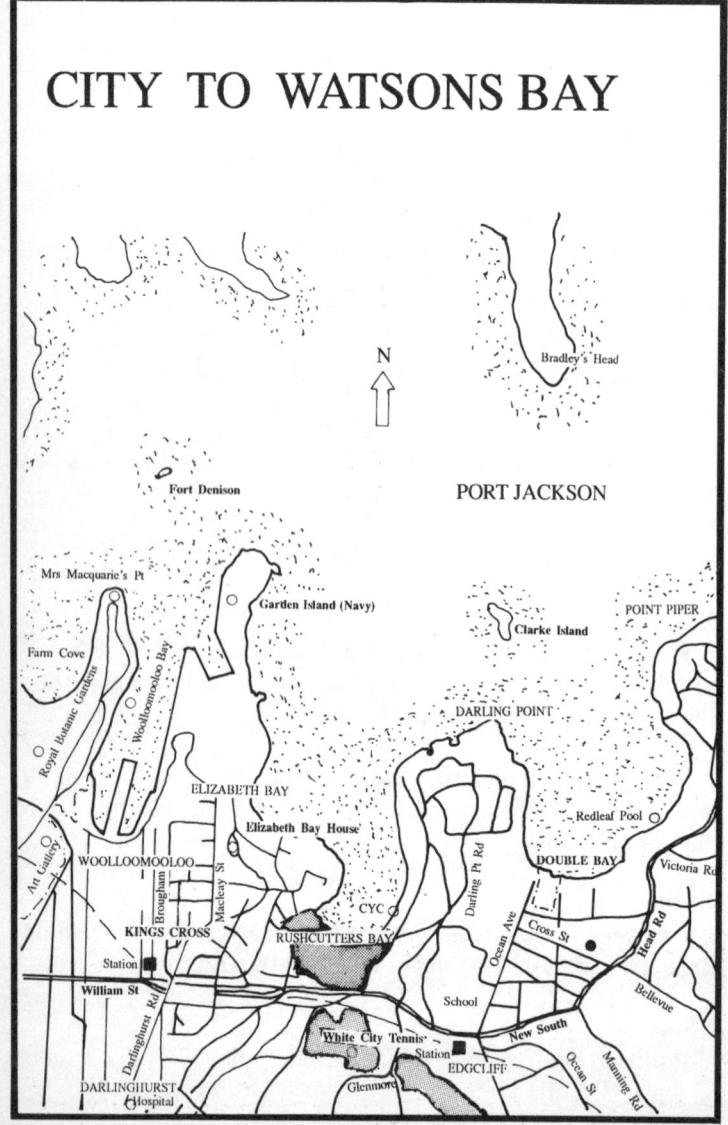

CITY TO WATSONS BAY

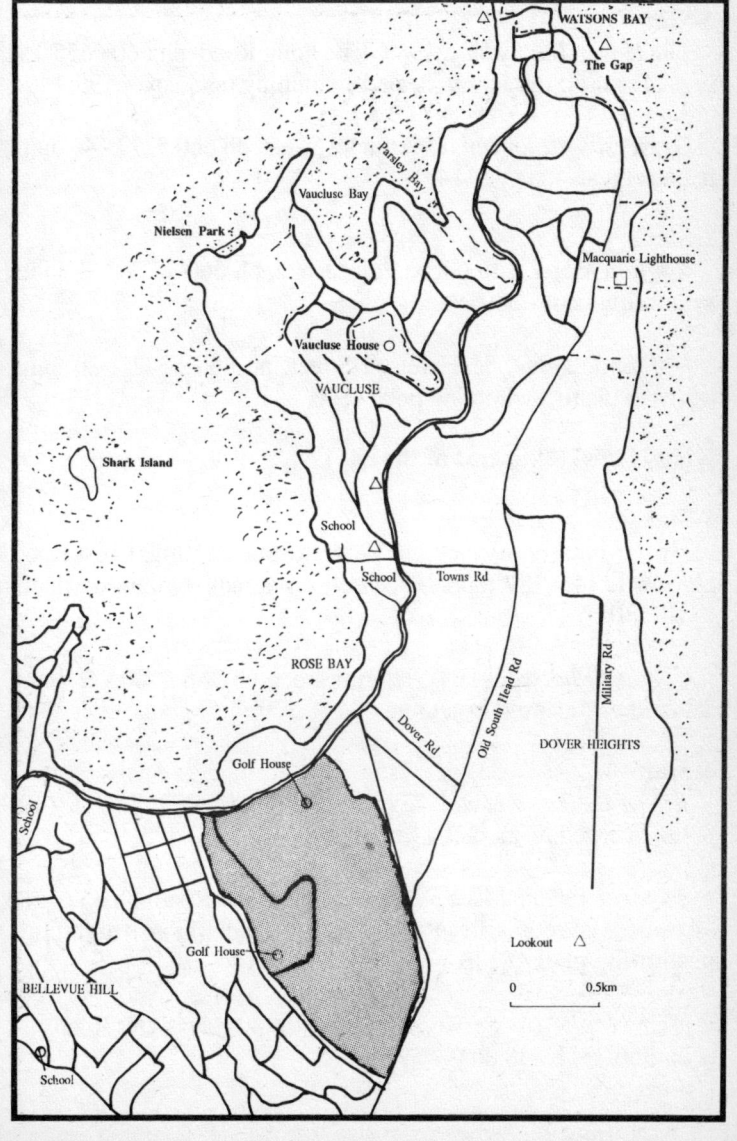

WATSONS BAY

The Gap

Parsley Bay

Vaucluse Bay

Nielsen Park

Macquarie Lighthouse

Vaucluse House ○

VAUCLUSE

Shark Island

School

School   Towns Rd

ROSE BAY

Dover Rd

Old South Head Rd

Military Rd

DOVER HEIGHTS

Golf House

School

Golf House

BELLEVUE HILL

School

Lookout △

0   0.5km

Medina Executive Apartments, 68 Roslyn Gardens, ph 356 7400 - 58 units - $120.

Glebe (3km west of the city)

3-Star

The Haven Inn Sydney, 196 Glebe Point Road, ph 660 6655 - 51 units, licensed restaurant, heated swimming pool, spa - $99-140.

University Motor Inn, 25 Arundel Street, ph 660 5777 - 45 units, licensed restaurant - $114.

2-Star

Rooftop Motel, 146 Glebe Point Road, ph 660 7777 - 39 units, swimming pool - $80.

Hereford Lodge, 51 Hereford Street, ph 660 5577 - 20 units, licensed bistro, swimming pool - $60.

Kings Cross (2km east of the city)

5-Star

Hyatt Kingsgate Sydney, cnr Victoria Street & Kings Cross Road, ph 356 1234 - 389 rooms, licensed restaurant, swimming pool - $210-230.

Century Radisson, 203 Victoria Street, ph 368 4000 - 5 suites, 291 rooms, licensed restaurant - $140-170.

4-Star

Top of the Town Motel, 227 Victoria Street, ph 361 0911 - 101 units, licensed restaurant, swimming pool - $150-175.

Bayswater Park Plaza Suites, 33 Bayswater Road, ph 357 7266 - 45 suites, 25 rooms, licensed restaurant, **Studebaker's nightclub, swimming pool - $135.**

Metro Motor Inn Serviced Apartments, 40 Bayswater Road, ph 356 3511 - 38 units - $95.

Claremont Inn, 5 Ward Avenue, ph 358 2044 - 64 units, licensed restaurant, heated indoor swimming pool, spa, sauna - $77.

Roslyn Gardens Motor Inn, 4 Roslyn Gardens, ph 358 1944 - 29 units - $69-85.

Kings View Motel, 30 Darlinghurst Road, ph 358 5599 - 68 units, unlicensed restaurant - $66.

3-Star
Hampton Court Hotel, 9 Bayswater Road, ph 357 2711 - 126 rooms - $98.

Crest Quality Inn, 111 Darlinghurst Road, ph 358 2755 - 210 rooms, licensed restaurant, cocktail bar, swimming pool - $95.

Lane Cove (9km north of the city)

4-Star
Metro Inn Riverview Apartments, 302 Burns Bay Road,
ph 427 4000 - 32 units, riverside location, heated swimming pool, sauna, squash - $178.

Country Comfort Motel, cnr Pacific Highway & Gatacre Avenue, ph 427 0266 - 43 units, unlicensed restaurant - $75.

North Sydney (4km north of the city)

4-Star
Northside Gardens, 54 McLaren Street, ph 922 1311 - 48 suites, 167 rooms, licensed restaurant, cocktail bar - $135.

3-Star
Centra North Sydney Motel, Blue Street, ph 955 0499 - 221 units, licensed restaurant, swimming pool - $109-130.

Milsons Serviced Apartments, 44 McDougall Street, ph 956 4601 - 16 suites - $120.

Potts Point (3km east of the city)

5-Star
Hotel Nikko Sydney, 81 Macleay Street, ph 368 3000 - 13 suites, 459 rooms, licensed restaurant, cocktail lounge, swimming pool - $280-315.

4-Star
Chateau Sydney Motel, 14 Macleay Street, ph 358 2500 - 2 suites, 94 units, licensed restaurant, cocktail lounge, heated swimming pool - $160-180.

Olims Sydney Hotel, 26 Macleay Street, ph 358 2777 - 4 suites, 114 units, licensed restaurant, cocktail lounge, pool - $160.

Florida Motor Inn, 1 McDonald Street, ph 358 6811 - 29 suites, 89 units, unlicensed restaurant, swimming pool, sauna - $109-121.

3-Star
The Dorchester Inn, 38 Macleay Street, ph 358 2400 - 14 units - $95-135.

Sheraton Hotel, 40 Macleay Street, ph 358 1955 - 18 suites, 46 units, licensed restaurant, cocktail bar - $99.

Randwick (6km east of the city)

4-Star
Medina Apartments, 63 St Marks Road, ph 399 5144 - 60 units, swimming pool, spa, sauna - $180.

3-Star
Gemini Motel, 65 Belmore Road, ph 399 9011 - 97 units, licensed restaurant - $99.

Esron Motel, cnr Dudley & St Pauls Streets, ph 398 7022 - 41 units, swimming pool - $58-68.

2-Star

Royal Hotel, Cuthill Street, ph 399 3006 - 19 rooms (no private facilities), licensed restaurant (a university pub, could be noisy Thurs-Sat) - $60-70.

Rushcutters Bay (3km east of the city)

3-Star

The Bayside Hotel, 85 New South Head Road, ph 327 8511 - 99 rooms, licensed restaurants, cocktail lounge - $150.

Rushcutter Travelodge Motel, 110 Bayswater Road, ph 331 2171 - 5 suites, 109 units, licensed restaurant swimming pool - $89-130.

St Leonards (6km north of the city)

4-Star

Glenview Hotel & Convention Centre, 194 Pacific Highway, ph 439 6000 - 67 units, licensed restaurant, swimming pool - $88-165.

Greenwich Inn, 196 Pacific Highway, ph 906 3277 - 25 units, unlicensed restaurant - B&LtB $75-79.

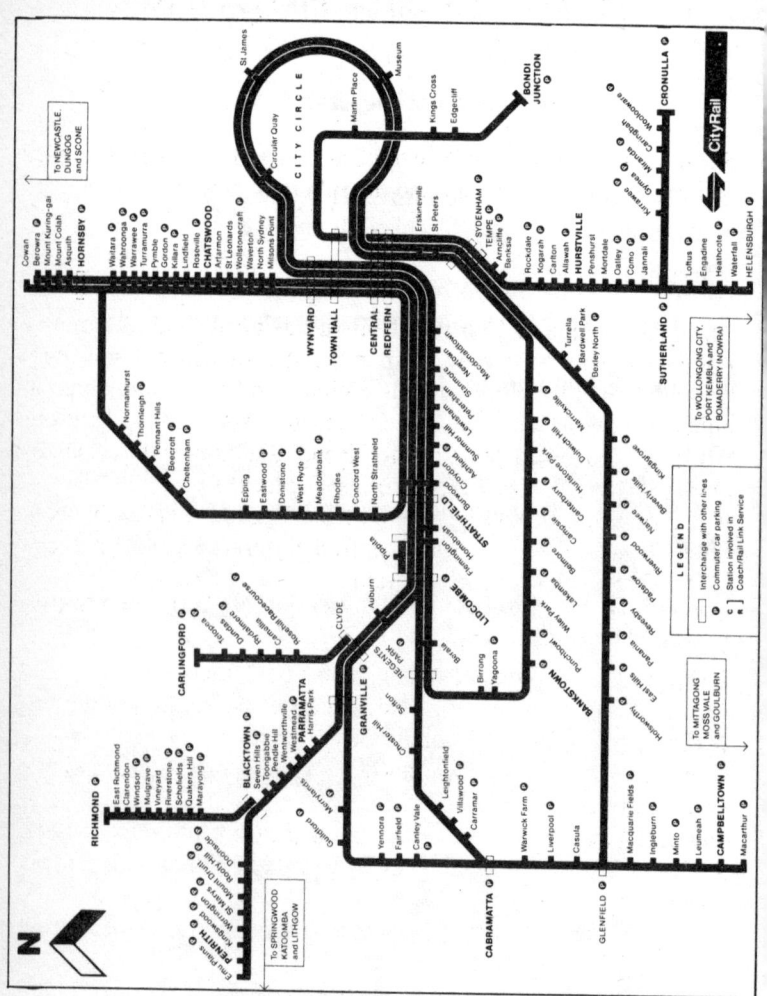

HOW TO GET AROUND

Sydney has an efficient public transport system, with buses, ferries and trains covering the city and the suburban areas.

TRAIN

The main station is **Central (Railway Square)** and all country trains begin their journey from here. All suburban trains pass through Central and Town Hall stations, and you can change at either to link up with the City Circle; to cross over the Harbour Bridge; or to board the train for Bondi Junction, which passes through Martin Place, Kings Cross and Edgecliff.

Central Station can be entered from Eddy Avenue, Elizabeth Street (best for suburban trains), or from the entrance road that runs of Pitt Street (best for country trains).

The stations in the City are:
Town Hall, Wynyard, Circular Quay, St James, Museum and Martin Place. These stations are all part of the underground network, and the first five form the City Circle.

Wynyard Station has two entrances - one in George Street and one in York Street.

Town Hall Station has two entrances on each side of George Street.

St James Station has entrances in Elizabeth Street and Queens Square.

Museum Station has entrances on both sides of Liverpool Street and one in Elizabeth Street.

Martin Place Station is well sign-posted, as is *Circular Quay Station*.

Tickets are purchased from a sales window before commencement of a journey, or you can use one of the machines on the city stations.

CityHopper tickets are available and allow unlimited, one-day rail travel around the City Circle, after 9am on weekdays and all day Saturday and Sunday. The ticket also includes Milsons Point, North Sydney, Martin Place and Kings Cross stations. The ticket costs **$2.20 adults, $1.10** children under 16, and is a very economical way of getting to the various city sights.

For details on train timetables, ph City-Rail, 131 500 (7am-10pm).

BUS

Sydney's buses are under the umbrella of State Transit, and full details of routes and schedules can be found in the A-K White Pages of the telephone book. Any other information you may need can be obtained by phoning the State Transit Bus & Ferry InfoLine on 131 315.

Generally speaking,
buses from the Eastern Suburbs terminate at either Central Railway or Circular Quay;
those from the North-western and Western Suburbs terminate at York Street (near the Queen Victoria Building) or Circular Quay;
and North Shore and Northern Suburbs bus routes end at Wynyard Park, near Wynyard Station, or outside the Queen Victoria Building.

On August 31, 1992, Sydney celebrated the opening of the latest aid to moving traffic, the Cahill Tunnel, which runs under the harbour. This has allowed one of the lanes on the Harbour Bridge to become a 'bus only' lane, and has cut down the travelling time for trips that involve crossing the harbour.

The opening of the Gore Hill Freeway in the city's northern suburbs has also caused the traffic to flow more smoothly, and it has shortened the trip from places such as North Ryde and Epping, to the city.

The Red Explorer Bus

The red Sydney Explorer bus is a great way to get around the city. It travels a 20km circuit to 26 different stops from 9.30am-9pm, every day except Christmas Day. Passengers can get on and off anywhere along the route, stay as long as they like at any stop, then catch the next Explorer to the next stop. If you miss the last Explorer bus, don't worry because your ticket is good on any State Transit bus within the Explorer route until midnight. The Explorer stops are:

1. Sydney Cove (Circular Quay)
2. Sydney Opera House
3. McMahons Point
4. Royal Botanic Gardens
5. Parliament House
6. Mrs Macquarie's Chair
7. Art Gallery of NSW
8. Kings Cross
9. Macleay Street
10. Elizabeth Bay House
11. Potts Point
12. Woolloomooloo Bay
13. William Street
14. The Australian Museum
15. Central Railway
16. Chinatown
17. Powerhouse Museum
18. Maritime Museum & Sydney Aquarium
19. Darling Harbour West
20. Chinese Garden
21. Queen Victoria Building
22. Wynyard
23. The Rocks
24. Village Green
25. Pier One
26. The Rocks Visitors Centre

Tickets can be purchased when boarding the bus, or beforehand from the NSW Travel Centre, 19 Castlereagh Street; Australian Pacific Tours, Shop 4, Overseas Shipping Terminal, Circular Quay

Sydney Explorer Bus Route

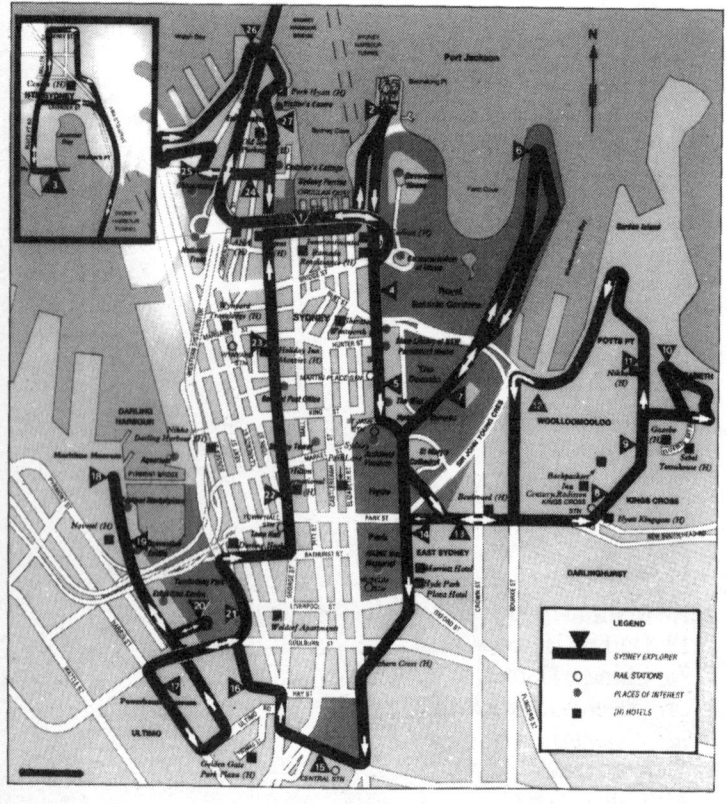

Circular Quay

West; CountryLink Rail Travel Centres; Sydney Tower, Centrepoint; or from a local travel agent. The fares are **$20 adult, $15 child, $45 family** (2 adults and 2 children).

The public bus system is supplemented by various local private bus companies, which usually connect outlying places to the closest railway station. If you cannot find the place you are looking for in the route maps in the Telephone Directory, you can contact the Association of Private Buses, ph 630 0511, and they will put you on to the company that services the area you wish to visit.

FERRY

Undoubtedly the most scenic way to travel, Sydney's ferries ply between Circular Quay and Watsons Bay, Rose Bay, Manly, Taronga Zoo, Cremorne, Mosman, Neutral Bay, Kirribilli, Hunters Hill, Meadowbank, Balmain and Darling Harbour. Full information on routes and schedules can also be found in the A-K White Pages of the telephone book.

Tickets for ferry travel are purchased at the ticket machines on the various wharves at the Circular Quay Ferry Terminal, either at the beginning or at the end of your trip. There are also change machines, so you don't have to worry about having the correct fare. You then use the ticket to open the exit gates.
  Sydney Ferries also operate cruises, which are also advertised in the A-K White Pages.

  The prices for the cruises are:
  River Cruise, daily 10am-12.30pm - **$16 adults, $12 child, $44 family.**
  Harbour Cruise, Mon-Fri 1-3.30pm, Sat-Sun, 1.30-4pm - **$16 adults, $12 child, $44 family.**
  Harbour Lights Cruise, Mon-Sat 8.9.30pm - **$14 adults, $10 child, $38 family.**

Tickets for the cruises can be purchased at the Ticket Office situated opposite the ferry wharves, underneath Circular Quay Railway Station.

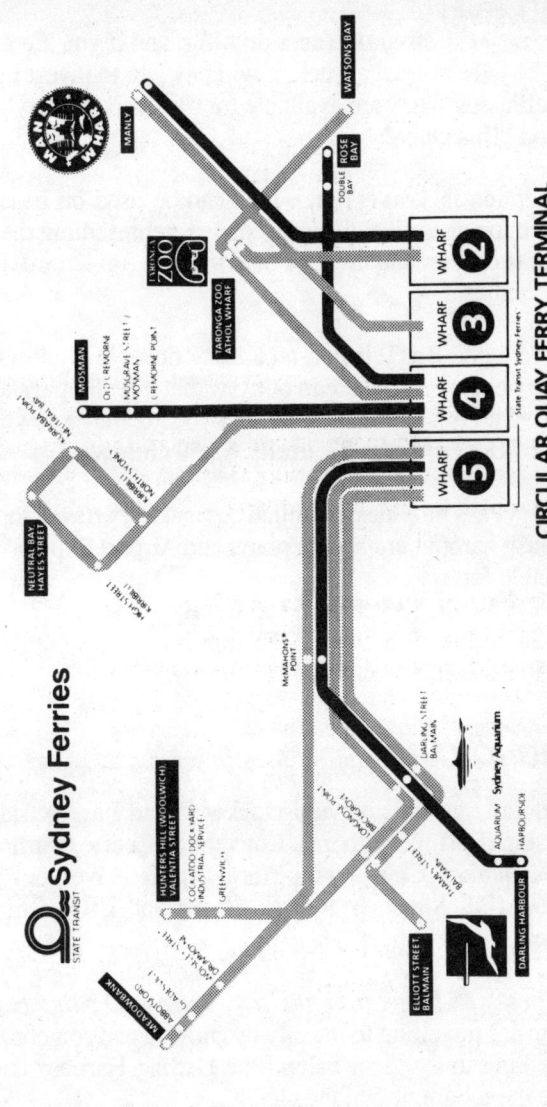

Sydney Ferries

STATE TRANSIT

CIRCULAR QUAY FERRY TERMINAL

*State Transit services are not available for journeys between Circular Quay and McMahons Point only.

Special Fares

There are **several discount fares on offer,** and if you are going to be in the city for at least a week, it will pay you to invest in one of the TravelPasses. They are available for "Train-Bus-Ferry", "Bus-Ferry" and "Bus Only".

Another option is **TravelTen,** which can be used on buses only. This ticket comes in five different colours, representing the length of the trip it covers, and must be inserted in the green machine on entering the bus.

Then there is the **BusTripper,** an all-day ticket that allows travel on as many buses as you like in one day, but it really pays to make a long trip with this ticket as the further you go, the more you save. The cost of BusTripper is **$7 adults, $3.50 children**.

The **SydneyPass** provides unlimited bus and ferry travel, including State Transit harbour cruises, Explorer and Airport Express. Passes are available for:
3 days - **$45 adult, $35 child, $125 family;**
5 days - **$65 adult, $55 child, $185 family;**
7 days - **$75 adult, $65 child, $215 family.**

THE MONORAIL

The monorail system runs anti-clockwise and has six stations - Harbourside (Darling Harbour), Convention Centre (Darling Harbour), Haymarket (Chinatown), World Square (Liverpool Street), Park Plaza (Pitt Street, near Park Street) and City Centre (Pitt Street, near Market Street).

It is the best way to get from the city centre to Darling Harbour, and if you are travelling to the city by car, you can sometimes find cheap parking in Pyrmont behind the Darling Harbour complex, then take the monorail into the city.

The fare for the monorail is **$2 for adults, $1 children,** whether you are going one stop or the complete circuit. You are not permitted to stay aboard for more than one circuit. The system operates daily - Mon-Thurs 7.30am-9pm, Fri-Sat 7.30am-11pm, Sun 8.30am-8pm.

TAXI

Sydney is well served by taxis and charges are set by the Department of Transport. *The main cab companies are:*
Taxis Combined Services, ph 332 8888;
RSL Cabs, ph 699 0144;
Legion Cabs, ph 289 9000;
Premier Radio Cabs, ph 897 4000;
Manly Warringah Cabs, ph 977 9111.

Specially outfitted cabs for people with disabilities are available, ph 339 0200, and must be booked in advance.

Taxis may be hailed in the street, hired at a taxi rank, or pick-up can be arranged by phone for an extra fee. Ranks in the city include
Central Station,
Circular Quay,
Park Street opposite the Town Hall,
and outside all major hotels.
If you hire a taxi in the city to take you over the bridge, $2 will be added to the bill even though there is no toll for travel south to north. This extra is added because the taxi driver has to pay the toll to come back over the bridge to return to the city, and may not get a fare going that way.

WATER TAXI

Two companies that operate water taxis are:
Taxis Afloat, ph 922 4252 ;
Aqua Cabs, ph 929 0477.
They will take you from any landing point to any landing point on the harbour, and also offer scenic cruises.

CAR

Renting a car is relatively cheap if you are travelling in a group, but **driving in the city is not really recommended.**

The one-way streets take a bit of getting used to, and parking is a problem. Street parking is extremely hard to find, and the parking station fees add a lot to the cost of your day out.

For travelling in the suburbs and outlying areas, a car is definitely the way to go.

| Tip |

When hiring a car it is important to check out what you are actually getting for your money.

Is the company offering unlimited kilometres?

Is the insurance cover adequate?

If you decide to drive interstate, can you drop the car off in another city, or do you have to drive back to Sydney?

Is the car entitled to NRMA (National Roads and Motorists Association) road service?

Ask for an all inclusive price so that you won't be hit with extra charges at the end of the rental period.

Here are a few names of rental companies and their reservation phone numbers:

Avis, ph 516 2877;

Betta Rent-A-Car, ph 331 5333;

Commuter Car Rental, ph 648 4399;

Hertz, ph 008 333 377;

National Car Rental, ph 332 1233;

Airport Rent A Car, ph 597 5433.

International and most overseas driver's licences are accepted, and a deposit, or credit card details, are required before pick-up. Other car rental companies are found in the A-K Yellow Pages of the Telephone Directory.

Traffic in Sydney drives on the left, and the speed limit in built-up areas is 60km/h.

Toll for Harbour Bridge and Tunnel

Both the Harbour Bridge (Bradfield Highway) and the Cahill Tunnel have a toll fee of $2 for southbound cars. It should be mentioned that the Tunnel is not an alternative to the Bridge. It is for traffic heading for the Airport and the eastern suburbs, and the Bridge is now for traffic to the city and the Western Distributor.

In recent years, a number of **roundabouts** have been installed and traffic already on the roundabout has right-of-way. The general driving rule is that cars have to give way to traffic on their right, but cars at a T-intersection have no right-of-way.

The NRMA has reciprocal arrangements with overseas and interstate automobile associations. The phone number for enquiries is 13 2132, and for road service, 13 1111.

The Harbour Bridge from North Sydney

A View of the City

EATING OUT

Sydney has a plethora of restaurants offering every type of cuisine imaginable. The harbour foreshores are liberally sprinkled with eating establishments, for there are not too many experiences that beat, or for that matter match, a leisurely brunch on a sunny weekend with the harbour and all its craft as a backdrop. *Unfortunately, though, you often have to pay 'over the top' for this indulgence.* With so much competition, you would expect that prices would have to be kept to a minimum, but there are apparently enough people to ensure that each restaurant is well-patronised, and indeed bookings are essential when a water view is offered.

Restaurants are classified as *'Licensed'* or *'BYO'*.
Licensed means that the establishment has a licence to sell alcohol; *BYO* means 'bring your own' wine, etc, because the restaurant does not have a liquor licence.

Some restaurants, although licensed, allow patrons to supply their own wine (not beer or spirits), which is usually less expensive than paying the mark-up on the wines that the restaurant is legally allowed to add. Then a *corkage fee* may be added which will be per bottle or per person, but the end result is usually still less expensive.
Alcohol can be purchased from the *bottle department* of a hotel, or from one of the many *bottle shop*s that abound in every suburb.

| Tip |

It is reasonable to say that the price of a bottle of wine in one of these shops would be less than half the price of the same wine in a restaurant.

All the experts agree that the best restaurant in Sydney, for food, service, presentation and locale, is **Berowra Waters Inn,** ph 456 1027. (Some believe it to be the best restaurant in Australia.) The suburb of Berowra Waters is a long way (about 45km) north of the city, and the fact that people will travel so far to patronise the Inn is testimony to the quality of the food and service. Unfortunately, you have to pay for what you get, and Berowra Waters Inn is also one of, if not the, most expensive of Sydney's eateries, with a **3-course meal** including coffee, but no alcohol or soft drinks, costing around **$85 per person.** Nevertheless, bookings are essential, and all major credit cards are accepted. Lunch is served from 12.30pm Fri-Sun, dinner from 7.30pm Fri-Sat.

At the other end of the scale is a Sydney landmark which has been around a very long time - *Harry's Cafe de Wheels,* Cowper Wharf Roadway, Woolloomooloo. It is not really a restaurant, not even a cafe, just a roadside stall, but everyone knows Harry's, and their real Aussie meat pies and peas, etc, handed to you on a paper serviette, are yummy! Eating a pie in this fashion is an art form which most Sydneysiders are born with, but when in Rome....!

As for everything between the above two extremes, following is a list of recommended restaurants, rated
Expensive (main course $15+),
Moderate (main course $10-$15)
Budget (main course under $10).

I have not included the restaurants in the large hotels as everyone knows that they exist, and are much the same the world over with regard to menus and prices.

Credit card abbreviations are: Amex = American Express; BC = Bankcard; DC = Diners Club; MC = Mastercard; V = Visa.

City and The Rocks

Bilson's, Upper Level, Overseas Passenger Terminal, Circular Quay West, ph 251 5600 - Licensed - good harbour views - French/Australian cuisine - **Expensive** - open Mon-Fri noon-2.30pm, Mon-Sat 7-10pm - Amex, BC, DC, MC, V.

Doyle's at The Quay, Lower Level, Overseas Passenger Terminal, Circular Quay West, ph 252 3400 - Licensed - good harbour views, outside tables - Seafood - **Expensive** - open Mon-Sun 11.30am-2.45pm, Mon-Sat 5.30-9.30pm, Sun 5.30-9pm - BC, DC, MC, V.

Bennelong, Sydney Opera House, Circular Quay, ph 250 7578 - Licensed - good harbour views - Modern Australian cuisine (basically that means a bit of everything) - **Expensive** - open Mon-Sat noon-2.30pm, Mon-Sat 5.30-7pm (pre-theatre) and from 8pm for a la carte - Amex, BC, DC, MC, V.

MCA Cafe, Museum of Contemporary Art, Quayside, Circular Quay, ph 241 4253 - Licensed - good harbour views, outdoor tables - Mediterranean-type cuisine - **Moderate** - open daily 10am-6pm, Tues-Sat 6-11pm - BC, MC, V.

Phantom of the Opera, 17-21 Circular Quay West, The Rocks, ph 247 2755 - Licensed - good views - Australian cuisine - **Moderate** - open Mon-Fri 11.30am-3pm, Sat-Sun 10am-noon, Mon-Sat 6-10pm - Amex, BC, DC, MC, V.

Imperial Peking Harbourside, 15 Circular Quay West, The Rocks, ph 247 7073 - Licensed - good views, outdoor tables - Chinese cuisine - **Moderate** - open daily noon-3pm, Sun-Thurs 6-11pm, Fri-Sat 6pm-midnight - Amex, BC, DC, MC, V.

Phillip's Foote, 101 George Street, The Rocks, ph 241 1485 - Licensed (it is actually a pub) - cook-your-own steaks, good salad bar, outdoor tables - **Budget** - open daily for lunch and dinner - Amex, BC, DC, MC, V.

Rockpool, 109 George Street, City, ph 252 1888 - Licensed - restaurant downstairs, oyster bar upstairs - modern Australian cuisine - **Expensive** - open Mon-Fri noon-2.30pm, Mon-Sat 6.30-10pm, oyster bar also Mon-Sat 10-11pm - Amex, BC, DC, MC, V.

Rossini Rosticceria, Shop W5, Circular Quay, ph 247 8026 - Licensed - good views, outside tables - Italian, cafeteria style - **Budget** - open daily 7-10.30am, 11am-4pm, 5-10.30pm - no credit cards accepted.

Paragon Cafe, 1st Floor, Paragon Hotel, Circular Quay, ph 241 3888 - Licensed - Modern cuisine - **Moderate** - open Mon-Fri noon-3pm, Mon-Sat 6.30-10pm - Amex, BC, MC, V.

Merrony's, 2 Albert Street, Circular Quay, ph 247 9323 - Licensed - Australian/French - **Moderate** - open Mon-Fri noon-2.30pm, Mon-Sat 5.45-11.45pm, Sun 5.45-10pm - Amex, BC, DC, MC, V.

Macquarie's, 123 Macquarie Street, City, ph 247 3210 - Licensed - Modern Australian - **Moderate** - open Mon-Fri noon-2.30pm, Mon-Sat 5.30-10pm - Amex, BC, MC.

EJ's, 143 Macquarie Street, City (lower ground floor), ph 247 8968 - Licensed - cuisine is a bit of everything from everywhere - **Moderate** - open for lunch only Mon-Fri noon-2.30pm - Amex, BC, DC, MC, V.

Claudine's on Macquarie, 151 Macquarie Street, City, ph 241 1749 - Licensed & BYO - Seafood/French - **Moderate** - open Mon-Fri 7.30-11.30am, noon-3pm, 5.30-8.30pm - Amex, BC, DC, MC, V.

Botanic Gardens Restaurant, once in the Gardens, follow the signs, ph 241 2419 - Licensed & BYO - good views - casual dining, outdoor tables - **Moderate** - open daily noon-3.30pm - BC, MC, V.

Central Park Bar & Grill, MLC Centre, Martin Place, City, ph 233 1094 - Licensed - Australian, outdoor tables - **Moderate** - open Mon-Fri noon-3pm, 5-8.30pm - Amex, BC, DC, MC, V.

Bridges, 4 Bridge Street, City, ph 221 5862 - Licensed - Southern Mediterranean cuisine - **Moderate** - open Mon-Fri noon-2.30pm, 6-9pm - Amex, BC, DC, MC, V.

Condor, 5 York Street, City, ph 299 8686 - BYO (no corkage fee) - Japanese cuisine, outdoor tables, very small - **Budget** - open daily 11.30am-midnight - no credit cards accepted.

Papillon, 71 York Street, City, ph 262 2624 - Licensed - French cuisine - **Expensive** - open Mon-Fri noon-3pm, Tues-Fri 6-9pm - Amex, BC, DC, MC, V.

King Street Curry House, 29 King Street, City, ph 299 7049 - BYO (no corkage fee) - Malaysian cuisine - **Budget** - open Mon-Fri noon-3pm, Tues-Fri 6-10pm - BC, MC.

Kamogawa, Corn Exchange Building, cnr Sussex & Market Streets, City, ph 299 5533 - Licensed - Japanese, with teppan bar, traditional rooms and conventional dining area - **Moderate to Expensive,** depending on locale - open daily 6.30-10am, 6-10pm, Mon-Sat noon-3pm, karaoke bar Mon-Fri 8.30pm-1am - Amex, BC, DC, MC, V.

Choys Jin Jiang, 2nd floor, Queen Victoria Building, City, ph 261 3388 - Licensed - Chinese - **Moderate** - open daily noon-3pm, Sun-Mon 5.30-10pm, Tues-Thurs 5.30-11pm, Fri-Sat 5.30pm-midnight - Amex, BC, DC, MC, V.

Ying's, 35 Goulburn Street, City, ph 281 2881 - Licensed - Cantonese seafood - **Budget** - open daily noon-4am - Amex, BC, DC, MC, V.

Chinatown (Haymarket)

Golden Harbour, 31 Dixon Street, ph 212 5987 - Licensed & BYO (corkage fee $4 per bottle) - Cantonese - **Budget** - open Mon-Fri 10am-4.30pm, 5.30-11pm, Sat-Sun 9am-4.30pm, 5.30pm-1am - Amex, BC, DC, MC, V.

Emperor's Garden, 96-100 Hay Street, ph 211 2135 - Licensed - Chinese - **Budget** - open daily 8am-2am - Amex, BC, DC, MC, V.

House of Guangzhou, 76 Ultimo Road, ph 281 2205 - Licensed - Chinese - **Budget** - open Mon-Fri 11.30am-3pm, Sat-Sun noon-3pm, daily 5.30pm-2am - Amex, BC, DC, MC, V.

Marigold Citymark, Levels 4 & 5, 683-689 George Street, ph 281 3388 - Licensed & BYO (corkage fee $1.50 per person) - Cantonese - **Moderate** - open daily 10am-3pm, 5.30pm-midnight - Amex, BC, DC, MC, V.

Bali Bagoes, 1st floor, Prince Centre, 8 Quay Street, ph 281 3017 - Licensed & BYO (corkage fee $1 per bottle) - Indonesian - **Budget** - open daily 11am-11pm - Amex, BC, DC, MC, V.

Jing May, 1st floor, Prince Centre, 8 Quay Street, ph 281 2387 - BYO - Chinese - **Budget** - open Mon-Tues, Thurs-Sun 11am-11pm - no credit cards accepted.

Malaya, 761 George Street, ph 211 0946 - Licensed - Malaysian cuisine - **Budget** - open daily noon-3pm, Mon-Sat 5-10pm, Sun 5-9pm - Amex, BC, DC, MC, V.

East of the city

East Sydney

Beppi's, cnr Yurong & Stanley Streets, ph 360 4558 - Licensed - Italian cuisine - **Expensive** - open Mon-Fri noon-3pm, Mon-Sat 6-11.30pm - Amex, BC, DC, MC, V.

Yutaka, 200 Crown Street, ph 361 3818 - Licensed & BYO (corkage fee $1 per person) - Japanese cuisine - **Moderate** - open Mon-Fri noon-2.15pm, Mon-Sat 6-10.45pm, Sun 6-10pm - Amex, BC. MC, V.

Tre Scalini, 174 Liverpool Street, ph 331 4358 - Licensed - Italian cuisine - **Expensive** - open Mon-Fri noon-2.30pm, Mon-Sat 6-10.30pm - Amex, BC, MC, V.

Fine Bouche, 191 Palmer Street, ph 331 4821 - Licensed - French cuisine - **Expensive** - open Mon-Fri noon-3pm, Mon-Sat 7-11pm - Amex, BC, DC, MC, V.

Ristorante Mario, 71-73 Stanley Street, ph 331 4945 - Licensed - Italian cuisine - **Expensive** - open Mon-Fri noon-3pm, Mon-Sat 6.30-11pm - BC, MC, V.

No Names, 2 Chapel Street, ph 360 4711 - BYO - Italian pasta and minestrone - **Budget** - open for lunch and dinner - no credit cards accepted. There are several *No Names* restaurants around Sydney, but this is the original, and most people think it is still the best.

Darlinghurst

Rogues Streetons, 16-18 Oxford Street, ph 332 1718 - Licensed - Australian, outdoor tables - **Expensive** - open Mon-Fri noon-3pm, Mon-Wed 7-11pm, Thurs-Sat 7pm-midnight, Sun 6.30-10pm - Amex, BC, DC, MC, V.

Chat Thai, 285 Liverpool Street, ph 361 5123 - Licensed & BYO (corkage fee $1.50 per person) - Thai cuisine, outdoor tables - **Budget** - open Mon-Fri noon-2.30pm, Sun-Thurs 5.30-10pm, Fri-Sat 5.30-11.30pm - Amex, BC, MC, V.

32 Bar & Grill, 32 Burton Street, ph 332 3232 - Licensed - the name says it all - **Moderate** - open Tues-Fri noon-3pm, Sun 11am-3pm, daily 6.30pm-midnight - Amex, BC, MC, V.

Metro Cafe, 26 Burton Street, ph 361 5356 - BYO - Vegetarian cuisine - **Budget** - open Wed-Fri 6pm-midnight, Sun 6-11pm - no credit cards accepted.

Geronimo's, 294 Crown Street, Darlinghurst, ph 331 3001 - BYO (corkage fee 50c per person) - Indian cuisine - **Budget** - open Thurs-Fri noon-2.30pm, Tues-Sun 6-11pm - BC, MC, V.

Taylor Square Restaurant, 2a Flinders Street, ph 360 5828 - Licensed & BYO - Brasserie - **Moderate** - open Mon-Sat 6.30-11pm, Sun 6-11pm - BC, MC, V.

Adriatic Grill, 201 Oxford Street, ph 360 4792 - Licensed & BYO - Mediterranean cuisine - **Budget** - open Mon-Sat 6pm-midnight - Amex, BC, MC, V.

Angkor Wat, 227 Oxford Street, ph 360 5500 - Licensed & BYO (corkage fee $1 per person) - Cambodian cuisine - **Budget** - open Tues-Fri noon-2.30pm, daily 6-11pm - Amex, BC, MC, V.

Oh Calcutta, 251 Victoria Street, ph 360 3650 - BYO - Indian cuisine - **Budget** - open Thurs-Fri 12.30-2pm, daily 6-10.30pm - Amex, BC, MC, V.

Kings Cross

The Last Aussie Fishcaf, 24 Bayswater Road, ph 356 2911 - Licensed - Seafood plus live music, outdoor tables - **Moderate** - open Mon-Sat 6-11.30pm - Amex, BC, DC, MC, V.

Hanaya, 42 Kellett Street, ph 356 4222 - Licensed - Japanese cuisine - **Moderate** - open Sun-Thurs 6-11pm, Fri-Sat 6pm-midnight - Amex, BC, DC, MC, V.

Bayswater Brasserie, 32 Bayswater Road, ph 357 2177 - Licensed - changing menu, outdoor tables - **Moderate** - open daily noon-midnight, Sat-Sun 9am-noon - BC, MC, V.

Han II, 227 Victoria Street, ph 331 3944 - Licensed - Korean cuisine - **Moderate** - open Mon-Fri noon-3pm, daily 6-11pm - Amex, BC, DC, MC, V.

Potts Point

Trianon Challis Avenue, 29 Challis Avenue, Potts Point, ph 358 1353 - Licensed - French, outdoor tables - **Expensive** - open Mon-Sat 7pm-midnight - Amex, BC, DC, MC, V.

Macleay Street Bistro, 73A Macleay Street, ph 358 4891 - BYO (corkage fee $2 per bottle) - steak/seafood, outdoor tables - **Moderate** - open Tues-Sun noon-3pm, 6.30-11pm - BC, MC, V.

La Strada, 95 Macleay Street, ph 358 1160 - Licensed - Italian cuisine - **Expensive** - open Mon-Sat 6-10.30pm - Amex, BC, DC, MC, V.

Antipodes, 44 Macleay Street, ph 358 1322 - Licensed & BYO (corkage fee $2 per person) - menu has just about everything - **Moderate** - open Mon-Sat noon-2.30pm, 6-11pm, Sat 8am-noon - Amex, BC, DC, MC, V.

Mezzaluna, 123 Victoria Street, ph 357 1988 - Licensed & BYO (corkage fee $3.50 per person) - Australian cuisine, outdoor tables, good views - **Moderate** - open Tues-Fri noon-3pm, Tues-Sat 6-11pm, Sun 11am-3pm, 6-10pm - Amex, BC, DC, MC, V.

Mere Catherine, 146 Victoria Street, ph 358 3862 - BYO - French cuisine - **Moderate** - open Tues-Sat 7pm-midnight - Amex, BC, MC, V.

Double Bay

George's, 419 New South Head Road, ph 327 3672 - Licensed & BYO - International cuisine, outdoor tables - **Moderate** - open daily from 8am for breakfast, noon-2.30pm, 5pm-midnight, Fri-Sat until 2am - Amex, BC, DC, MC, V.

Twenty-One Espresso, 21 Knox Street, ph 327 2616 - Licensed & BYO - Middle European cuisine, outdoor tables - **Budget** - Amex, BC, MC, V.

Bukhara, 55 Bay Street, ph 363 5510 - Licensed & BYO (corkage fee $1 per person) - Indian cuisine, outdoor tables - **Moderate** - open Thurs-Sat noon-2.30pm, Tues-Sun 5.30-10.30pm - Amex, BC, DC, MC, V.

Cleveland, 63 Bay Street, ph 327 6877 - Licensed - Szechuan/Vegetarian cuisine - **Expensive** - open daily noon-3pm, Sun-Thurs 6-11pm, Fri Sat 6pm-midnight - Amex, BC, DC, MC, V.

Cafe Donini, 46 Cross Street, ph 328 7142 - Licensed & BYO (corkage fee $3 per bottle) - Italian cusine, outdoor tables - open daily 10am-midnight (supper served from 10.30pm).

North of the city

North Sydney

Armstrong's, 1 Napier Street, ph 957 3011 - Licensed - Australian cuisine, outdoor tables - **Expensive** - open Mon-Fri noon-4pm, Mon-Sat 6-10.30pm - Amex, BC, MC, V.

L'Incontro, 196 Miller Street, ph 957 2274 - Licensed - Italian cuisine, outside tables - **Expensive** - open Mon-Fri noon-3pm, Mon-Sat 6-10.30pm - Amex, BC, DC, MC, V.

Imperial Eagle Peking, 146 Arthur Street, ph 954 1988 - Licensed - Northern Chinese cuisine, outdoor tables - **Budget** - open daily noon-3pm, 6pm-late - Amex, BC, DC, MC, V.

Arizona, 110 Walker Street, ph 954 0488 - Licensed - Mexican cuisine - **Budget** - open Mon-Fri noon-midnight, Mon-Sat 6pm-midnight - Amex, BC, DC, MC, V.

Crows Nest

La Goulue, 17 Alexander Street, ph 439 1640 - BYO (corkage fee $2 per person) - French cuisine - **Expensive** - open Tues-Sat from 6.30pm - Amex, BC, DC, MC, V.

Rangoon Racquet Club, 70 Alexander Street, ph 906 4091 - Licensed - Indian, Sri Lanka, etc - **Moderate** - open Mon-Fri noon-3pm, Mon-Sat 6-10.30pm - Amex, BC, DC, MC, V.

The Red Centre, 70 Alexander Street, ph 906 4408 - Licensed - Pizzas - **Budget** - open Mon-Fri 11am-11.30pm, Sat 5-11.30pm - Amex, BC, MC, V.

La Grillade, cnr Albany & Alexander Streets, ph 439 3707 - Licensed - French cuisine, outdoor tables - **Expensive** - open Mon-Fri noon-3.30pm, Mon-Sun 6.30-10.30pm - Amex, BC, DC, MC, V.

Montezuma's, 51 Alexander Street, ph 901 3533 - Licensed - Mexican cuisine - **Moderate** - open daily noon-3pm, 5.30-11pm - BC, MC, V.

Neutral Bay

Fiorentino, 24 Young Street, ph 908 1320 - Licensed - Italian cuisine - **Expensive** - open Mon-Fri noon-3pm, Mon-Sat 6-11pm - Amex, BC, MC, V.

Cafe Sante, The Grove, 5/174 Military Road, ph 953 0569 - BYO (corkage fee $1 per bottle) - Australian cuisine, outdoor tables - **Budget** - open daily 9am-6pm, Wed-Sat 6.30-10pm - BC, MC, V.

Karma Indian Brasserie, 24 Young Street, ph 953 9870 - Licensed & BYO (corkage fee $1.50 per person) - Indian cuisine - **Budget** - open Mon-Fri noon-2.30pm, daily 6-11pm - Amex, BC, DC, MC, V.

Mosman

Mosman Seafood Cafe, 886 Military Road, ph 969 3841 - Licensed & BYO (corkage fee $1.50 per person) - **Moderate** - open Mon-Fri noon-3pm, Mon-Sat 5.30-10.30pm, Sun noon-9pm - Amex, BC, DC, MC, V.

Mosman Malaysian Restaurant, 523 Military Road, ph 969 9275 - BYO (no corkage fee) - Malaysian and Thai cuisine - **Budget** - open daily 5-11.30pm - Amex, BC, MC, V.

Boronia House, 624 Military Road, ph 969 2099 - Licensed - French cuisine - **Expensive** - open Mon-Sat 6.30pm-midnight - Amex, BC, DC, MC, V.

5 Nippers, 634 Military Road, ph 960 2443 - Licensed & BYO (corkage fee $1.50 per bottle) - seafood/steak - **Moderate** - open Wed-Fri from noon, Tues-Sun 6-9.30pm - Amex, BC, DC, MC, V.

Algiers, 543a Military Road, ph 969 9676 - BYO (no corkage fee) - North African/Mediterranean - **Budget** - open daily 6pm-late - Amex, BC, DC, MC, V.

Cafe Paradiso, Shop 2, 5 Spit Road, ph 968 2828 - BYO (no corkage fee) - Italian - **Budget** - open Tues-Sun noon-midnight - BC, MC, V.

Fresh Ketch, 77A Parriwi Road, ph 969 5665 - Licensed - Seafood, good views - **Expensive** - open Mon-Sat noon-2.30pm, 6-9.30pm, Sun noon-8.30pm - Amex, BC, DC, MC, V.

Balmoral

Beaches, 51 The Esplanade, Balmoral Beach, ph 969 7704 - Licensed & BYO (corkage fee $1.50 per person) - Australian cuisine, good views - **Moderate** - open Mon-Fri noon-3pm, Mon-Sat 6.30-10pm - Amex, BC, DC, MC, V.

The Bathers Pavilion, 4 The Esplanade, ph 968 1133 - Licensed - Australian cuisine, on the beach front, outdoor tables - **Expensive** - Amex, BC, MC, V.

West of the city

Glebe

The Mixing Pot, 178 St John's Road, ph 660 7449 - Licensed & BYO (corkage fee $1.50 per person) - Italian cuisine, outdoor tables - **Expensive** - open Mon-Fri noon-2.30pm, Mon-Sat 6-10pm - Amex, BC, DC, MC, V.

Darling Mills, 134 Glebe Point Road, ph 660 5666 - Licensed & BYO (corkage fee $2.50 per person, or $3 per bottle) - International cuisine - **Expensive** - open Tues-Fri noon-3pm, daily 6-10.30pm - Amex, BC, DC, MC, V.

Rose Blues, 23 Glebe Point Road, ph 552 2105 - BYO (corkage fee $1 per bottle) - extensive menu, outdoor tables - **Budget** - open daily 9am-midnight - BC, MC, V.

Tanjore, 34 Glebe Point Road, ph 660 6332 - BYO (corkage fee $1 per bottle) - Indian cuisine - **Budget** - open Tues-Sun noon-3pm, daily 5.30-11pm - Amex, BC, DC, MC, V.

The Abbey, 156-160 Bridge Road, ph 660 4792 - Licensed - Italian cuisine in a converted church - **Expensive** - open Mon-Sat 6pm-midnight - Amex, BC, DC, MC, V.

Newtown

Thai Land, 74-78 King Street, ph 516 1127 - BYO - **Budget** - open Mon-Fri noon-2.30pm, daily 6-10.30pm - Amex, BC, MC, V.

The Pensione Sydney, 25-27 Georgina Street, ph 550 1700 - BYO (corkage fee $2 per person) - Australian, outdoor tables - **Expensive** - open Wed-Sat 6.30-10.30pm - Amex, BC, MC, V.

Singapore Gourmet, 520 King Street, ph 550 6453 - BYO (no corkage fee) - Singaporean cuisine - **Budget** - open daily 5-10pm - no credit cards accepted.

Thai Pothong, 298 King Street, ph 550 6277 - Licensed & BYO (corkage fee $1 per person) - **Budget** - open Mon-Fri noon-3pm, Sun-Thurs 6-10.30pm, Fri-Sat 6-11pm - Amex, BC, DC, MC, V.

Indian Village, 194 King Street, ph 516 1358 - BYO - **Budget** - open daily 6-11.30pm - BC, MC, V.

Taverna To Steki, 2 O'Connell Street, ph 516 2191 - Licensed Fri-Sun, BYO Wed-Thurs (corkage fee $1.50 per person) - Greek cuisine - **Budget** - open Wed-Sun 6.30-10pm - BC, MC, V.

Annandale

Princess Nisha's, 215 Parramatta Road, ph 569 8884 - Licensed & BYO (corkage fee $1 per person) - Indian cuisine - **Budget** - open Tues-Thurs & Sun 6-10pm, Fri-Sat 6-11pm - BC, MC, V.

Villani's Brasserie, 127 Booth Street, ph 660 6652 - Licensed & BYO - Italian cuisine - **Moderate** - open Mon-Sat 5.30-11pm - Amex, BC, MC, V.

Sushi Bar Rashai, 241 Parramatta Road, ph 560 3007 - Japanese cuisine - **Budget** - open Tues-Sun 6-10.30pm - Amex, BC, MC, V.

Leichhardt

La Rustica, 435 Parramatta Road, ph 569 5824 - Licensed & BYO (corkage fee $2 per bottle) - Italian cuisine - **Moderate** - open Mon-Sat noon-3pm, 6-10pm - Amex, BC, DC, MC, V.

Antica Osteria, 153 Norton Street, ph 564 2198 - BYO - Italian cuisine, live music - **Moderate** - open Mon-Fri noon-2.30pm, Mon-Sat 6-10pm - BC, MC, V.

Numero Tre, 159 Norton Street, ph 560 9129 - BYO (corkage fee 50c per person) - Italian cuisine, outdoor tables - **Moderate** - open Tues-Sun 6-10.30pm - BC, MC, V.

Balmain

The Manor House, 393 Darling Street, ph 810 4914 - Licensed - International cuisine - **Expensive** - open Mon-Fri noon-3pm, Mon-Sat 6.30-10.30pm - Amex, BC, DC, MC, V.

Le Bich, 386 Darling Street, ph 555 1068 - BYO - Vietnamese cuisine - **Budget** - open Tues-Sun 6-10.30pm - BC, MC, V.

Manjit's, 360 Darling Street, ph 818 3681 - BYO - Indian cuisine - **Moderate** - open Mon-Fri noon-2.30pm, daily 5.30-11.00pm - Amex, BC, DC, MC, V.

Riverview Hotel, 29 Birchgrove Road, ph 810 1151 - Licensed - International cuisine - **Expensive** - open Wed-Fri noon-3pm, Tues-Sat 7-10pm - BC, MC, V.

Jiyu No Omise, 342 Darling Street, ph 818 3886 - Licensed & BYO - Japanese cuisine - **Moderate** - open daily 6.30-11pm - Amex, BC, DC, MC, V.

Jewel of India, 9 Beattie Street, ph 810 5008 - Licensed & BYO (corkage fee $1 per person) - Indian cuisine, outdoor tables - **Budget** - open daily 5.30-10.30pm - Amex, BC, DC, MC, V.

Cruising Restaurants

Captain Cook Cruises, ph 251 5007, have lunch and dinner options. Cruise 2 is the *Captain Cook Luncheon Cruise*, which departs Darling Harbour at 11.55am. The cruise lasts 1 1/2 hours and includes a Buffet Luncheon featuring Sydney rock oysters, Tasmanian trout, rare roast beef, ham, chicken, fresh salads, fruit platters and Australian cheeses - **$36 adult, $29 child.**

Cruise 5 is the *Captain Cook Showtime Dinner Cruise* called "Under The Southern Cross" and features a 3 course limited a la carte dinner and show. The cruise leaves from Wharf 6 Circular Quay at 7pm. The cruises on Tues, Wed, Thurs & Sun finish at 9.30pm, but on Fri and Sat they continue until 11pm, and offer dancing with the showtime band. **The cost is $72**, and reservations are essential.

The John Cadman Cruising Restaurant cruises every night of the year and departs Wharf 6 Circular Quay at 7.30pm, and Jeffrey Street Wharf, Kirribilli at 7.45pm. It returns at 11pm. The a la carte menu is prepared by international chefs, and there is a selection of Australian and imported wines. **Cost of the dinner cruise is $72,** and reservations are essential, ph 922 1922.

Sail Venture Cruises, have luncheon and dinner cruises on their Big Cats, with changing menus. The luncheon cruise departs Darling Harbour Aquarium Wharf at 12.15pm (returning at 2.25pm) and Campbells Cove, Circular Quay, at 12.35pm (returning at 2.05pm) - **$35 adult, $18 child.**

The dinner cruise departs Darling Harbour at 7pm (returning at 10.10pm) and Campbells Cove at 7.30pm (returning at 9.45pm) - **$48 adult, $25 children**.
For reservations and enquiries, ph 262 3595.

Matilda Cruises serve lunch on their two-hour harbour cruises, which leave Darling Harbour Aquarium Wharf at 11.30am and 1.30pm, Campbells Cove Circular Quay at 11.45am and 1.45pm, and Taronga Zoo at 12.45pm and 2.45pm. **The cruises cost $22 adult, $12 children,** and an **Aussie Bar-B-Q lunch cooked on board costs an extra $8.50.** Reservations are necessary, ph 264 7377.

Matilda Cruises also operate the *Solway Lass,* a tall ship, which has a luncheon sail departing daily from Darling Harbour Aquarium Wharf at 12.15pm (boarding at noon) and returning at 1.45pm - **$35 adults, $18 children.** The dinner cruise *Dine Under-Canvas,* sails Fri and Sat, boarding at 6.30pm, sailing at 7pm, and returning at 10pm - carvery dinner, with fully stocked bar and wine cellar - **$45 adults.** Bookings are essential, ph 264 7377.

Bounty Cruises have lunch and dinner cruises aboard the tall ship *Bounty,* and they always guarantee that part of the cruise will be under sail. The cruises leave from Campbells Cove Wharf, where you can also inspect the *Bounty,* which is a replica of the one that Captain Blight sailed on and was built for the movie *Mutiny on The Bounty.* The lunch cruise departs on Sat, Sun and public holidays at 12.30pm, and the dinner cruise on Fri and Sat (and Sun of a long weekend) at 7pm. Both cruises offer **buffet-style meals and cost $45 adult,** with 50% discount for children 5-15.Children under 5 years sail free. For reservations, ph 247 1789.

Don't think for one moment that the above lists all the restaurants in Sydney. It is little more than the tip of the iceberg. Often you will find restaurants in the same street as the one listed here, which we have not included. The above does, however, give you somewhere to start. On weekends, it is a wise idea to phone ahead and book a table.

In case you are wondering about the availability of a Big Mac, be reassured that there are nine *McDonald's* in the city, and more than seventy sprinkled throughout the suburbs.

Pizza Hut has two city branches, and about thirty-five in the suburbs; and while "the Colonel" only has one *KFC* in the city, the suburbs are blessed with seventy-six outlets.

ENTERTAINMENT

As mentioned in the Introduction chapter, the Friday edition of *The Sydney Morning Herald* has the comprehensive "Metro" lift-out which lists what's on at all of Sydney's night spots.

It would be lengthy and boring to list all the venues in the city and suburbs, so we took a survey amongst a group of Sydney ragers and the following are their favorites.

NIGHT CLUBS

 City

Julianas, Hilton International Hotel, 259 Pitt Street, ph 266 0610.
  Hours: Tues-Sat, 9pm-3am
  Cover charge: Tues-Thurs free entry
          Fri $10
          Sat $10 9-10pm, $15 after 10pm.
  Age Group: 25 - 30 years.

Bar Luna, Jackson's on George, 176 George Street, ph 247 2605.
The Club is upstairs in the restaurant.
  Hours: Tues-Sat, 10pm-5am (restaurant service ceases 9.30pm).
  Cover charge: $5 after 10pm, Fri-Sat.
  Age Group: 18 years+.

Harbourside Brasserie, Pier One, Millers Point, ph 252 3000.
  Hours: Mon-Fri 6pm-2am, Sat 6pm-4am, Sun 6pm-10pm, dinner to 11pm.
  Live Entertainment: 7 nights
  Cover charge: $7-$20 depending on act.
  Dinner and show: $45
The Harbourside brasserie has two cocktail bars and commands sweeping views of Sydney Harbour.

Paragon Hotel, cnr Loftus & Alfred Streets, ph 241 3522.
Hours: Fri-Sat, noon-5am (restaurant service ceases Fri 9.30pm, Sat 9pm - restaurant is also open Mon-Thurs).
Cover charge: Sat $10 after 9pm.
Age Group: Fri - business crowd; later - 18 years+;
Sat - 18-30 years

Orient Hotel, cnr Argyle & George Streets, ph 251 1255.
Hours: Fri-Sat 9.30pm-3am (entertainment every night of the week but hours on other nights are shorter).
Cover charge: free entry
Age Group: 20-30 years.
Nightclub and live bands set out over three spacious floors.

Neo Pharaoh, cnr King & Sussex Streets, ph 299 3777 (office hours 299 8777).
Hours: Mon-Sat 6pm-3am or 4am. Restaurant is open 6pm-10 or 11pm, and dinner includes cover charge.
Cover charge: Mon-Thurs $10
Sat-Sun $15
After 8.30pm $5.
Age Group: Wednesday 19-20 years (Wednesday is casual night)
Thursday 19-30 years (Jazz night)
Other nights 25-30 years.

Darling Harbour

Bobby McGees Conglomeration, 377 Harbourside Festival Marketplace, Darling Harbour, ph 281 3944.
Hours: Mon-Fri 8pm-2.30am, Sat 8pm-3.30am. The restaurant is open for lunch and dinner every day, and lunch on Sunday.
Cover charge: Wed $5
Thurs-Sat $10
Age Group: varied.

Sydney Show Club, cnr Pyrmont & Allen Streets, ph 552 2722.
  Hours: Nightly, dinner from 7pm, showtime 8.30pm-9.40pm,
  second show 11pm, open until 3am.
  Cover charge: Dinner includes show: set menu $50 per person
                                      a la carte $75 per person
              Second show: plus supper $20.00 per person
              show only $11 cover charge
  Age Group: 25 years+

East of the City

Kings Cross

Site Nite Club, 171 Victoria Street, ph 358 6511.
  Hours: Thurs-Sat 11pm-4am, Sun 7pm-12am
  Cover charge: $7.00
  Thur night: 70's night
  The site is renowned for its theme nights, and is a fun place to
  dance.
  Attached bar - Soho bar - cafe and bar open noon-3am

Tom Tom Club, 22 Bayswater Road, ph 358 4676.
  Hours: Sun-Fri, dinner from 6pm, Sat 5pm, Mexican cuisine.
  Entertainment 7 nights, 10pm-late
  Entertainment ranges from rock to acoustic, dance bands and
  funk/rock. Saturday night is Jungle, hard rock, Sunday DJ.
  Cover charge: applicable after 10pm.
  Age group: 20-35 years
  Monday is to become Fiesta night with Maracas, Mambos, etc
  Formerly known as the Kardohmah Cafe.

Studebakers, 33 Bayswater Road, ph 358 5656.
  Hours: Tues-Fri 5pm-2am, Sat 8pm-3am, Sunday 5pm-midnight
  complimentary supper 5pm-9pm.
  Cover charge: Tues - $10, ladies' drinks free; Wed-Thur - $6
              Fri-Sat - $8, after 8pm $12
  Studebakers is set up as a 1950s American style cafe, with waiters
  and waitresses dressed to suit the era.
  Age group: 20-35 years

Darlinghurst

Kinselas, 383 Bourke Street, 331 2699 (Box office and general enquiries ph 331 3299, 331 6200).
Hours: Mon-Sat 5pm-3am, Sun 3pm-12am, dinner is light cafe food from the bar. Each bar is situated on a different floor.
Cover charge: Club bar - no cover charge
Nightclub - cover charge from $5 - $20
Comedy and cabaret shows
Age group: all ages
This building was once Kinsela's Funeral Parlour.

Rogues, 16 Oxford Street, ph 332 1718.
Hours: Wed-Sat 9pm-4am, restaurant from 6pm
Cover charge: $10, membership first priority
Age group: 20-35 years

Paddington

The Freezer, 11 Oxford Street, Paddington, ph 332 2568.
Hours: Nightly 9pm-3am, Dinner ceases at 10pm
Cover charge: variable
Age Group: 18-35 years

Potts Point

Tunnel Night Club, 1 Earl Place, ph 358 1519.
Hours: Wed-Thurs 8pm-3am, Fri 6pm-4am, Sat 8pm-5am
Happy hour: 6pm - 2 half price drinks and hot and cold buffet.
Cover charge: Fri-Sun - $10
Wed-Thurs - $8
Age group: 25 years+

Test Tube Factory, 118 Macleay Street, ph 358 1122.
Hours: Mon-Sat 5:30pm-7am, Sun 5pm-12, restaurant 6pm
Cocktail bar and Nightclub
Cover charge: free entry
Age group: 18-35 years

Shots of tequila, sambucca, etc, are served in test tubes, the waitresses are dressed as nurses, and the interior is done with fluorescent paint to add to the scene.

Bondi Junction

Players, 209 Oxford Street, ph 389 5051.
Hours: Mon-Sat 8am-3am, Sun 11am-3am, dinner served till 3am, a la carte menu.
Happy hour: Mon-Sat before 10pm
Cover charge: free entry to nightclub
Age Group: 25-40 years
Players is situated on three floors and the nightclub gets going around 11pm after the Happy Hour.

Coogee

Selina's, Coogee Bay Hotel, 253 Coogee Bay Road, ph 665 0000.
Hours: Mon-Fri, Sat-Sun 8pm-3am, garden bar, restaurant from 6pm, bistro.
Sat-Sun - local and international bands
Cover charge: $6-$7 - local bands
$20-$25 - international bands
One of the most popular venues to see local and international bands.

North of the city

Chatswood

The Great Northern Hotel, 522 Pacific Hwy, 419 4555.
Hours: Mon-Sat 10am-12am, Sun 12am-10pm, dinner ceases at 9pm.
Live entertainment nightly, except Tuesday,
Cover charge: $5-$10, cocktail bar, beer garden, public bar.
The Northern is fast becoming the place on the North Shore for live music with local bands taking the stage.

Manly

The Old Manly Boatshed, Pig & Whistle, 40 The Corso,
ph 977 4443.
Hours: Mon-Sun 6pm-3am, dinner till 10pm in restaurant.
Live entertainment nightly downstairs in the Pig & Whistle,
Cover charge: $5-$7.

North Sydney

Metropolis, cnr Walker & Mount Streets, ph 954 3599.
Hours: Mon-Fri, Mon: noon-3am, Tues 8:30pm-5am,
Wed - Functions,
Thurs 8:30pm-3am, Fri noon-5am, Sat noon-3am, dinner Fri-Sat
from 7:30, bookings advised.
Cover charge: $10
Tues - lunacy night 18-20 years
Thurs - bands
Age group: 18-25 years

Blueberrys Brasserie, 107 Mount Street, ph 954 4919.
Hours: Mon-Thurs noon-3am, Fri noon-5am, Sat 6pm-5am,
lunch dinner noon-midnight.
Cover charge: Free entry
Age group: 19-35 years
Frequented by the Advertising crowd who work in the vicinity.

Cremorne

Steps Night Spot, 305 Military Road, Cremorne, ph 909 8888.
Hours: Tues 9pm-3am, Wed 9pm-12, Thurs-Sat 9pm-3am.
Cover charge: Free Entry
Age Group: 18-35 years (Thurs - 18-23 years)
Steps is located in the Metropole which has a large pool hall and
Minskys cocktail/piano bar.

Epping

Tracks Nightclub, 58 Beecroft Road, ph 876 1305.
  Hours: Tues-Wed 7pm-3am, Thurs-Sat 8pm-3am,
  dinner Bistro from 6pm.
  Cover charge: Nightclub Mon-Thurs free before 8pm
                                    Fri-Sat - $5
  Age group: 18-40 years

BARS & BISTROS

City

King Georges Tavern, cnr King & George Streets, ph 232 3144.
  Hours: Mon-Thur noon-2am, Fri noon-5am, Sat 6pm-5am,
  lunch and dinner (service ceases at 8.30pm).
  Happy Hour: Mon-Thurs 5pm-6.30pm, Fri 5pm-7pm.
  Nightclub: Fri 10pm-3am, Sat 9pm-5am
  Blue Bar: Fri live music
  Cover charge: Free Entry
  Age Group: all ages

On Tuesdays nights during school holidays, the tavern becomes
completely non-alcoholic, and a good night out is had by the under
18 fraternity. **No one over 18 is admitted.**

Brooklyn Hotel, 225 George Street, ph 247 6808.
  Hours: Mon-Fri 7am-midnight, Sat 4pm-midnight
  Happy Hour: 5pm-8pm promotional, Bar Snacks available
  Age group - Weekdays: business crowd
                        Weekends: younger crowd
  Nightclub - sometime in 1993

Lucy's Tavern, 54 Castlereagh Street, ph 221 3908.
  Hours: Mon-Thurs 10am-11pm, Fri-Sat 10am-2am
  Happy Hour: Fri 5pm-7pm & Sat 8pm-10pm
  Nightclub: Fri-Sat 8pm-3am
  Strip floorshow night: Wednesday

Cover charge: Free entry
Age group: 25-35 years (well known but you can find better).

Marble Bar, Hilton Hotel, Pitt Street, ph 266 0610.
   Hours: Mon-Thurs 4pm-11pm, Fri 4pm-2am, Sat 5pm-2am
   Happy Hour: Mon-Fri 4pm-5pm.
   Night Club and live bands
   Cover charge: Fri-Sat $5
The Marble bar was built by George Adams, founder of Tatts Lotto.
When the Hotel was being refurbished by the new owners, the
Marble Bar was dismantled stone by stone and rebuilt on the
completion of the Hotel that stands today.

Arizona, 150 Day Street, ph 261 4444.
   Hours: Mon-Fri noon-11pm, lunch and dinner.
   Sat-Sun 4pm-11pm.
   Happy Hour 5pm-7pm
   Cover charge: Free entry
   Live entertainment: Thurs-Sat
   Age Group: 25-40 years (not a young crowd)
Set with a Western theme. The floor is scattered with the discarded
shells of peanuts, which are located around the bar in barrels to eat
at your leisure. The bar runs various interesting competitions, e.g.
swallowing the mescal worm which is found at the bottom of a
bottle of mescal tequila, without drinking the tequila.

Customs House, Ramada Hotel, 30 Pitt Street, ph 259 7000.
   Hours: Mon-Thurs 10am-10pm, Fri 10am-11pm
   (closed weekends). Lunch is served from noon-2pm, there is
   no dinner service.
   Happy Hour: 4-5pm
The bar is at the rear of the hotel and opens onto Macquarie Place
Park where, in summer, a crowd of business people spend their
Friday evenings.

Woolloomooloo Bay Hotel, 2 Bourke Street, ph 357 1177.
   Hours: Mon-Sat 10am-11pm, Sun 11pm-9pm, bistro lunch
   and dinner 12pm-9pm.
   Live entertainment Fri-Sun

Cover charge: Free entry
Fri: 7.30-11pm - live music
Sat: 7:30-11pm - piano bar
Sun: 5:30-9pm - live music

The Woolloomooloo is a great place to spend a Sunday afternoon in summer. The patrons spill onto the pavement outside whilst the band is playing.

Darling Harbour

Craig Brewery Bar & Grill, Festival Market Place, Darling Harbour, ph 281 3922.
Hours: Mon-Wed 10am-noon, Thurs-Sat 10am-3am.
Dinner - cook your own steaks on the barbecue.
Happy Hour: Mon-Fri 5:30-8:00pm
Nightclub: 8pm-late
Cover charge: Fri-Sat $10 after 9pm
Age Group: 18-35 years

Pumphouse Tavern Brewery, 17 Little Pier Street, Darling Harbour, ph 281 3967.
Hours: Mon-Fri 11am-late, dinner till 9pm, nightclub & live bands.
Cover charge: Free entry
Age Group: 18-30 years

The pumphouse is known for the fabulous boutique beers available on tap.

East of the city

Kings Cross

Oz Rock Cafe, 274 Victoria Street, Kings Cross, ph 360 7300.
Hours: Mon-Thurs 11am-midnight, Fri-Sat 11am-3am, dinner till 10pm.
Cover charge: Thurs-Sat $10 - live entertainment (Sat nightclub)
Age Group: 18-35 years

The Oz Rock has five floors which range from rock memorabilia, to a nightclub to a cafe.

Bourbon & Beefsteak, 24 Darlinghurst Road, Kings Cross, ph 358 1144.
  Hours: 24 hrs, 7 days a week, dinner 7.30-10.30pm
  Happy Hour: every day 4-7pm
  Pianist: 4:30-9pm
  Jazz: 9pm-midnight
  Rock & Roll: 9pm-midnight
  Disco: Fri-Sat 10pm-6am
  Cover charge: Fri-Sat after 11pm.
  Age Group: All ages
The Bourbon and Beefsteak is an institution. Nearly every Sydneysider has visited the Bourbon at least once.

Darlinghurst

Burdekin Hotel, 2 Oxford Street, ph 331 3066.
  Hours: 11am-2pm, lunch & dinner 7.30-10.30pm

Hard Rock Cafe, 121-129 Crown Street, ph 331 1116.
  Hours: Sun-Thurs noon-midnight, Fri-Sat noon-2am
  Minimum charge in restaurant is $6 per person.
  Age Group: All ages

Glebe

The Harold Park Hotel, cnr Wigram Road & Ross Street, ph 692 0564.
  Hours: Mon-Sat 10am-midnight, Sun 10am-10pm
  Happy Hour: Mon-Thurs 5-6pm.
  Mon: Comedy - $5
  Tues: Literary Readings - $5
  Wed & Thurs: Theatre Play - $5
  Fri & Sat: Comedy - $10 (Politics in Park Fri 6-7pm - $2)
  Sun: Readers on Stage
  Restaurant Thurs-Sat: Theatre Comedy Musical - dinner and show $30; show only $10-$15

Paddington

London Tavern, 85 Underwood Street, ph 331 6192 (restaurant),
331 1637 (bar), 331 3213 (office).
Hours: Mon-Thurs 11am-11pm, Fri-Sat 10am-11:15pm
Happy Hour: 6:30-7:30pm; Thurs Beer Bust - cheaper beer
Dinner 6pm-10pm
Pool Tables and card machines available.
Age Group: all ages

Woollahra

Lord Dudley Hotel, Jersey Road, ph 327 5399.
Hours: Mon-Thurs 11am-11pm, Fri 11am-12am,
dinner 6.30pm-9pm.

South of the city

Surry Hills

Dolphin Hotel, 412 Crown Street, ph 357 5614.
Hours: 10am-12am
Happy Hour 1-3pm (generally beer)
Garden bistro serving lunch and dinner in the beer garden
(dinner 6pm-9pm)

North of the city

North Sydney

McGettigan's Bar & Bistro, 77 Berry Street, ph 922 7489.
Hours: Mon-Sat 11am-late, lunch 11am-2.30pm
Live entertainment and disco nightly
Cover Charge: Fri-Sat nights $5
Age group: 18-30 years

Mosman

Bridgepoint Tavern, 555 Military Road, ph 968 1355.
Hours: Sun-Wed 11am-midnight, Thurs-Sat 11am-2am,
restaurant *Food Point* noon-12am
Happy Hour: Thurs 8-11pm
Sun: Live Jazz
Thurs-Sat: Nightclub
Cover charge: $5 Fri-Sat
Age Group: 18-25 years

Chatswood

Rosie O'Grady's Tavern, 821 Pacific Highway, Chatswood,
ph 412 4411.
Hours: Mon-Tues 10am-midnight, Wed-Sat 10am-3am,
lunch noon-3pm
Happy Hour: Wed 6pm-midnight
Night Club: Mon-Wed, Fri-Sat. *Cover charge:* $5
Live Entertainment: Thurs. *Cover charge:* $6
Age group: 18-30 years

PUBS

City

Lord Nelson Brewery Hotel, 19 Kent Street, ph 251 4044.
Hours: Mon-Sat 11am-11pm, dinner 6pm-10pm
The Lord Nelson brew their own beer and have 5 unique beers from
which to choose.

Mercantile Hotel, 25 George Street, The Rocks, ph 247 3570.
Hours: Mon-Thurs 10am-midnight, Fri-Sat 10am-1am
Live Entertainment: Every night except Tuesday; Sat & Sun
afternoon.
The Mercantile is frequented by Irish travellers and is known as the
Irish Pub. It has an Irish flavour and St Patricks Day, March 17 is
a big day for the Mercantile. They even serve green beer!

The Hero of Waterloo Hotel, 81 Lower Fort Street, ph 252 4553.
   Hours: Mon-Sat 10am-11pm, Sun 10am-10pm, snack bar served
   over the counter.
Museum downstairs shows a tunnel which runs down to the harbour. This pub is the oldest continuous trading pub in Sydney. Built in 1843.

East of the city

Paddington

Royal Hotel, 237 Glenmore Road, ph 331 2604.
   Hours: Mon-Sat 10am-midnight, Sun noon-10pm;
   restaurant Mon-Sat noon-11pm, Sun noon-9pm
   Happy Hour: Tues 7pm-9pm.

Double Bay

Royal Oak Hotel, 28 Bay Street, ph 363 3935.
   Hours: Mon-Fri 10am-midnight, Sun 10am-10pm.
   Restaurant bistro 5:30pm-midnight
This pub is frequented by many country folk as well as their city counterparts.

Watson's Bay

Watson's Bay Hotel, 10 Marine Parade, ph 337 4299.
   Hours: Mon-Sat 10am-11pm, Sun 10am-10pm. Lunch 12-3pm
   Beer garden overlooking Sydney Harbour.

North of the city

Neutral Bay

The Oaks, 118 Military Road, ph 953 5515.
   Hours: Mon-Sat 10am-midnight, Sun noon-10pm,
   lunch and dinner noon-9pm.
The Oaks has three bars, and a beautiful beer garden surrounding

a very large, old, oak tree. Barbecues are available to cook your own steaks, or you can choose something already prepared.

West of the city

Balmain

Exchange Hotel, cnr Beattie & Mullins Streets, ph 810 1171.
  Hours: Mon-Sat noon-midnight, Sun noon-6pm.
  Dinner to 9pm, snack bar.
  The Safari cocktail bar is upstairs, and pool rooms are available.

The London Hotel, 234 Darling Street, ph 555 1377.
  Hours: Mon-Sat 11am-midnight, Sun noon-10pm.
  Dinner 6pm-10pm a la carte.

JAZZ VENUES

Soup Plus, 383 George Street, City, ph 299 7728.
  Hours: noon-midnight, Jazz 7:30-midnight
  Cover charge and 3-course meal: $23
  Cover charge (without meal): $4.

The Real Ale Cafe, 66 King Street, City, ph 262 3277.
  Hours: Mon-Fri noon-1am, Sat 6pm-1am, dinner 6pm-11pm,
  closed Sundays
  Cover charge: $5-$15.
Good value for lunch and dinner plus 140 imported beers (special beers cheaper prices noon-7pm).

Strawberry Hills Hotel, 453 Elizabeth Street, Surry Hills,
  ph 698 2997.
  Hours: Mon-Thurs 11am-midnight, Fri-Sat 11am-12.30am,
  Sun noon-10.30pm
  Restaurant noon-3pm, 6-9.30pm.
  Contemporary Jazz Tues-Wed 8.30-11.30pm - $6-10
  Thurs - Jazz 8.30-11.30pm - around $5
  Fri - Jazz 7pm-12.30am (no cover charge)

Sat - Jazz 8pm-12.30am (no cover charge)
Sun - Jazz from 3-6pm, 7-10.30pm (no cover charge)

THE CLASSICS

The Sydney Opera House is **the** venue in Sydney for Opera, Ballet, and performances by the Sydney Symphony Orchestra.

The newly refurbished Sydney Town Hall is also the scene of musical evenings. The "Metro" has the information on programs, locations and times.

THEATRES

Sydney has a vibrant theatre scene, and the local talent compares favorably with the rest of the world.

The large theatres have cocktail bars for pre-show or intermission drinks, and most of them have banned smoking in these areas, as well as in the auditoriums themselves. Some theatres have restaurants attached, where service is geared to getting patrons into the theatre on time, and there are a few theatre-restaurants, where you watch the show either while eating dinner, or at least from the same chair.

Then there are the small theatre groups, and local dramatic and musical societies, whose performances are quite professional and you may see a star in the making for half the price required when he or she makes the big time. For example, **NIDA,** the National Institute of Dramatic Art (where Mel Gibson learnt his craft) presents plays at The Parade Theatre at 125 Anzac Parade, Kensington, ph 697 7613, opposite the main entrance to the University of New South Wales. **Prices are around $14,** not much more than you pay to see Mel in a movie.

Half-tix

Speaking of prices, Sydney has a **Half-tix booth** in the middle of Martin Place that sells tickets to major venues at half price on the day of the performance.

It is open between noon and 6pm Monday to Saturday, and it's cash only, with no telephone bookings.

Major Theatres

Sydney Opera House has two theatres -
the *Drama Theatre*, which seats 544,
and the *Playhouse*, which seats 398.

The Box Office is open Mon-Sat 9am-8.30pm, and charge telephone bookings may be made by phone, dial 250 7777. There are several eateries at the Opera House itself, or you can choose from the dozens in the area of Circular Quay.

Her Majesty's Theatre, 107 Quay Street, ph 212 3411, is close to Central Railway Station and within walking distance of the restaurants of Chinatown.

The Theatre Royal, MLC Centre, King Street, ph 231 6111, is in the heart of the city.

The Ensemble Theatre, 78 Mc Dougall Street, Milsons Point, ph 929 8877, is situated in the Lower North Shore and has its own restaurant.

The Wharf Theatre, Pier 4, Hickson Road, Millers Point (The Rocks), ph 250 1700, also has a restaurant, ph 250 1761.

Belvoir Street Theatre, 25 Belvoir Street, Surry Hills, ph 699 3444, doesn't have a restaurant, but does have a licensed bar offering light snacks before and after the show.

Seymour Theatre Centre, cnr Cleveland Street & City Road, Chippendale, ph 692 3511, has three theatres - the *York*, *Everest* and *Downstairs*, and a very good restaurant, ph 692 4138. There is also a coffee and snack bar in the upstairs foyer.

The Footbridge Theatre, Parramatta Road, Glebe, is actually in the grounds of Sydney University. It doesn't have a restaurant of its own, but there are plenty nearby in Glebe.

Marian Street Theatre, 2 Marian Street, Killara, ph 498 3166, is home to the Northside Theatre Company, and has a good restaurant, although with a limited menu.

Glen Street Theatre, Glen Street, Frenchs Forest, ph 975 4044, has Sorlies Restaurant which offers either a set menu pre-show dinner, or you can choose an a-la-carte dinner.

Small Theatres

Stables Theatre, 10 Nimrod Street, Kings Cross, ph 361 3817.
Kent Street Theatre, 420 Kent Street, City, ph 529 9190.
Bay Street Theatre, 75 Bay Street, Glebe, ph 692 0977.
New Theatre, 542 King Street, Newtown, ph 519 6999.
Pilgrim Theatre, 262 Pitt Street, City, ph 261 8981.
Iron Cove Theatre, cnr Darling & Denison Streets, Rozelle.
Enmore Theatre, 116 Enmore Road, Enmore, ph 550 3666.

These small theatres may not have a current presentation when you are in town, and others not mentioned here may have something that you would be interested in seeing. Check "Metro" for details.

Theatre Restaurants

Sydney Show Club, cnr Pyrmont and Allen Streets, Darling Harbour, ph 552 2722.
The Argyle Tavern, Argyle Street, The Rocks, ph 247 7782.
Dirty Dick's Theatre Restaurant, 313 Pacific Highway, Crows Nest, ph 929 8888.
Bankstown Theatre Restaurant, Bankstown Civic Centre, cnr Chapel & Rickard Roads, Bankstown, ph 707 9766.
Billboard Dinner Theatre, 220 Railway Parade, Kogarah, ph 588 6266.
Ramsgate Chinese Theatre Restaurant, 209 Ramsgate Road, Ramsgate, ph 529 3422.

Burning Log Restaurant, 632 Old Northern Road, Dural,
ph 651 1955.

Rock Concerts

The main venue for these is the *Sydney Entertainment Centre*, near Chinatown.

Another possibility is the *Hordern Pavilion* at the Showground, and if the person or group is a big, big star, the promoters may decide to use the actual Showground itself to accommodate the expected thousands of screaming fans. This latter choice involves a lot of praying that it won't rain.

The Sydney Entertainment Centre is also used for ice shows, tennis tournaments, boxing matches, etc.

CINEMAS

The main cinema area in the city is in George Street, between Park and Liverpool Streets. Here is found:
Village Cinema Centre, 545 George Street, ph 264 6701, with 6 cinemas;

Hoyts Centre, 505 George Street, ph 267 9877, with 7 cinemas;

Greater Union, 525 George Street, ph 267 8666, with 4 cinemas.
Greater Union also has the *Pitt Centre*, 232 Pitt Street, ph 264 1694, with another 3 cinemas.

Other cinemas in the city are:
Dendy in Martin Place, ph 233 8166;
Mandolin, 150 Elizabeth Street, ph 267 1968,
Encore Cinema, 64 Devonshire Street, ph 281 1788.

Hoyts also has cinema complexes in Bankstown, ph 796 4199; Brookvale, ph 938 4511; Pagewood, ph 349 7199; and Parramatta, ph 635 8499.
Village suburban complexes are at Blacktown, ph 621 5400; Double Bay, ph 327 1003; and Parramatta, ph 633 3766.

Greater Union cinemas can be found at Hurstville, ph 580 0044; Miranda, ph 540 5477; Mosman, ph 969 1988; and Parramatta, ph 633 2555.

Independent suburban cinemas include:
Academy Twin, 3a Oxford Street, Paddington, ph 0055 20248;
The Walker, 121 Walker Street, North Sydney, ph 0055 20249;
Valhalla, 166 Glebe Point Road, ph 660 8050;
Stanmore Cinema Centre, 200 Parramatta Road, ph 569 0488;
Avalon Hayden, 39 Old Barrenjoey Road, Avalon, ph 918 2789;
Cremorne Hayden, Military Road, Cremorne Junction,
ph 908 1654;
Beverly Hills Twin, 449 King Georges Road, Beverly Hills,
ph 580 3178;
Bondi Plaza United, 500 Oxford Street, Bondi Junction,
ph 389 5877;
Collaroy Twin, Pittwater Road, Collaroy, ph 971 8668;
Cronulla Cinema, Cronulla Plaza, Cronulla, ph 523 0555;
Hornsby Family Cinema, 155 Pacific Highway, ph 476 3777;
Mecca Movie City, 28 Station Street, Kogarah, ph 587 4444;
Manly Twin Cinemas, opposite Manly Wharf, ph 977 0644;
The Ritz, 43 St Paul's Street, Randwick, ph 399 9840;
Roseville Cinema, 112 Pacific Highway, Roseville, ph 416 8555.

As a general rule, Tuesday is half-price night at all cinemas, although some offer discounts on other nights as well. Also, many of the suburban cinemas have combined with local restaurants to provide dinner/show tickets at reduced prices.

GAMBLING VENUES

Sydney does not, as yet, have a casino, which is really a bit odd because there are plenty of other places to go if you feel like a flutter. Firstly there are the **Clubs** - Leagues Clubs, RSL (Returned Servicemen's League) Clubs, Bowling Clubs, Worker's Clubs, Golf Clubs - which all have poker machines, and most have keno.

Of course, it is not compulsory to play the pokies, and in fact, a lot of people don't, they go to the club to get a reasonably priced meal, and enjoy whatever entertainment is on offer. This varies from imported acts to cabaret shows with local talent, to movies, to chook raffles (yes, you do actually win a chook, or should I say a dead chicken).

Every suburb has one or more clubs, but if you are a first-time visitor to Sydney, I suggest that you stick to the suburban League Clubs. They are bigger, brighter, busier, and you can experience a good cross-section of Sydney life.

The following may seem like a list of teams that compete for the local Winfield Cup Rugby League Premiership, and in fact it is, because they were the original reason for the clubs:

Balmain Leagues Club, 138 Victoria Road, Rozelle, ph 555 1650.
Canterbury Bankstown Leagues Club, 26 Bridge Road, Belmore, ph 759 8733.
Cronulla Sutherland Leagues Club, Captain Cook Drive, Woolooware, ph 523 0222.
Eastern Suburbs Rugby League Club, 97 Spring Street, Bondi Junction, ph 389 1011.
Manly-Warringah Rugby League Club, 563 Pittwater Road Brookvale, ph 939 6722.
North Sydney Leagues Club, 20 Abbott Street, Cammeray, ph 955 6101.
Parramatta Leagues Club, 15 O'Connell Street, Parramatta, ph 683 1888.
St George Leagues Club, 124 Princes Highway, Kogarah, ph 587 1022.
South Sydney Leagues Club, 263 Chalmers Street, Redfern, ph 319 4156.
Western Suburbs Leagues Club, 115 Liverpool Road, Ashfield, ph 797 6955.

Although the clubs are there primarily for the use of members, **visitors are always made welcome,** as long as they are suitably dressed - no thongs, a collar with a shirt, and in the evening, long pants are preferred. Those dress rules are of course for men. Women must be 'decently' attired. Also, remember to sign the visitor's book in the foyer.

The clubs also have TAB (Totalizator Agency Board) facilities and SKY Channel television. This means that you can study the form guide in the comfort of a well-appointed club with a cold glass of whatever you fancy, place bets on your favourite horses, watch the race live, then collect your winnings (or tear up your ticket). Perhaps I should mention that SKY Channel is only available to TAB agencies and registered clubs.

If you are not into the club scene you can, of course, place your bets at the local TAB agency, and they are in every suburb, but there is no atmosphere.

Alternatively you can venture out of doors and actually watch the horses, or dogs, go round at the track. Sydney's racetracks are very attractive, with good parking facilities, lots of grassed areas, plenty of bars, take-away food outlets, and restaurants, and the choice of investing your money on the Tote, or with a bookmaker. Children are welcome, and on a beautiful Sydney day it can be a great family day out.

The horse-racing venues are:
Randwick Racecourse, Alison Road, Randwick, ph 663 8400.
Canterbury Racecourse, King Street, Canterbury, ph 799 8000.
Rosehill Racecourse, James Ruse Drive, Rosehill, ph 682 1000.
Warwick Farm Racecourse, Hume Highway, Warwick Farm, ph 602 6199.

Races are held every Saturday and Wednesday at one of the above courses.
The first race is usually around 12.30, but during January and February the first race starts around 2.30pm. These are called *Twilight Meetings,* as the last race is around 6.30pm. The daily newspapers have details of race times, starters and jockeys, comprehensive form guides, TAB numbers and post positions.

Harness-racing venues are:

Harold Park Paceway, Ross Street, Glebe, ph 660 3688. Meetings are held on Tuesday and Friday nights, and first race is 7pm.

Bankstown City Paceway, 178 Eldridge Road, Bankstown, ph 708 4111. Meetings are held on Monday nights, and first race is 7pm.

Fairfield Paceway, Fairfield Showground, ph 604 4559.
   Meetings are not held on a regular basis, so either phone the club or look in the newspapers for forthcoming races.

Greyhound racing is held at *Wentworth Park*, Wentworth Park Road, Glebe, ph 660 6232. Meetings are held every Monday and Saturday nights and the first race is 7.30pm.

Shoppers in Hyde Park

SHOPPING

Sydney has a large shopping area in the city centre, stretching from Park Street in the south to Martin Place, with shops along George, Pitt and Castlereagh Streets. The section of Pitt Street between King and Market Streets is a pedestrian mall, with many arcades connecting it to both Castlereagh and George Streets.

The closest railway station to the city centre is Town Hall, and *it is possible to walk from Town Hall Station to the MLC Centre in Martin Place without venturing out of doors*. This is a great bonus on a rainy day. It is rather a convoluted route, but there are signs pointing you in the right direction. Basically, from the station take the arcade under the Queen Victoria Building to Grace Bros, then from the first floor of GBs take the overpass to Centrepoint, then travel across the Imperial Arcade, Glasshouse and Skygarden shopping centres to the King Street overpass, and, voila, you are in the MLC Centre. Of course, if the weather is warm and sunny, forget this option and stroll through the Mall.

Shops are normally open Mon-Wed 9am-5.30pm, Thurs 9am-9pm, Fri 9am-6pm, Sat 9am-5pm, but this is not a hard and fast rule. Many shops are now open on a Sunday, both in the city and the suburbs, and some of the suburban supermarkets are opening until late at night six days a week, and until around 6pm on Sundays. *The shops in the tourist areas are always open seven days a week.*

SOUVENIRS

If you are only interested in buying souvenirs, such as cuddly koalas and kangaroos, T-shirts, etc, it is probably best to head for the tourist areas, such as **The Rocks** and **Darling Harbour.**

Other 'typically Sydney' souvenirs are found in the range of goods at the Done Art & Design Shops at The Rocks, Darling Harbour, Skygardens, Queen Victoria Building and Mosman. Ken Done is a local artist who produces very colourful works of art featuring the harbour, the bridge, the opera house, koalas, kangaroos, etc. These paintings are reproduced on material and his wife, Judy, designs a spectacular range of sportswear, swimwear, homewares, bags, stationery - in fact, just about everything you can think of can be found in their shops.

Buying Opals

If you have your heart set on some **opal jewellery,** you should grab your passport and airline ticket and head for a duty free store, or a jewellery shop that has a 'Tax Free for Overseas Visitors' sign in the window. In the case of opals, which are mined in Australia and set in jewellery locally, there is no duty, therefore in both establishments you would be saving the sales tax only (approx 30%).

Australia produces more than 90% of the world's opals, and the three main areas where they are found are Lightning Ridge in NSW which produces the Black Opal; Quilpie, where the Queensland Boulder Opal originates; and Coober Pedy in South Australia, which has the White or Milk Opal.

When buying opals there are a few terms you should know:
Solid Opal - this is the most valuable, and is good for investment purposes. The more colourful and complete, the greater its value.

Doublet - this is comprised of slices of opal glued together, and is of medium value. It has no investment value.

Triplet - slices of opal covered with quartz, perspex or glass, this is the least expensive and has no investment value.

If your pocket can't stretch as far as a solid opal, but you still would like a piece of opal jewellery, remember that anything that is glued can come unstuck, and that condensation can form under perspex or glass. The less expensive types of opal are not suitable for rings, unless you are going to remember to take them off every time you wash your hands.

DEPARTMENT STORES

David Jones

David Jones has two stores in the city - one bounded by Elizabeth, Market and Castlereagh Streets, the other diagonally opposite on the corner of Market and Castlereagh Streets. The Elizabeth Street store is devoted mainly to ladies' wear, except for the Lower Ground Floor (haberdashery, books, records, CDs, pharmacy, confectionery, wool, fabrics and restaurant); the 5th Floor (toys, children's wear and sporting goods) and the 6th Floor (manchester).

The Market Street store is known as the men's store, but it also has the Food Hall on the lower ground floor, and stocks travel goods, and small and large electrical appliances and furniture. Both stores have the same phone number - 266 5544.

David Jones is considered to be one of the most beautiful stores in the world, and was designed by the same person who later designed the refurbishment of Harrods in London along the same lines.

David Jones stores are open Mon-Fri 9am-5.30pm (Thurs to 9pm), Sat 9am-4pm, and all major credit cards are accepted.

Grace Bros

Situated on the corner of George and Market Streets, Grace Bros is more of a family store and sells literally everything under one roof. It has seven floors of shopping and is open Mon-Wed 8.30am-5.30pm, Thurs 8.30am-9pm, Fri 8.30am-6.30pm, Sat 8.30am-4pm, Sun 10am-4pm, ph 218 2111.

CITY SHOPPING CENTRES

The Queen Victoria Building

The QVB was built in 1898 in the Byzantine style, and originally housed the city markets. Bounded by George, Market, York and Druitt Streets, its prosperity was shortlived, and it fell into disrepair. At one stage it was used as part offices and part Municipal Library, and the partitions that succeeded in making the building into a rabbit warren were actually nailed onto the beautiful tiled floors. Both the inside and outside of the building were decidedly tacky, and in 1959 there was much debate about demolishing the entire structure and building another shrine to modern architecture. Fortunately, common sense prevailed, the wreckers were not allowed to move in, but it was not until 1982 that a 99-year lease was granted and over $75 million invested to restore the building to its original state.

It is a magnificent building, and Pierre Cardin, on a visit to Sydney, christened it "the most beautiful shopping centre in the world". But, it is not only a shopping centre, there are a lot of things to see, all with a royal theme, in keeping with the name of the building. It even has replicas of the Crown Jewels on the top level.

The Royal Automata Clock 'performs' on the hour between 9am and 9pm daily, and you need to get there early to see the moving Royal Pageant. (It is a good idea to keep a firm grip on your handbag and wallet while waiting in this crowd.)

The QVB is open seven days a week. Apart from the range of boutiques and specialty shops, there are several restaurants and cafes, both in the QVB and in the underground walkway to Grace Bros.

Centrepoint

Advertised as being "in the heart of the city", Centrepoint is located on Pitt Street Mall, beneath Sydney Tower, and connects Grace Bros with David Jones. It has 170 shops on four levels, including hairdressers, beauticians, leather shops, jewellery and accessory outlets, boutiques, and several coffee shops and takeaways. The lifts for the Sydney Tower are found on the elegant Gallery Level of Centrepoint.

The lower ground floor is the Centrepoint Tavern, a good spot for a quick lunch, or a happy-hour drink.

Centrepoint is open daily, but not all the shops are open outside normal shopping hours (Mon-Sat).

Imperial Arcade

The Imperial runs between the Pitt Street Mall and Castlereagh Street, and has 114 specialty shops on 3 levels. It is also connected to Centrepoint.

Glasshouse on The Mall

Located in the heart of the Pitt Street Mall, the Glasshouse has three floors of shopping, with the usual collection of boutiques, etc.

Skygarden

A very up-market shopping experience, Skygarden has three levels of prestigious shops under a huge crystal dome. The mosaic entrance arch is made of thousands of Venetian glass tiles, and depicts the day and night theme of the complex. The top dining level is nothing to write home about.

Strand Arcade

The Strand opened in 1892 and is an olde worlde walk-through with mosaic tiled floor and Victorian architecture. It connects Pitt Street Mall with George Street and is open Mon-Fri 9am-5.30pm, Sat 9am-4pm.

Mid City Centre

This centre connects Pitt Street Mall and George Street, and is between the Strand Arcade and Grace Bros. It has four levels of shopping with over 40 fashion boutiques, more than 50 specialty shops, and first class restaurants and coffee shops.

MLC Centre

The MLC Centre has entrances from Martin Place, Castlereagh Street and King Street, and has fashion boutiques, coffee shops and restaurants, and the Theatre Royal. The outdoor cafes overlooking Martin Place are popular lunchtime places.

Royal Arcade

Located under the Sydney Hilton Hotel, the Royal Arcade is between Market and Park Streets, and connects Pitt and George Streets. It has a range of rather expensive shops, typical of those found in hotel arcades.

Darling Harbour

Harbourside Festival Marketplace has 200 shops from boutiques to souvenirs, sportswear to art, and restaurants, cafes and bars. It is a bazaar for overseas visitors rather than the Sydneysiders.

SUBURBAN SHOPPING CENTRES

Most suburbs have a shopping centre of some kind, although many consist of a supermarket, butcher, greengrocer and a few specialty shops, such as a haberdasher, a hardware outlet, delicatessen, etc.

Then there are suburbs that have giant shopping complexes with branches of one or both major department stores and many specialty shops.

Following is a list of these:

Bankstown Square Shopping Centre, North Terrace, Bankstown, ph 790 0751.

Blacktown Westpoint Marketown, Patrick Street, Blacktown, ph 621 3333.

Bondi Junction Plaza, 500 Oxford Street, Bondi Junction, ph 387 3333.

Burwood Westfield Shoppingtown, Burwood Road, Burwood, ph 744 9596.

Carlingford Court Shopping Centre, cnr Pennant Hills & Carlingford Roads, ph 871 4111.

Castle Tower, cnr Old Castle Hill Road & Eric Felton Street, Castle Hill, ph 634 4911.

Chatswood Chase, 91 Archer Street, Chatswood, ph 419 6255.

Chatswood Westfield Shoppingtown, cnr Anderson Street & Victoria Avenue, Chatswood, ph 412 1555.

Hornsby Northgate Shopping Centre, cnr Florence & Hunter Streets, Hornsby, ph 477 5111.

Hurstville Westfield Shoppingtown, cnr Cross Street & Park Road, Hurstville, ph 570 6333.

Liverpool Westfield Shoppingtown, Macquarie Street, Liverpool, ph 602 6633.

Macquarie Shopping Centre, cnr Herring & Waterloo Roads, North Ryde, ph 887 3011.

Miranda Westfield Shoppingtown, 600 The Kingsway, Miranda, ph 525 6344. (This is now the largest shopping centre in the Southern Hemisphere.)

Mount Druitt Square, North Parade, Mount Druitt, ph 625 7177.

Pagewood Westfield Shoppingtown, cnr Wentworth Avenue & Bunnerong Road, ph 344 6766.

Parramatta Westfield Shoppingtown, 159 Church Street, ph 633 1588.

Roselands Shopping Centre, Roselands Drive, Roselands, ph 750 0533.

Warringah Mall, Pittwater Road, Brookvale.

MARKETS

The Rocks Market

Every Saturday and Sunday, at the end of George Street in The Rocks, a sail-like canopy transforms the area into a Portobello Road. It is not an exceptionally large market, but it has many interesting articles for sale, and the Victorian terraces and old warehouses that surround it contribute to a holiday atmosphere year round. Nearby there are plenty of cafes, outdoor food stalls and pubs.

Paddys Markets

The original Paddys Markets were at Haymarket, near Chinatown (hence the name of the area).

Now there are two locations:
Parramatta Road, Flemington, open Fri 11am-3.30pm, Sun 9am-4.30pm;
Garden Street, Redfern (near Redfern Railway Station), open Sat-Sun 9am-4.30pm.

There are over 1000 stalls in each location selling fashion garments, footwear, jewellery, household and electrical goods, takeaway foods, fresh fruit and vegetables, poultry, seafood, and heaps and heaps of souvenirs. Paddys is the biggest market in Australia, and for further information, phone the Hotline - 11 589.

Parklea Markets

These markets are at the corner of Sunnyholt and Old Windsor Roads in Parklea, an outer suburb of Sydney. It is a big market with a wide variety of merchandise, and is worth a visit if you happen to be in the neighbourhood.

Paddington Village Bazaar
Located at the corner of Oxford and Newcombe Streets, Paddington, in the grounds of the Uniting Church, this bazaar is held on Saturdays 10am-4pm, ph 331 2646. There are over 250 stalls offering all types of clothing, crafts, jewellery and food.

Balmain Saturday Market
Held in the grounds of St Andrew's Congregational Church, corner Darling Street and Curtis Road, Balmain, every Saturday 9am-4.30pm, ph 818 2674.

Fishing off Mrs. Macquarie's Point

SPORT AND RECREATION

Swimming

The closest public swimming pools to the city centre are
North Sydney Olympic Pool, Alfred South Street, Milsons Point,
ph 955 2309;
Andrew (Boy) Charlton Pool, The Domain, Woolloomooloo,
ph 358 6686;
Prince Alfred Park Swimming Pool, Chalmers Street, Surry Hills
(near Central Railway Station), ph 319 7045.

With so many beaches close to the city, and most having a protected
swimming area, why go seeking a chlorine environment?

Golf

Following is a list of golf clubs in alphabetical order where visitors
are most welcome, not only to play golf, but to use the facilities of
the club houses as well. These clubs are in close proximity to the
city centre and most are located south of the city towards and to the
east of the Airport. So you can have a game of golf, grab a beer and
a snack, and have a flutter on the poker machines, though this is
not compulsory.

Balgowlah Golf Club, 506 Sydney Road, Balgowlah, ph 948 1900
   9 hole course - par 66 for 18 holes - 4650 metres (18 holes)
   Green fees: $9 for 9 holes; $14 for 18 holes
   Club and buggy hire is available and prices vary according to
standard of clubs, etc.
The course is open daily, but it is necessary to book ahead. Time
sheets are kept so you are guaranteed to get an exact time for tee
off.

Bondi Golf Club, 5 Military Road, North Bondi, ph 30 3170
   9 hole course -par 56 for 18 holes - 2526 metres (18 holes)
   Green fees: $8 for 9 or 18 holes

Club hire: $18

Buggy hire: $2 - no electric buggies as it is too hilly.

Members play till 11.30am Tues, till 1pm Sat-Sun, visitors welcome other times. It still is wise to phone ahead.

Bonnie Doon Golf Club, Banks Avenue, Pagewood, ph 349 2101

18 hole course - par 72 - 6000 metres

Green fees: $50

Club hire: $20 full set

Buggy hire: $30 motorised; $2 pull buggy

Visitors are welcome on weekday afternoons, but it is best to phone ahead.

Cammeray Golf Club, Park Avenue, Cremorne, ph 953 1522

9 hole course - par 66 for 18 holes - 4610 metres (18 holes)

Green fees: $9 for 9 holes; $15 for 18 holes

Club hire: $9, includes buggy.

Concord Golf Club, Majors Bay Road, Concord, ph 743 6111

18 hole course - ACR 72, par 71 - 6213 metres

Green fees: $50 for 18 holes

Club hire and buggy hire is available, phone the club professional, Kyle Francis, on 743 0265.

Overseas and interstate visitors are restricted to Mondays and Thursdays.

Eastlake Public Golf Links, Gardeners Road, Kingsford, ph 663 1374

18 hole course - par 70 - 5482 metres

Green fees: $12 Mon-Fri; $13 Sat-Sun

Club hire: $13 includes buggy hire

Members play till 1pm on Sat-Sun. It is best to book ahead by phoning the Pro Shop, 662 6453.

The Lakes Golf Club, King Street, Mascot, ph 669 1311

18 hole course - par 73 - 6269 metres

Green fees: $90 for overseas visitors; $60 for interstate visitors

Club hire: $25

Buggy hire: $25 (electric)

Visitors are welcome on Mon and Thurs, but bookings are essential. Residents of Australia must be members of a golf club.

Lane Cove Country Club Ltd, River Road, Northwood, ph 427 6631
  9 hole course - par 64 for 18 holes - 4033 metres
  Green fees: $9 for 9 holes; $12 for 18 holes
  Club hire: $8, includes buggy hire
Advance bookings must be made for every day by phoning the Pro Shop, 428 1316.

Moore Park Golf Club, cnr Cleveland Street & Anzac Parade, Moore Park, ph 663 3791
  18 hole course - par 71 - 5790 metres
  Green fees: $15 Mon-Fri; $18 Sat-Sun
  Club hire: $20
  Buggy hire: $30 drive buggies; $4 pull buggies.

St Michael's Golf Club, Little Bay, ph 311 0621
  18 hole course - par 71 - 5808 metres
  Green fees: phone for current fees for visitors.
  Club hire: $20 full set
  Buggy hire: $25 per motorised cart; $3 per hand buggy

Tennis

Tennis courts abound in Sydney's suburbs and most have lights for night play. Pages of available courts can be found in the L-Z Yellow Pages of the Telephone Directory, appropriately enough under Tennis Courts For Hire.

For spectators, the NSW Tennis Open is played at White City in Rushcutters Bay.

Lawn Bowls

There are bowling clubs in almost every suburb of Sydney, and one in the city. Bowling clubs are famous for their hospitality, and visitors are warmly welcomed. It is necessary, of course, to phone ahead to find out what days are reserved for social play, and to organise for a set of bowls. Bowling clubs are listed in the Yellow Pages of the Telephone Directory under *Clubs - Bowling*. If you are not sure which club is the closest to where you are staying, you could contact the Royal NSW Bowling Association, ph 283 4555.

Ten Pin Bowling

The bowling centres close to the city are:

AMF Bowling Centres at 815 Pacific Highway, Chatswood, ph 411 5222; and Condamine Street, Balgowlah, ph 948 7656.

Rushcutter Bowl, Bayswater Road, Rushcutters Bay, ph 361 0558.

Other centres can be found in the A-K Yellow Pages of the Telephone Directory under Bowling - Indoor.

Ice Skating

The closest ice rink to the city is *Macquarie Ice Rink Pty Ltd* in the Macquarie Shopping Centre, North Ryde, ph 888 1100.

Roller Skating

The closest roller skating rink to the city is *Majestic Rollarink*, 49 New Canterbury Road, Petersham, ph 569 3233.

Horse Riding

Centennial Park Horse Hire, RAS Showground, Driver Avenue, Moore Park, ph 332 2770, has horses for hire daily 9am-5pm. Centennial Park and adjoining Queens Park have a combined area 220ha (543 acres) - more than enough room to have a decent ride.

Cycling

Centennial Park Cycles, 50 Clovelly Road (near Avoca Street), Randwick, ph 398 5027, are open seven days and are close to Centennial Park. They hire out bikes at reasonable prices.

Boating

It should be noted that a licence is required to drive any mechanically driven vessel capable of speeds 10 knots or more. There are several places around the harbour foreshores where bare boats can be hired. Here are a few names and addresses:

Abbotsford Point Boat Hire, 617 Great North Road, Abbotsford, ph 713 8621.

Australian Sailing School & Club, The Spit, Mosman, ph 960 3077.

Balmoral Marine Hire Boats, 2 The Esplanade, Balmoral, ph 969 6006.
Catamaran Hire, The Spit, Mosman, ph 960 3077.
Drummoyne Boat Hire, Birkenhead Point Marina, Drummoyne, ph 819 6111.
Eastsail, d' Albora Marinas, New Beach Road, Rushcutters Bay, ph 327 1166.
It's A Breeze Yacht Charter, The Spit, Mosman, ph 960 3999.
Rose Bay Windsurfer School, 1 Vickery Avenue, Rose Bay, ph 371 7036.

Scuba Diving
Gear can be hired and dives arranged from the following:
Dive 2000, 2 Military Road, Neutral Bay, 2089.
Deep 6 Diving Pty Ltd., 169-171 Pittwater Road, Manly, ph 977 5966; 86-88 Bayswater Road, Rushcutters Bay, ph 361 4481.
Pro Dive, 227 Victoria Road, Drummoyne, ph 819 7711; 10 Belgrave Street, Manly, ph 977 4355.
Moby Dive, Shop 288, Manly Wharf, Manly, ph 976 3297.

SPECTATOR SPORTS

Football (March-October)
Rugby League is played on Saturdays and Sundays at various suburban grounds and at the Sydney Football Stadium, near the Showground.
Rugby Union is played on Saturdays at suburban grounds and at their headquarters at Concord Oval.
Soccer is played on Saturdays at various suburban grounds and Sydney Athletic Field, Anzac Parade, Kensington, ph 662 4390.
Australian Football is played on Saturdays at suburban grounds, and the Sydney Swans play their home games in the Victorian competition at the Sydney Cricket Ground.

Cricket (October-March)
The Cricket Ground, near the Showground, is home to International matches and NSW home ground in the Sheffield Shield competition. Grade matches are played on suburban grounds.

Baseball (October-February)

The Sydney Blues is the local team in the National Baseball League and their home games are played at the Parramatta Stadium. The teams in the local competition play at various suburban venues, and for information on games, times, etc, contact Garry Everson at the NSW Baseball League on 552 4635.

Basketball (April-October)

Sydney's team in the National Basketball League (NBL) is *The Kings,* and they play their home games at the Sydney Entertainment Centre. Contact the recorded Show Information line on 11 582, or enquiries, 211 2222 for dates of the Kings' games.

Horse Racing

See Entertainment.

STATE SPORTS CENTRE

The Centre is in the suburb of Homebush, and can be reached from Parramatta Road by taking Birnie Avenue, Homebush Bay Drive, or Underwood Road. It is a multi-purpose venue designed to present a full spectrum of events. The design enables the Centre to be used as: a competition venue for sporting events of State, National and International standard, and a training centre for these athletes; a sports education centre; and a venue for concerts, seminars, exhibitions, etc

The Arena, within *the Sports Hall,* is the focal point of the State Sports Centre, and is capable of staging a wide range of sports from gymnastics to showjumping, fencing to indoor cricket. It has seating for 5000, and a clear floor area of 57m x 38m.

Also in the Sports Hall is the *Hall of Champions* which honours Sydney's champs in many sports.

The State Softball Centre has four fields, two of which are suitable for day and evening games.

The State Hockey Centre has two synthetic pitches. Pitch No 1 has 2 grandstands and grassed banks to accommodate over 6000 people, computerised electronic scoreboard, 5 light towers, the Eva

Redfern Memorial Lounge, public amenities (including toilet facilities for the disabled), food and drink outlets and full media facilities.

There are also outdoor netball courts, training centres and plans for many more sporting facilities. When Sydney finally hosts the Olympic Games, the Centre on Homebush Bay will become world famous.

For information about current programs at the Centre, phone their 24-hour Information line, 746 2855.

A common sight off Sydney's beaches

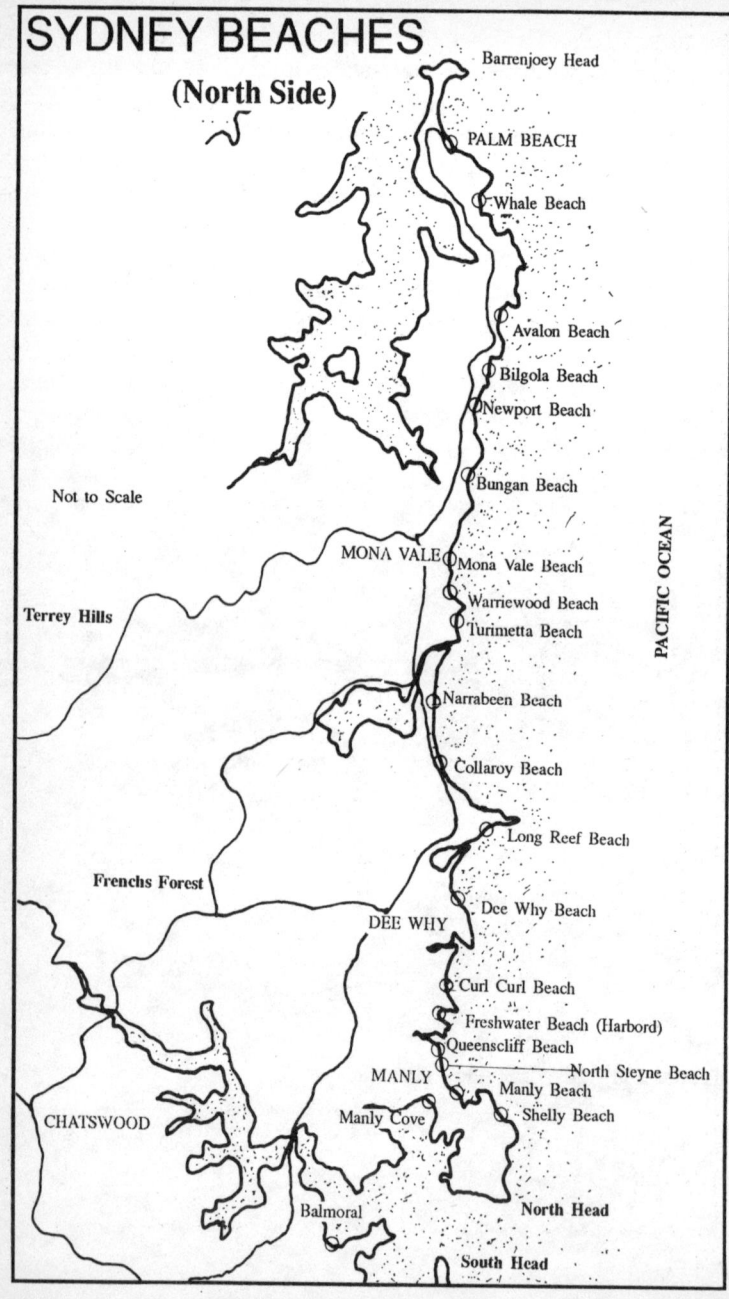

SYDNEY BEACHES
(North Side)

Barrenjoey Head

PALM BEACH

Whale Beach

Avalon Beach

Bilgola Beach

Newport Beach

Bungan Beach

MONA VALE — Mona Vale Beach

Warriewood Beach

Turimetta Beach

Narrabeen Beach

Collaroy Beach

Long Reef Beach

Dee Why Beach

Curl Curl Beach

Freshwater Beach (Harbord)

Queenscliff Beach

North Steyne Beach

Manly Beach

Shelly Beach

Not to Scale

Terrey Hills

Frenchs Forest

DEE WHY

MANLY

Manly Cove

CHATSWOOD

Balmoral

North Head

South Head

PACIFIC OCEAN

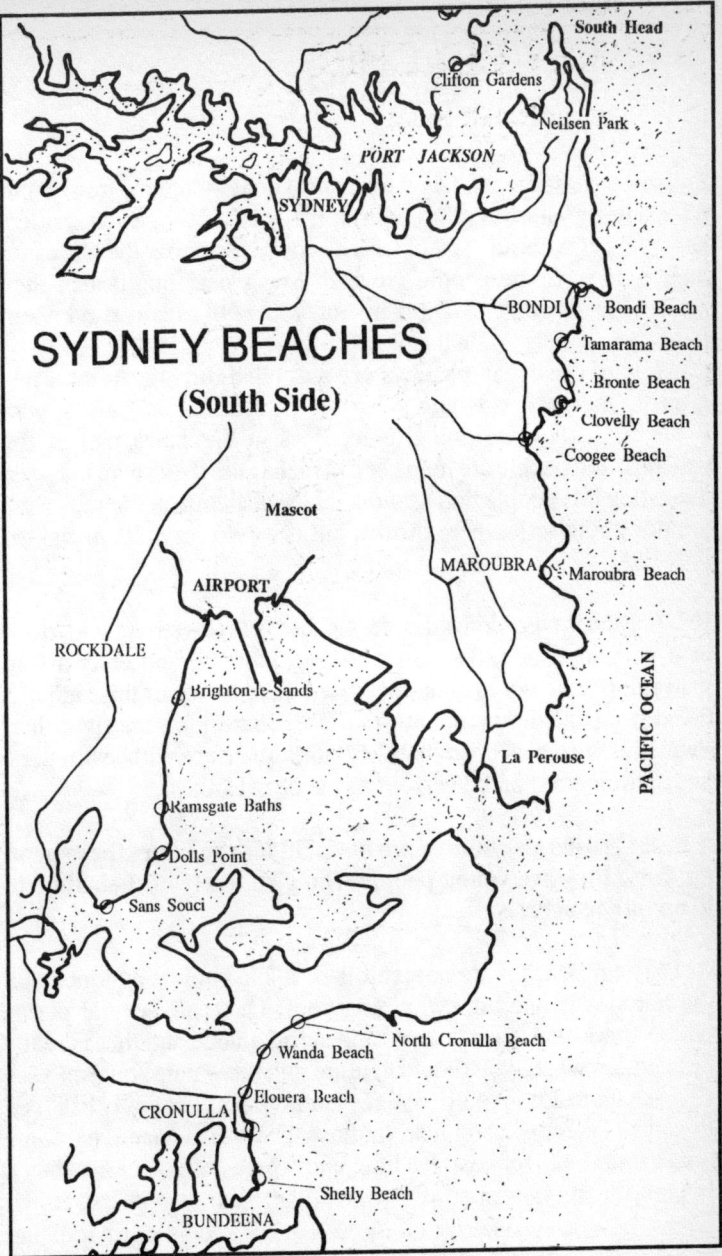

SYDNEY BEACHES

(South Side)

South Head
Clifton Gardens
Neilsen Park
PORT JACKSON
SYDNEY
BONDI
Bondi Beach
Tamarama Beach
Bronte Beach
Clovelly Beach
Coogee Beach
Mascot
MAROUBRA
Maroubra Beach
AIRPORT
ROCKDALE
Brighton-le-Sands
PACIFIC OCEAN
La Perouse
Ramsgate Baths
Dolls Point
Sans Souci
North Cronulla Beach
Wanda Beach
Elouera Beach
CRONULLA
Shelly Beach
BUNDEENA

BEACHES

Sydney's coastline stretches for approximately 65km, from Palm Beach in the north, to Cronulla in the south. Most Sydneysiders have their 'favourite' beach, which is not necessarily the closest to their homes. Some people grew up living near one beach, then moved as an adult to another, but you will usually find them returning to their original haunt.

Most of the ocean beaches are patrolled during the summer months on weekends and school holidays. The lifesavers, who know what they are doing, erect flags in the safest part of the beaches, and people are requested to make sure they swim between these flags. If people don't, and get into difficulties, the lifesavers are not going to let them drown, but it would serve them right if they did.

If the beach is considered unsafe, e.g. because of a strong undertow, or a very high tide, the lifesavers will close it, and erect a sign warning people not to enter the water. Take notice of this sign and decide to spend the day somewhere else. Boardriders are given their own stretch of beach, so that they don't interfere with swimmers, and swimmers should keep out of the board area.

Lifesavers in this country are not paid for the hours they spend on duty, they are young people who give freely of their time to keep our beaches safe.

Harbour beaches are not patrolled. It must not be assumed that the harbour is one big swimming pool. There are several places where shark-nets have been strung across inlets, and these are the only places where you should venture into the water. You won't see one, but there are sharks in Sydney Harbour. It is generally believed that old sharks that can't fend for themselves in the open sea, come into the harbour for easy feeding, and what could be easier than a human thrashing around. Of course, there are also sharks in the ocean, but the surf patrols on these beaches keep a sharp lookout, and sound alarms if a shark is sighted. You may not have caught a wave all day, but if a shark alarm sounds it is incredible how quickly you can get yourself back on the beach.

Having said all that, there has not been a shark attack in Sydney since 1963, when two children were taken whilst swimming in Middle Harbour.

OCEAN BEACHES

Listed below are the beaches stretching from Palm Beach in the north to Bundeena in the south.

The attributes listed are:

Dressing Shed, which normally will include shower and toilets.

Patrolled which is normally in summer on weekends and school holidays (i.e. from the first weekend in October to Easter the following year). Beaches are not patrolled in winter. The patrols tend to be within the vicinity of the surf club.

Pool, Rock pool suitable for children.

Surf suitable for *board and body surfers*.

Normally all the beaches back onto a park or a reserve, and there are clear directions from the major road as to how to get to the beach. Most beaches tend to be topless, among the over 25s in the main, usually after 11am until the sun starts to wane.

Palm Beach, about 1.5 hours drive from the city centre (Bus no 190 from Wynyard). A beach mainly frequented by the wealthy and yuppy set, Surf Club, Dressing Shed, patrolled, surfers and board, pool south end, off Barrenjoey Road.

Whale Beach, Surf Club, Dressing Shed, patrolled, surfers and board, pool south end, off Barrenjoey Road. Bus 190 from Wynyard, Bus 193 from Avalon (infrequent service).

Avalon Beach, Surf Club, Dressing Shed, patrolled, surfers and board, pool south end, off Barrenjoey Road. Bus 190 from Wynyard, Bus 191 from Newport.

Bilgola Beach, Surf Club, Dressing Shed, patrolled, surfers and board, off Barrenjoey Road. Bus 190 from Wynyard, Bus 191 from Newport.

Newport Beach, Surf Club, Dressing Shed, patrolled, surfers and board, off Barrenjoey Road. Bus 187 from Wynyard.

Bungan Beach, Surf Club, patrolled, board, off Barrenjoey Road. Scantly clad on this beach. Bus 187 from Wynyard.

Mona Vale Beach, top end not patrolled (Bongin Bongin), Surf Club, Dressing Shed, patrolled, surfers and board, north end, off Barrenjoey Road. Bus 157 from Manly, Bus 185 from Wynyard (peak hour).

Warriewood Beach, Surf Club, Dressing Shed, patrolled, surfers and board, off Pittwater Road. Bus 157 from Manly.

Turimetta Beach, board, not patrolled, off Pittwater Road. Bus 157 from Manly

Narrabeen Beach, Surf Club - north end, Dressing Shed, patrolled, surfers and board, off Pittwater Road. Bus 182-190 from Wynyard, Bus 155, 157 from Manly.

Collaroy Beach adjoins Narrabeen Beach, Surf Club, Dressing Shed, patrolled, surfers and board, pool southern end, off Pittwater Road. Bus 182-190 from Wynyard, Bus 155, 157 from Manly.

Collaroy Basin, surfers, little swell, off Pittwater Road.

Long Reef Beach, Surf Club, Dressing Shed, patrolled, surfers and board, off Pittwater Road. Bus 177 from Wynyard (peak hours), Bus 136, 157 from Manly.

Dee Why Beach adjoins Long Reef Beach, Surf Club, Dressing Shed, patrolled, surfers and board, pool south end, Howard Street via Pittwater Road. Bus 177 from Wynyard, Bus 136, 157 from Manly.

Curl Curl Beach, Surf Club, Dressing Shed, patrolled, surfers and board, pool south end, via Oliver Road off Pittwater Road. Bus 139 from Manly.

Freshwater (Harbord) Beach, Surf Club, Dressing Shed, patrolled, surfers and board, pool north end, via Oliver Road, off Pittwater Road. Bus 139 from Manly.

Queenscliff Beach, Surf Club, Dressing Shed, patrolled, surfers and board, pool north end, off Pittwater Road. Bus 136, 139 from Manly.

North Steyne Beach adjoins Queenscliff Beach, Surf Club, Dressing Shed, patrolled, surfers and board, off Pittwater Road. See Manly chapter for travel information.

Manly Beach adjoins North Steyne Beach, Surf Club, Dressing Shed, patrolled, surfers and board, off Pittwater Road.

Between Shelly Beach and Manly Beach there is a pool at Fairy Bower.

Shelly Beach, surfers, off Darley Road. Sheltered area with little swell.

On the south side of the Harbour we have the following beaches:

Bondi Beach, Surf Club, Dressing Shed, patrolled, surfers and board, sanctioned topless area south end, pool at the south end, via Bondi Road off Old South Head Road.

An internationally famous beach, Bondi attracts more than 40,000 on any given sunny Sunday afternoon. The 1km strip of beach has a long history of development since the local government authority gained control of it in 1881. By 1907 it was very popular with the neck-to-knee fraternity, although bathing time was limited to half an hour to avoid loitering. In 1928, the Bondi Beach Pavilion was built and then contained changing rooms for 1200 people, turkish baths, shops, a gymnasium and a ballroom. Today it is a community centre.

Surf life saving had its origins here and at nearby Bronte, with these clubs claiming to be the world's oldest. Surf Carnivals are often held at the beach, but the standard of the surf depends on the wind, and can range from enormous waves one day, to a mill-pond the next.

Tamarama Beach, Surf Club, Dressing Shed, surfers and board, off Bronte Road. Bus 378 from Central Railway.

Bronte Beach, Surf Club, Dressing Shed, patrolled, surfers and board, pool south end, off Bronte Road. Bus 378 from Central Railway.

Clovelly Beach, Dressing Shed, swimming, pool, off Clovelly Road. Bus 339 from Millers Pt-Wynyard.

Coogee Beach, Surf Club, Dressing Shed, patrolled, surfers and board, pool, south end, off Coogee Bay Road. Bus 304 from Town Hall, Bus 372 from Central Railway, Bus 373 from Circular Quay.

Maroubra Beach, Surf Clubs - north and south ends, Dressing Shed, patrolled, surfers and board, via Fitzgerald Ave off Anzac Parade. Bus 377, 396 from Circular Quay, Bus 395 from Central Railway.

Wanda Beach, Surf Club, Dressing Shed, patrolled, surfers and board, off Kingsway. Train to Cronulla, walk to beach.

Elouera Beach adjoins Wanda Beach, Surf Club, Dressing Shed, patrolled, surfers and board, off Kingsway. Train to Cronulla, walk to beach.

North Cronulla Beach adjoins Wanda and Elouera Beaches, Surf Club, Dressing Shed, patrolled, surfers and board, pool south end, off Kingsway. Train to Cronulla, walk to beach.

Cronulla South Beach, Surf Club, Dressing Shed, patrolled, surfers and board, pool north end, off Kingsway. Train to Cronulla, walk to beach.

Shelly Beach, Dressing Shed, patrolled, surfers and board, pool south end, off Cronulla Street. Train to Cronulla, walk to beach.

HARBOUR BEACHES

There are hundreds of coves and bays around the harbour, but we are only including the following, which have shark-proof nets, changing facilities, takeaway food outlets, and picnic areas. Obviously the beaches on the harbour do not have waves, unless a large ship sails past and you get the backwash.

Clifton Gardens, Chowder Bay. The bay is two bays north-east of Taronga Park Zoo, and not easy to get to by public transport. There are two choices - Bus nos 182 or 184 from Wynyard to Mosman Junction, then Bus 235 to Clifton Gardens (but the latter is an infrequent service); Bus 247 from Wynyard to Taronga Zoo, get out at Thompson Street and follow the signs.

Balmoral, Hunter's Bay. This is quite a pretty beach and is divided into two by Rocky Point, a tree-covered rocky outcrop. Balmoral is very popular and has takeaway food bars as well as coffee shops and an up-market restaurant, the Bathers Pavilion. The rotunda on the beach is used for many shows on summer evenings, the Shakespeare on the Beach programs in particular have a large following. Take Bus no 238 from Taronga Zoo, Bus no 257 from Chatswood, or Bus no 233 from Mosman Wharf.

Manly Cove, Manly. The swimming enclosure is adjacent to Manly Wharf, where the ferry from Circular Quay docks. For more information see the section on Manly. Take Bus no 144 from Chatswood, or Buses 169, 172, 173 from Wynyard.

Nielsen Park, between Vaucluse Road and Greycliffe Avenue, Vaucluse, is in the eastern suburbs. During the summer swimming season (October to April) a sharkproof net is erected at Shark Beach. Experience has shown that this net must be taken down during the colder months because it cannot withstand the winter storms and heavy seas. There are dressing sheds and showers for swimmers, and a kiosk is situated opposite the beach. Bus no 325 operates between Edgecliff Station and Nielsen Park. There is no parking available in the park.

BOTANY BAY BEACHES

Botany Bay was the place where Captain James Cook landed, and where Captain Phillip was sent to begin the new colony. Phillip, unable to find a fresh water supply, sailed further north to Sydney Harbour. Now, Botany Bay is a densely populated area, and if you arrived in Sydney by air, you have already spotted it. Kingsford Smith Airport is situated on the shores of Botany Bay.

Botany Bay also has its share of sharks, so if you feel like a swim, stick to one of the following.

Brighton-le-Sands Baths, off Grand Parade. It has wire netting for protection though the rest of the Lady Robinson Beach is not protected and is frequented by swimmers. There are dressing sheds. Bus 302-3 from Circular Quay, Bus 478 from Rockdale.

Ramsgate Baths, opposite Ramsgate Road and off Grand Parade, shark proof net, dressing sheds. These baths abut Cook Park. Bus 302-3 from Circular Quay, Bus 478 from Rockdale.

Dolls Point Baths off Russell Avenue abut a Reserve. They have a shark proof net and dressing sheds. Bus 302-3 from Circular Quay, Bus 476 from Rockdale.

Sans Souci Baths off Clareville Avenue have a shark net and dressing sheds. Bus 302-3 from Circular Quay, Bus 477 from Rockdale.

Bundeena
Below Botany Bay is Port Hacking. Cronulla is on its northern side with Bundeena on the southern side bordering the Royal National Park. They are linked by a ferry service. Surrounding Bundeena are a number of very pleasant yet small beaches which have little swell and are suitable only for swimming. The beaches are Hordens, Gunyah and Jobbons. They have no safety nets and are not patrolled.

CITY SIGHTS

It is not possible to see the sights of the city of Sydney in one day on a walking tour, even if you are super-fit. Apart from the distance, Sydney is not a flat city, and the hills would slow you down. By taking advantage of **The Sydney Explorer** bus you could catch a glimpse of everything, but you still wouldn't have time to appreciate what you saw. It is best to allot at least a few days for the city itself before you spread your wings to the outer attractions. So this guide is set out in areas, perhaps you should allow one day per area.

CIRCULAR QUAY AND THE ROCKS

Sydney Harbour Bridge

Affectionately known to Sydneysiders as 'The Coathanger' the Sydney Harbour Bridge dominates the city skyline. It is 503m long, and was completed in 1932 after nine years in the making. It was built from either shore, and when the two halves met they were only 7.6cm (3 inches in the old measurements) out of alignment! The Bridge opened with a piece of drama. The dignatories were lined up, the Premier, Jack Lang, stepped forward to cut the ribbon, and up rode Captain de Groot on a noble steed. He slashed the ribbon with his sword, and all and sundry stood speechless, at least for a few seconds. The miscreant was apprehended, the ribbon was rejoined, and the ceremony continued.

In August, 1992, came the opening of the long-awaited harbour tunnel. I am sure that the Premier had a few anxious moments as he stepped forward with the scissors, maybe a touch of *deja vu*, but nothing happened and everything went according to plan. I really think that a few Sydneysiders were a little disappointed that we seem to have lost some of our larrikin spirit.

A nice touch to the opening of the tunnel was that the first person to cycle through was Sir Rupert Oppenheimer, not only one of the greatest cyclists in Australian sporting history, but also the first person to cycle over the bridge sixty years before. The grand old man admitted afterwards that the rise at the end of the tunnel was slightly daunting, but he was clearly moved by the rousing ovation he received.

The Cahill Tunnel has now become a way of life, and by taking the cars that are driving to the eastern suburbs, it has certainly reduced the peak hour traffic snarls on the bridge. You can't walk through the tunnel but you can walk over the bridge, and you can climb up the south-east pylon for some of the best harbour views. The pylon is open Tues-Sat 10am-5pm (every day during school holidays) and admission is $1 adult, 50c children.

Sydney Opera House

The magnificent performing arts complex is situated on Bennelong Point, which was named by Governor Phillip after an Aboriginal he befriended, taught English, and actually took back to England. This spot is apparently where Bennelong had his humpy.

Shrouded in controversy during its construction, Sydney Opera House was finally completed in 1973, and has since become almost the symbol of Australia. Instantly recognisible anywhere because of its unique architecture, it can only really be appreciated when seen as part of its surroundings. Then it seems to become another form of sea-going craft, and it is does not take too much imagination to picture it joining the other sail boats on the harbour.

The Opera House has four theatres, four restaurants and six bars, and is surrounded by wide walkways. Details of current programs are published in the daily newspapers, and the Box Office is open Mon-Sat 9am-8.30pm and two hours prior to the start of a Sunday performance. Phone bookings may be made up to seven days prior to the performance, and the booking clerk will advise when payment must be made, or you can use your credit card.

Guided tours are available daily 9am-4pm. They last one hour and **cost $8.50 adult, $5.50 child**. There are also tours on Sundays only that take visitors backstage, 9am-4pm. They cost $12 and are unsuitable for children under 12.

Bus no 438 travels down George Street to the concourse; Bus no 440 travels from the concourse up George Street. Circular Quay Railway Station is the closest stop for train passengers.

Circular Quay

It doesn't seem to matter when you visit the Quay, there are always lots of people around, but it is on weekends and holidays that you have the added colour and noise of all the buskers. From men playing classical pieces on violins, to little kids belting it out on a range of brass instruments, to aborigines and (non aborigines) playing didgeridoos and teaching people to perform kangaroo and emu dances - it's all great entertainment.

There's people waiting for ferries to take them to Manly or the Zoo for the day; people hurrying to catch their train at the railway station; some buying tickets for harbour cruises; some fishing in the doubtful water near Wharf 5; others, the well-dressed ones, are beginning their walk around to the Opera House for a ballet or opera matinee; and those with suitcases are probably taking off on an exotic cruise on the ship moored at the Overseas Terminal.

Circular Quay Railway Station, although not underground, is part of the City Circle, and the Cahill Expressway on top of the railway takes traffic from the Bridge to the Eastern Suburbs and Macquarie Street.

Museum of Contemporary Art

The MCA is the Art Deco building on the waterfront around from Wharf 5. It formerly housed the Maritime Services Board and when the board moved to new premises, there was some talk of levelling this imposing structure. Then it was realised that it would be the perfect place for the J.W. Power collection of contemporary art, which had been left to the University of Sydney many years before. Now the museum is run as a non-profit company jointly by the University and the NSW Government.

The museum's brochure says, "This is a museum about the beautiful under our noses, the unusual, the weird and wacky in the visual, electronic, sound and tactile world we all live in." And that just about sums it up! The museum is open Wed-Mon 11am-7pm, and **admission is $6 adult, $4 child under 16, $15 family,** ph 252 4033. Entrance is from the Quay or from George Street.

The MCA Store in George has an incredible range of books, magazines, posters, etc, and the MCA Cafe next to the Quay entrance is worth a visit in itself, and why not? It is managed by

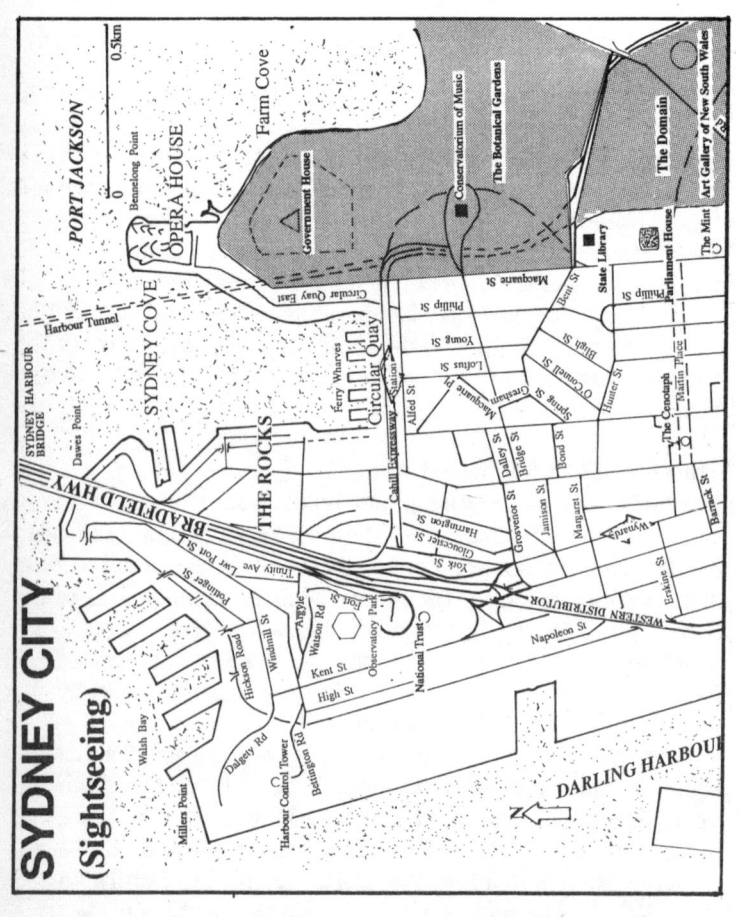

SYDNEY CITY (Sightseeing)

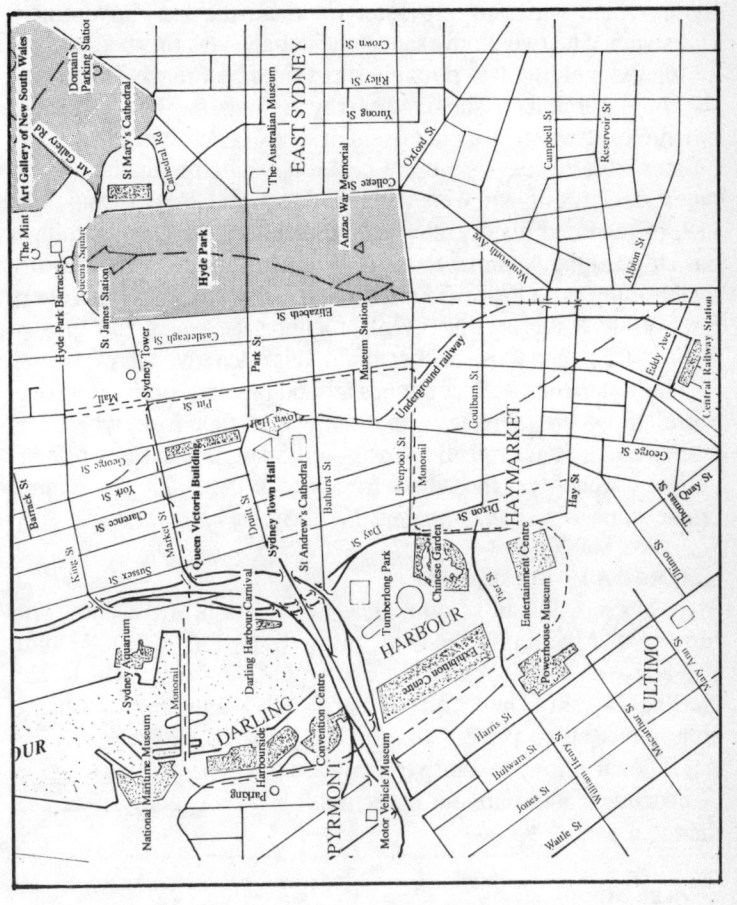

the people from the award-winning restaurant, Rockpool, which is nearby at 109 George Street, The Rocks.

Cadman's Cottage

Continuing along the waterfront, the cottage is situated in a reserve on the corner of Argyle Street. It is the oldest remaining house in Sydney, and was home to John Cadman, the last Government Coxswain. The two-storey sandstone cottage was finished in early 1816, and building was possibly supervised by Francis Greenway, the convict architect, who lived nearby. At that time the house stood two metres from the water, on a small sandy beach, and had a wharf on its northern side. Its present position resulted in the late 1840s when ten acres of land were reclaimed to form Circular Quay. The lack of recorded history, artefacts or detailed plans of the cottage has stopped the National Parks & Wildlife Service from restoring the building as an historical museum. It is presently a NPWS shop, ph 247 8861, and has plenty of brochures on walks and trips in Sydney parks and those further afield. It is open seven days a week.

The waterfront walk continues around the back of the Overseas Terminal, where there are many tour offices, and from where bus tours depart, to Campbell's Cove, with many restaurants in converted storehouses; the wharf from which the _Bounty_ and other cruise ships depart; and the Park Hyatt Sydney Hotel.

The Rocks Visitors Centre

Steps beside Cadman's Cottage lead up to George Street, and if you turn right at the top of the steps and walk past the Sailors' Home you arrive at The Rocks Visitor Centre, ph 247 4972 or The Rocks Hotline 11 606. The Centre is open daily 9am-5pm, and has a continuous video presentation on the growth of Sydney from a small penal colony to a thriving modern city. There are also heaps of brochures and maps for attractions all over Sydney as well as the local area.

George Street

Continuing along George Street, there are many old historic buildings and pubs, and on the weekends the Bridge end of the street is closed off and The Rocks markets are held (see Shopping section).

Before the markets, on the right hand side, you can take a walk through a building, past the restaurant, Pancakes on The Rocks, ph 247 6371 (which never closes, but is a bit expensive for what you get), to Hickson Road, and visit **The Earth Exchange**, a geological and mining museum, ph 251 2422. There are three floors of interactive exhibits, from the time of formation of the lands to mining for gold, opals, crystals and many other minerals. The Minerals and Energy Information Centre is on the first floor, and from them you can pick up a fossicker's licence. On the top floor there is a cafe/restaurant, Guthries, with great views of the harbour. The Earth Exchange is open daily (except Christmas Day and Good Friday) 10am-5pm, and **admission is $7 adult, $5 child.**

Westpac Museum
From Hickson Street, retrace your steps to George Street, walk past the Old Sydney Parkroyal Hotel, then turn up Playfair Street. Here at no 6-8 is the Westpac Museum, ph 251 1419, which traces the history of the bank from its beginnings in 1817 as the Bank of NSW, up to the present day of technological banking. There are also temporary exhibitions featuring subjects as diverse as the Royal Flying Doctor Service and Antarctica. The museum is open Mon 1.40-4pm, Tues-Fri 10.30am-4pm, Sat 1-4pm, Sun noon-4pm. By the way, Playfair Street bends to the left, and straight ahead from the museum is Atherden Street, with four terrace houses. It is the shortest street in Sydney.

The Rocks Square
The square is in the middle of Playfair Street (which is closed to traffic) and this area has many outdoor eateries, jazz or rock bands, little shops, and several lanes leading here, there and everywhere. Following Playfair Street to its end brings you to Argyle Street.

The Rocks Puppet Cottage
The cottage is situated in Kendall Lane, and can be reached from George Street through a lane at no 77. It is open 10am-5pm Wed-Sun, ph 241 2902. There are hundreds of puppets on display, and shows are held at 11am, 12.30pm, 2pm and 3.30pm on weekends, and other days during school holidays. **Admission is free,** and the cottage is sponsored by the Sydney Cove Authority.

The Rocks Walking Tours

The office, and the departure point for the tours, is at 39 Argyle Street, ph 247 6678. There are three tours Mon-Fri, at 10.30am, 12.30pm and 2.30pm, and two tours Sat-Sun at 11.30am and 2.30pm, and it is wise to ring beforehand to make sure there are vacancies. The tours last about an hour and a quarter, and could be classified as 'strolls', so don't be put off if your fitness level is not what is should be. Every aspect of the history of The Rocks is covered, and changes made over the years are highlighted. **Costs are $7 adults, $4.50 children 10-16, children under 10, free.**

Clocktower Square

The square is the building on the corner of Argyle and Harrington Streets with the clocktower, and it contains several souvenir shops, a Japanese restaurant, and **The Rocks Opal Mine**, ph 247 4974. Here you can not only buy tax-free opals, you can dig for them! There is a mine shaft elevator which really does seem to travel down to the depths of the earth, then the door opens and an old mine tunnel appears with 'miners' busy at work. It's good fun even if you are not interesting in buying opals, and is open seven days.

The Argyle Centre

Housed in restored warehouses, the Argyle Centre has a good selection of art and craft shops, galleries and gift shops, and an excellent coffee shop. The Centre is open seven days, and there is an old-timer who sings real Colonial songs on the weekends. He knows more verses of *Click Goes The Shears* than anyone I have ever heard.

A few doors up Argyle Street from the Centre is **The Argyle Tavern**, which is open daily 11.30am-3pm, 7.30-10.30pm, ph 247 7782. This is a real Aussie theatre-restaurant, that serves good old fashioned tucker (food) with large helpings of fun and laughter.

Millers Point

Millers Point is the suburb on the other side of the Harbour Bridge, and Bradfield Highway which crosses it, to The Rocks. It can be reached by following Hickson Road from the Park Hyatt Sydney Hotel around the base of the south-east pylon of the Bridge to Dawes Point; by following George Street to its end, then walking

THE ROCKS

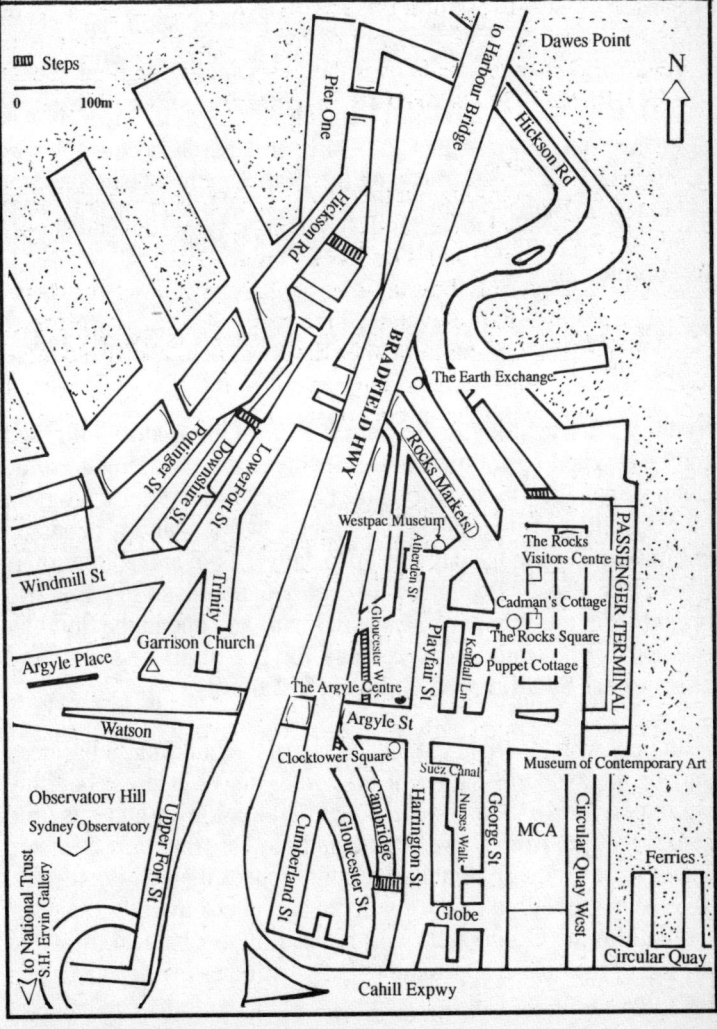

Steps

0   100m

N

Dawes Point

to Harbour Bridge

Hickson Rd

Pier One

Hickson Rd

BRADFIELD HWY

Downshire St

Lowcroft St

The Earth Exchange

Rocks Market(s)

Westpac Museum

PASSENGER TERMINAL

Windmill St

Trinity

Atherden St

The Rocks Visitors Centre

Cadman's Cottage

Gloucester W

Playfair St

Kendall Ln

The Rocks Square

Garrison Church

Puppet Cottage

Argyle Place

The Argyle Centre

Argyle St

Watson

Clocktower Square

Suez Canal

Museum of Contemporary Art

Observatory Hill

Sydney Observatory

Upper Fort St

Cumberland St

Gloucester St

Cambridge

Harrington St

Nurses Walk

George St

MCA

Circular Quay West

Ferries

to National Trust
S.H. Ervin Gallery

Globe

Circular Quay

Cahill Expwy

down steps to Hickson Road; or by continuing along Argyle Street and passing under the Bradfield Highway.

The closest attraction to the Bridge is **Pier One**, a three-level structure which was full of shops when it was first opened, but is now visited more for its restaurants - *Harbour Watch*, *Water's Edge* and the *Harbourside Brasserie*, which is also a nightclub. Pier One does have a large amusement arcade, a book shop, and some galleries where artists work, but they are not always there.

The **Holy Trinity (Garrison) Church** is in Argyle Street. It was built in 1848 and is called the Garrison Church because it was compulsory for the soldiers of the 50th Regiment stationed at Dawes Point Battery to attend the morning service. There is a leaflet available for purchase ($2) at the rear of the church which details its complete history.

Argyle Place, the little park just up the street, is Sydney oldest village green.

Sydney Observatory is on Watson Road, Observatory Hill, and can be reached by following Argyle Street, then walking up some steep steps. The Observatory, ph 217 0485, has a regular program of exhibitions, films, talks and night viewings, and a hands-on exhibition. During the day it is open daily 2-5pm and admission is free. It is also open nightly, except Wednesdays, and has two programs in the Winter (6.30 and 8.30pm) and one in the Summer (8.30pm). **Bookings are necessary for the night sessions, and charges are $5 adults, $2 children, $12 family.**

You may wonder about the ball on top of the building. It has been part of the synchronisation of time in Sydney since the building was erected in 1858. In the early days of the colony, a gun was fired at exactly 1pm from Dawes Point, and another from Fort Denison. These were for the ships in the harbour to check their chronometers. To enable the settlers in the colony to also check their time-pieces, the ball on the Observatory was hoisted by mechanical means to the top of the pole at approximately five minutes to one, then when the guns fired, the ball dropped back to the bottom. The ball still fulfils its function, but it is now lost from the view of most of the people in the city because of the skyscrapers in between.

The **S.H. Ervin Gallery** is in the National Trust Centre, almost next door to the Observatory. The building was erected in 1815 as a military hospital, then for many years was home to one of Sydney's leading girls' high schools.

The Gallery has changing exhibitions, and for current programs and entry charges phone 258 0174.

THE BOTANICAL GARDENS AND MACQUARIE STREET

The Botanical Gardens
The Gardens are a popular lunchtime spot for city workers, and weekends see many family picnics. They are situated on the edge of Farm Cove, where the early colonists first tried to grow vegetables.

As you enter through the gate near the Opera House and climb the slight slope, the enormous castle to your right is **Government House**, the residence of the Governor of NSW. The building at the end of the driveway leading from Government House is the **Conservatorium of Music**, which was originally the Governor's stables.

Signposts point the way to **Mrs Macquarie's Chair**, a rock outcrop where the Governor's wife apparently sat to watch for ships arriving from England. The island fort you can see is **Fort Denison**, also known as Pinchgut, because the island was used for a short time as a place of punishment for erring convicts. The fort was built as part of Sydney's defences, and has recently come under the jurisdiction of the National Parks and Wildlife Service, as part of Sydney Harbour National Park. Tours of Fort Denison are run by Hegartys, ph 247 2733, and leave from Wharf 6, Circular Quay. They run on Tues-Sun at 10am, 12.15pm and 2pm, and **cost $8.50 adult, $6 child, $24 family.**

The walkway around the water leads to the visitors centre and shop, a kiosk, and a restaurant; and signposts show the way to the herbarium and the pyramid glasshouse. There are two exits near the pyramid, one on to Macquarie Street, the other leads to the Art

Gallery. The gardens are open daily 8am to sunset, ph 231 8125.

Art Gallery of New South Wales

The Art Gallery is in Art Gallery Road, in the Botanic Gardens and faces The Domain. It is a spectacular building, and houses a vast contemporary collection of Australian, European and Asian Art, and a fine collection of Aboriginal paintings and artifacts. Many special exhibitions are held at the Gallery, and for recorded information on current exhibits phone 225 1790. Free guided tours of the Gallery are available - check at the information desk on your left as you walk into the gallery through the vestibule. There is no charge for admission to the Gallery and its permanent collection, but a fee is levied for special exhibitions.

There is a restaurant and a coffee shop, and the Gallery is open daily, except Christmas Day and Good Friday, 10am-5pm.

The Domain

The Domain is the large grassed area between the Art Gallery and the Public Library. It is a peaceful park setting for soap box orators on Sundays, and the venue for a number of Sydney's free summer-time open-air concerts, such as Opera In The Park.

State Library of New South Wales

The original, imposing building of the Library faces Shakespeare Place, on the corner of Macquarie Street, and the new section has been built behind, but can also be entranced from Macquarie Street.

The Library contains the nation's finest collection of Australian history, and an excellent Reference Library. The new wing contains the latest technology for reading and learning. The information desk has a self-guided tour sheet which has information on every part of the library, and is worth obtaining.

There is a restaurant and a bookshop, and the Library is open Mon-Fri 9am-9pm, Sat 9am-5pm, Sun 11am-5pm, and admission is free, ph 230 1414. The Library has changing exhibitions, usually of an historic nature, and information on current programs can be obtained from a recorded information phone line, 0055 21068 (0055 calls are time-charged).

Parliament House

Situated in Macquarie Street, Parliament House is open to visitors, and they can even attend a session. Parliament generally sits from mid-February to early May, and from mid-September to early December, on Tues, Wed and Thurs. For information on hours, ph 230 2111.

The Mint

Sydney Hospital is between Parliament House and The Mint Museum, which was once a wing of Governor Macquarie's Rum Hospital. The 1850s earned the building its name for it was here that gold sovereigns were coined. Now it is a museum of decorative arts, coins and stamps. It is open Thurs-Tues 10am-5pm, Wed noon-5pm, and there is no admission charge, ph 217 0333.

Hyde Park Barracks

The Barracks is a Georgian building, designed by convict architect Francis Greenway, and intended as accommodation for convicts when it was built in 1819. It now houses an impressive collection which shows how the convicts spent their daily lives, where and how they slept, ate and worked.

The Barracks also has the Greenway Gallery, which has changing exhibitions of historical and cultural interest. The Barracks Cafe is in the original confinement cell area and has an imaginative menu, but it's a bit on the expensive side.

The Historic Houses Trust of New South Wales has control of the Barracks which is open daily (except Christmas Day and Good Friday) 10am-5pm, ph 223 8922. **Admission is $5 adults, $3 children, $12 family.**

Francis Greenway also designed St James' Anglican Church on the other side of the street from the Barracks.

St Mary's Cathedral

The Cathedral is a magnificent example of revival Gothic architecture in Hawkesbury sandstone. Begun in 1866, after a fire destroyed the previous church, the workmen laid down their tools in 1928, after 62 years of work. The twin spires over the southern nave were never added, giving the exterior an unfinished look, but the interior is beautiful and fascinating, with its soaring vaults, gargoyles, side altars and statues.

The outstanding feature is the stained glass windows which have scenes from the life of the Blessed Virgin Mary, and the early days of the Catholic Church in Australia. Below is a crypt where the Catholic Archbishops of Sydney are interred, and next door is a small museum, formerly the Chapter Hall, open Wed-Fri 10am-4pm, Sat-Sun noon-5pm, ph 220 0465.

The museum is in the earliest building still standing on the site. Built in Gothic Revival style between 1843 and 1845, the Chapter Hall was to form part of a Benedictine Monastery planned to include the original cathedral. The monastery was never completed. The Chapter Hall was commissioned by John Bede Polding, the first Archbishop of Sydney, and since its construction it has been used as a meeting hall, classics school and general purpose hall. It is classified by the National Trust.

The main exhibition of the museum is the Australian Catholic Church from before European settlement to the present day. Guided tours of the Museum, which can include the Cathedral and crypt, where there are graves of pioneer priests and archbishops, are available. There is a small admission fee to the museum.

Another attraction of the Cathedral is its world-famous choir which sings every Sunday at the 10.30 Mass.

Hyde Park
Opposite Hyde Park Barracks is Queen's Square with an imposing statue of Queen Victoria, and adjoining that is Hyde Park and the beautiful Archibald Fountain.

Hyde Park is bounded by Queen's Square, College Street, Liverpool Street and Elizabeth Street, with Park Street running through the centre, and changing its name to William Street as it crosses College Street.

At the Queen's Square end of the park there are entrances to the underground St James Station from Macquarie Street, Elizabeth Street (at the end of Market Street) and Queen's Square. At the Liverpool Street end of the park there are entrances to the underground Museum Station from Elizabeth Street (at the end of Bathurst Street) and near the corner of Elizabeth and Liverpool Streets. Near here is also the **Anzac War Memorial** with the tomb of the Unknown Soldier.

The Australian Museum

The Museum is at 6 College Street, and is open daily, except Christmas Day, 10am-5pm. **General admission to the museum is $4 adult, $1.50 child, $8 family, but for special temporary exhibitions there may be an extra fee. Half-price admission is available on Saturdays, and there is no charge after 4pm each day.** The Museum Alive Line, ph 339 8181, gives all details of current attractions, special programs for children, etc, and gives information on guided tours and any query you could possibly have.

The Australian Museum is recognised as one of the top museums in the world, and has a bookshop and restaurant.

Parking

It is not really recommended that you take your car to the city if you intend to visit several places. Wherever you find a place to park, you will be walking quite a distance away from it, then have to retrace your steps to pick it up. There is very limited long term street parking, and although there are parking stations in The Rocks area (behind the Regent Hotel), it could end up costing you more for the car than for your day out.

Another alternative is the council-run **Domain Parking Station,** which is entered from Sir John Young Crescent, east of St Mary's Cathedral.

This station is open Mon-Sat 7am-midnight, Sun 10am-6pm, and **charges are:**

Mon-Fri, 1st hour $4, 2nd hour $3, 3rd hour $3, 4th hour $3, then $1 per hour up to **a maximum of $17; Sat-Sun $6 per day.**

There is a moving underground footway from the parking station to the intersection of St Mary's Road, Prince Albert Road and College Street, in the front of the Cathedral. Privately owned parking stations in other parts of the city are more expensive than the Domain.

| Tip |

Take notice of the closing times of the Domain station because there is a fine of $40 if you have to ring the emergency number and get someone to open the station to get your car.

CITY CENTRE

Though principally a shopping area, there are a few sites worth visiting.

Martin Place

A traffic thoroughfare until 1973, Martin Place, or Martin Plaza as it is sometimes called, is a wide pedestrian mall that stretches for five blocks, from George Street to Macquarie Street. At the George Street end near the GPO is **the Cenotaph,** where a Military Memorial Ceremony takes place every Thursday at 12.30pm. It is near the Cenotaph that Sydney's official Christmas Tree is erected.

Between Pitt and Castlereagh Streets, near the MLC Centre, there is a sunken amphitheatre where free lunchtime entertainment is staged Mon-Fri, noon-2pm.

Near the Elizabeth Street crossing is Halftix, where you can pick up half priced tickets for that evening's theatre performances.

The entrance to Martin Place Railway Station is between Phillip and Macquarie Streets.

Sydney Tower

The Tower soars over 300m above the city, and is the highest public building in the Southern Hemisphere. It is located above the Centrepoint Shopping Complex, bounded by Pitt, Market and Castlereagh Streets. From the Market Street foyer take the lift to the Podium Level, then board one of three double-decker lifts that will take you to the Observation Level (Level 4). Here there are high-powered binoculars, an illuminated display of Sydney Harbour's water traffic, a tourist booking and information service, audio and guided tours.

Level 3 has the highest coffee lounge in Australia; Level 2 has a self-service revolving restaurant; and Level 1 has an a la carte up-market restaurant.

The Observation Level is open daily 9.30am-9.30pm, Sat til 11.30pm.

The Queen Victoria Building

There is more information on this restored building in the Shopping chapter, but even if you aren't interested in shopping, you should call in and have a look. It is not just a shopping centre, it is a remarkable building, with Style.

Sydney Town Hall

Situated on the corner of George and Druitt Streets, the Town Hall was built between 1868 and 1889 in French Renaissance style. Its concert hall houses a pipe organ which ranks with the biggest and best in the world. The Sydney City Council administrative offices occupy the modern tower block at the rear of the building. The Town Hall was given a face-lift in time for Sydney's Sesquicentenary in 1992. Prior to 1842, Sydney had not received city status.

The Town Hall is open Mon-Fri 9am-5pm, ph 265 9230. The main hall is the venue for classical musical concerts.

Town Hall Railway Station has entrances to the underground on both sides of George Street.

St Andrew's Cathedral

The Cathedral has twin towers reminiscent of York Minster, and is the oldest cathedral in Australia. The foundation stone was laid on May 17, 1837 by Governor Bourke. Work stopped in 1842 due to lack of funds, as the colony had financial problems because of a three year drought. The Cathedral was finally completed in 1868.

There was a lot of drama during its construction, including a change of architects, and the inside of the church had to be completely turned around as in the original plans, the back door opened onto the main George Street. It is possible to buy a book detailing the history of this beautiful Cathedral.

DARLING HARBOUR

Darling Harbour is Sydney's newest area, and is nearly half the size of the Sydney Business District at 54ha (133 acres). It was originally a shipping and storage area for the Port of Sydney, but the advent of container ships sounded its death knoll and it became nothing more than an eyesore.

After years of planning, wrangling amongst civic authorities, and the investment of millions of dollars, Darling Harbour has become the entertainment centre of Sydney and something for the city of which to be proud.

There is always something on at Darling Harbour. Every weekend there is some program of entertainment, and almost every yearly festival or show has changed its venue to this central area - the Home Show, the Boat Show, Navy Week, Music Festivals, Book Fairs, Antique Fairs, the list goes on. For information on special events when you are in town, phone the Darling Harbour Infoline on 0055 20261 (24 cents for 26 seconds max).

How to Get There

By monorail, the closest station is near the corner of Pitt and Market Streets. The monorail operates from 7am Mon-Fri, from 8am Sat-Sun.

By Rocks Darling Harbour Shuttle Bus, which runs daily at 20 minute intervals, 10am-5.30pm, from Circular Quay along George Street to the Aquarium and Harbourside.

Bus no 469 runs from Central Railway to Prince Alfred Hospital via Darling Harbour, Mon-Fri 9.34am-2.34pm.

By Sydney Ferries from Circular Quay to the Aquarium, via Balmain. The trip takes 22 minutes, and ferries leave every 45 minutes from Wharf 5. *Matilda Cruises* also run ferries from Circular Quay to the Aquarium and adjacent to Harbourside, leaving every 30 minutes 10.15am-5pm ($3 per trip).

By Sydney Explorer Bus, which stops at Harbourside and the Chinese Gardens.

By Train - the nearest stations are Town Hall, from where you can walk down Market or Bathurst Streets then across Pyrmont Bridge; and Central Station, from where you can catch Bus 469, or take any bus travelling north along George Street and alight at Chinatown.

Parking

Although several thousand car parking spaces are available on the western side of Darling Harbour off Quay Street, adjacent to the Sydney Entertainment Centre; off Murray Street behind Harbourside; and off Darling Drive under the Sydney Exhibition Centre, it is an expensive operation to park your car for a whole day, so the best advice is to leave the car at home, or at a railway station on the outskirts of the city.

Getting around Darling Harbour

Of course, you can walk from attraction to attraction, but if you have small children, or elderly people with you, there are a couple of alternatives.

The People Mover train operates daily to all parts of the site, with major stops at the Aquarium, The Chinese Garden and Harbourside - $2.50 adults, $1.50 children.

Jolly Boat Rides operate a shuttle service Sat-Sun and school and public holidays, 11am-4pm, between the Aquarium steps and Harbourside - $1.60 adults, $1 children.

Taxis

If you have overstayed your visit and missed all the public transport available, there is always the option of grabbing a cab. Taxi Ranks are located at the Convention Centre entrance (rear of Harbourside off Darling Drive), in front of Sydney Entertainment Centre, and at all the hotels.

Darling Harbour Super Ticket

Several of the attractions at Darling Harbour have banded together to offer reductions in the form of the Darling Harbour Super Ticket, which can be purchased at any of the information booths at Darling Harbour, the Sydney Aquarium, the Monorail, the Chinese Garden, or at Matilda Cruises.

The cost is $35.50 adults, $19.50 children under 12, which sounds a bit expensive, but this is what you receive:

A two hour Matilda Harbour Cruise.

Entry to Sydney Aquarium.

A ride on the Monorail.

A visit to the Chinese Gardens.

10% off shopping voucher for use at Harbourside.

A BBQ lunch at the Craig Bar and Bistro. (Or, you can use this section of the ticket for lunch on the Matilda Cruise.)

When you add all that, the ticket is definitely worth considering. Also, all sections of the ticket can be used on the one day, or you can used some sections on that day, and the rest are good for three months from the date of issue.

Now that you know how to get there, how to get around, how to leave, and all about the Super Ticket, let's see what there is to see and do.

Sydney Aquarium

The Aquarium is located near the city end of Pyrmont Bridge, and is one of the largest and most spectacular in the world. The numerous tanks and tunnels allow the visitor to experience life on the ocean floor, with hundreds of different species of marine life. There are also displays of river systems, crocodiles, rocky shores, and the Great Barrier Reef. A touch pool allows you to finally get your hands wet.

The Aquarium is open daily 9.30am-9pm, and **admission is $12.90 adult, $6.50 child, $36.00 family (2 adults and up to 3 children),** ph 262 2300.

Australian National Maritime Museum

The museum, at the western end of Pyrmont Bridge, is dedicated to helping people understand and enjoy Australia's ongoing involvement with the sea. Among craft moored at the museum are yachts, warships, tugboats, and a refugee boat.

Free guided tours of the Museum building are available at regular intervals throughout the day, and booking must be made at the Information Counter on arrival. Audio tours are also available from the Information Counter - **$3 adults, $5 for 2 adults sharing, $2 children.**

The museum has a programme of changing exhibitions, and information can be obtained by phoning the recorded information Hotline 0055 62 002 (time charged), or for general information, ph 552 7777. Jigglers restaurant, ph 281 0866, has light meals and hearty snacks and is fully licensed. There is also a library and a shop with a wide range of nautical gifts. The museum is open daily (except Christmas Day) 10am-5pm, and **admission is $7 adult, $3.50 child, $17.50 family.**

Harbourside

Harbourside Darling Harbour is a shopping centre with 200 shops that include 54 waterfront restaurants and food places. There are no department stores, and many of the shops sell for the tourist trade although there are branches of fashion shops that seem to find their way into every shopping centre in Sydney.

Harbourside shops have longer trading hours than in any other complex in the city - Mon-Sat 10am-9pm, Sun 10am-6pm - the restaurants, of course, stay open longer.

Australian Motor Vehicle Museum

The building next to Harbourside is the **Convention Centre**, and for people that are interested in cars, motoring and associated memorabilia, their next stop would be the Australian Motor Vehicle Museum, 320 Harris Street, a short walk from the Convention Centre Monorail Station. Here there is a spectacular array of classic machines from the earliest to the latest, with lots of hands-on exhibits, in an historic old Woolstore building. The museum and carpark cover almost 4ha on two levels, and even has a place where you can 'park' the kids under supervision.

The Cadillac Cafe is available for roadside snacks, and the bookshop stocks everything ever written about cars, and some out-of-the-ordinary souvenirs. The museum is open daily 10am-5pm, and **admission is $7 adults, $4 children, $17 family.**

The Powerhouse Museum

While you are in Harris Street, you should walk away from the water to no 500 and The Powerhouse Museum, Australia's largest museum. Created from the shell of an old Sydney power station, the museum is alive with dynamic exhibitions, hands-on fun and special performances. There is so much to see that some people spent the whole day wandering through this incredible exhibition. Tours, talks, films, performances, demonstrations and workshops are continually happening, and there is the Switch Cafe and a kiosk when you need sustenance. As always, there is a souvenir/book shop, but this one offers some way-out merchandise.

The Powerhouse Museum is open daily (except Good Friday and Christmas Day) 10am-5pm, and **admission is $5 adults, $2 children, under 5 free.**

Back at Darling Harbour proper, the **Exhibition Centre** is the next group of buildings, and information on the current shows is available from the Infoline.

In front of the centre is Tumbalong Park, and from there it is a short walk to the next attraction.

The Chinese Garden

The Garden was specially designed by landscape architects from Guangdong Province, and is the largest and most elaborate outside China. It covers a full hectare, and has a two-storey pavilion above a system of lakes and waterfalls. It is a serene retreat from the madcap and mayhem of the waterfront.

The Garden is open daily 8.30am-sunset and **admission is $2 adults, 50c children, $4 family.**

Across Pier Street from the Chinese Garden is the one hundred year old **Pumphouse Tavern and Brewery**, and next to that is the **Sydney Entertainment Centre**. Chinatown is opposite the main entrance to the Centre, in Harbour Street.

Darling Harbour Sports

A multi-sports centre along from the Chinese Garden, Darling Harbour Sports has as its address, cnr Day & Bathurst Streets, ph 212 1666. The facilities of the sports centre are available for hire, and casual rates are as follows:

Tennis - $20 per hour
Basketball - half court $15 per hour; full court $30 per hour
Volleyball - $15 per hour
Netball - half court $15 per hour; full court $30 per hour
Gym - $10 per workout

The centre is open daily 6am-11pm (courts are floodlit in the evening), and the gym hours are: Mon, Wed, Fri 6am-8.30pm; Tues, Thurs 6am-10pm; Sat, Sun 9am-5pm. Phone the centre for details of aerobic sessions.

There is a also a restaurant offering suitable fare.

Darling Harbour Carnival

Circling back towards Pyrmont Bridge from the sports centre you come to a temporary attraction, Darling Harbour Carnival. The area is leased by the Carnival on a month to month basis, as the land is eventually going to be used for more development.

The Carnival has a roller coaster, dodgem cars, the Disco Train,

The Tri-Star, a go-cart circuit, and lots of bright lights and atmosphere. It really fits in well with the rest of Darling Harbour, and it seems a shame that it may disappear. Don't blame me if it has gone when you visit.

It is presently open Fri from 6.30pm, Sat-Sun and all public and school holidays from 10.30am, and stays open while there are still people around - sometimes to 2 or 3am. **Rides range from $2 to $3,** and if you want to ring beforehand, the number is 281 7804.

Harbourside Darling Harbour

The City from Gladeville

SUBURBAN SYDNEY

NORTH

Although the Lower North Shore harbour front now contains some of the most valuable and exclusive real estate in Australia, it was originally the burial ground of the infant colony because it was considered to be far enough away to stop the spread of disease.

HOW TO GET THERE
Obviously, whatever form of transport is used, visitors must first cross the Sydney Harbour Bridge.

By Train
Trains from Central Station pass through Town Hall, Wynyard and Milsons Point to North Sydney. If you are on a train that is going to travel the City Circle, you must change trains at Town Hall or Wynyard for one on the Northern Line.

After North Sydney, the service continues through many suburban stations to Hornsby including Chatswood and Gordon. Hornsby is on the main northern line out of Sydney and one can link up with trains to Newcastle, and points further north.

There is no rail service to the Lower North Shore suburbs, but most of the buses that travel to them can be joined at North Sydney Station.

By Bus
Buses to the Lower North Shore begin in Carrington Street, at Wynyard Station. There are several to choose from, but there is a route map there, and a ticket machine. Some buses travel via North Sydney Station, while others take the Freeway and exit the Bridge on Military Road.

By Car
There are signs on all roads leading from the city that direct you to the Bridge or the Cahill Expressway. Once on the Bridge, Lane 1 has an exit for Lavender Bay, Milsons Point, and access under the

Bridge to Kirribilli; Lanes 1 and 2 allow cars to exit to North Sydney, and Lane 2 also allows travel to the next exit for Crows Nest and Manly. (Falcon Street turnoff).

To reach Military Road, and the suburb of Neutral Bay, follow the signs leading to Manly. Lane 4 also has an exit for Neutral Bay and Kirribilli, but I don't think this is as easy to follow so, I suggest you avoid it.

Further on after the Falcon Street turnoff, Lanes 3 and 4 bring you into Epping Road (Lane Cove) and you can turn off to the left to join the Pacific Highway which is the main artery north and crosses over the expressway.

By Ferry
Ferries leave from Circular Quay Wharf 4 for the Lower North Shore suburbs. Buses meet the ferries to take passengers to the main street, Military Road.

ATTRACTIONS
On the western side of the Bridge are the suburbs of **Milsons Point** and **Lavender Bay**. Milsons Point is home to North Sydney Olympic Pool, and the now inoperative Luna Park. Lavender Bay has harbourside parkland, from where you can get great photographs of the Harbour.

The suburb of **North Sydney** rivals the Sydney CBD for skyscraping office blocks, and has a few large shopping areas, and numerous restaurants. North Sydney is really a mid-week place, as the service industry is geared for the office worker rather than the resident. This, of course, does not apply to the several good night spots (see Entertainment).

On the eastern side of the Bridge lies **Kirribilli** and the stately mansions, *Admiralty House*, Sydney residence of the Governor-General, and *Kirribilli House*, Sydney residence of the Prime Minister. These two imposing buildings can be seen from the Harbour, and about twice a year they are opened for public inspection. Even if you are lucky enough to be in Sydney that particular weekend, think twice about going to view them for the queues of locals extend for blocks. By the way, Admiralty House is the one closest to the Bridge. Also in Kirribilli is the *Ensemble Theatre*. This area is dotted with at least 6 private secondary schools.

Neutral Bay is the first suburb over the Bridge if you have used the Expressway, and the main street is lined with designer shops and restaurants. The side streets on the right hand side lead to the Harbour and open parklands, and there are many interesting old Federation homes. The side streets on the left lead to the suburb of **Cammeray** and Long Bay, part of Middle Harbour.

Military Road, still with door-to-door shops and restaurants, continues through **Cremorne Junction** to **Spit Junction**, where Spit Road branches off towards Manly, and Military Road continues on its way to **Mosman**, where the biggest attraction has to be the Zoo. There is a lovely walk along the foreshores of the Harbour between Cremorne Point Wharf and Mosman Bay Wharf.

Taronga Park Zoo has Australia's best collection of native and exotic animals, and was recently voted NSW's best tourist attraction. Its address is Bradley's Head Road, ph 969 2777, and the main entrance is there, but the Zoo is only a 12 minute ferry ride from Circular Quay. There is a ZooLink ticket which combines rail travel, ferry and zoo entrance, and a ZooPass ticket is available from the ticket office at Circular Quay, but you have to do some arithmetic to work out if these are practical. It is not possible to give prices of the ZooLink tickets here, because it would vary from station to station, and depend on the distance travelled in getting to Circular Quay Station.

However, the **ZooPass costs $17 adult, $8.70 child, with no combination ticket for a family.** The pass includes the ferry to the Zoo, a bus ride up to the main entrance, and admission fee. The individual costs of each of these are:

Ferry to Zoo - $5.20 adults return, $1.60 child.
Bus to top entrance - $1.20 adult one-way, 60c child.
Entry to Zoo - $13.50 adult, $6.00 child.
$31.50 family (2 adults + 2 children)
$26.50 family (1 adult + 3 children)
$5.00 extra child.

It doesn't take a mathematical genius to work out that travel from the Quay and Zoo entrance for two adults and two children is cheaper without using the ZooPass, because of the family entrance fee to the Zoo. It should perhaps be mentioned here that the Zoo is built on a hill. If you get transport to the top entrance, you actually walk down the hill to the wharf as you visit the different animal exhibits, therefore you would not need to catch a bus back down the hill.

The ZooLink ticket (the one that includes rail travel) would probably be a good buy though, and get better the further you had to travel to arrive at the Quay. Still, find out the cost from the station you would be departing, and do your homework.

There is another alternative for getting from the Zoo wharf to the main entrance and that is the Aerial Safari, which offers great views of the Harbour as it rises to the top, and costs $2.50 adult, $1 child one-way.

You can, of course, enter the Zoo by the gate near the wharf, but then you will be walking up hill the whole time you are there, and you'll really need the bus or the Aerial Safari for the trip back to the wharf.

Don't let all the above put you off, though, because it really is a great zoo. The views are stupendous, and the animals are well-cared for and look sleek and healthy. There is a rainforest aviary to walk through; a nocturnal house full of creatures that you don't usually get to see; seal shows at 1.15 and 3.15pm every day; a large aquarium; a good restaurant; and lots of places to buy snacks.

Taronga is open every day, including Christmas Day, 9am-5pm, ph 969 2777 (or for recorded information, ph 9692295).

From Mosman, is it also a short drive, or you can get a bus, to **Balmoral Beach**. If you head back to Spit Junction, and turn right down Spit Road, you will come to **The Spit**, the entry to Middle Harbour and the famous, or infamous, Spit Bridge, which opens to allow tall-masted boats to pass through into Middle Harbour, where they moor. There are set times for the opening of the bridge, but for the unwary driver it will be an uncomfortable delay. On the other hand, for people on harbour cruises, it is fascinating to see the giant piece of the bridge lift skyward.

Once through The Spit, the road goes up a sweeping hill, then a right turn leads through the suburb of **Balgowlah** to **Manly** and **the beaches**, which are detailed in a separate chapter.

Following the traffic north of the Sydney Harbour Bridge the road passes through the suburbs of **Willoughby** to **Chatswood** and the leafy suburbs of the area described as the Upper North Shore - very much an executive class homeowner's belt. To the immediate west of Chatswood Shopping Centre left off the Pacific Highway along Fullers Road is the *Lane Cove National Park* which provides a welcome haven for picnickers. It is very much a family outing place with river boat rides, canoe hire, swimming areas and outdoor cooking facilities. You should enquire as to where the shark net is posted for swimming, ph 412-1811. **Chatswood** Shopping Centre is one of the major shopping areas in Sydney. Extending east from the Railway Station down Victoria Avenue for about 2km up to a cross street called Neridah Street, the area is a very busy retail

Entrance to Taronga Park Zoo

sector. There are a number of shopping centres in this area - Wallaceway, Lemon Grove, Grace Bros, Westfield Shoppingtown and Chatswood Chase housing David Jones and Grace Bros. Further to the West of Chatswood is the Macquarie Shopping Centre at **North Ryde** which was developed by Grace Bros. It and Chatswood are responsible for the demise of the shopping centre at **Gordon** and its change to a more upmarket boutique styled centre. (Further Shopping Centres are listed in the Shopping Chapter.) There are no special attractions until one comes to the Ku-ring-gai Chase National Park detailed in the Manly section.

EAST

Travelling to the inner eastern suburbs may seem that you have never left the city because, in fact, you haven't. It is just that most of the streets have changed their names. For example, Park Street in the city becomes William Street as you cross College Street., then Bayswater Road as you pass through Kings Cross, then New South Head Road as you depart Rushcutters Bay.

HOW TO GET THERE

By Train
The Eastern Suburbs line commences at Town Hall and runs to Martin Place, Kings Cross, Edgecliff and Bondi Junction.

By Bus
Buses to the eastern suburbs leave from Circular Quay and Railway Square. Routes service the main areas of Maroubra, Randwick, Waverley, Bondi including Bondi Beach, and Vaucluse/Dover Heights going through such places as Double Bay and Woollahra to get there, as well as Oxford Street, and Anzac Parade.
Some Specifics -
To Bondi Beach - from Circular Quay: 380, 389
                    - from Railway Square: None.
Get the train to Bondi Junction then the 391 to the Beach.

To Randwick Racecourse - from Central Railway: 372; 395, 393 go via Anzac Parade and you will have to walk a little way. They also pass the University of New South Wales which overlooks the Racecourse.

From Circular Quay: 373; 394, 396 same as for the 394, 396.

To Double Bay - from Circular Quay, 324, 325.
To Vaucluse -   Stay on the 324; and for Vaucluse House take the 325.

By Car

Drive up William Street from the Australian Museum. At the top of the street, turn left to Darlinghurst Road to tour **Kings Cross,** or take the freeway straight ahead for **Rushcutters Bay** where *White City Tennis Courts* are, and also *the Cruising Yacht Club* which organises the Sydney to Hobart Yacht Race.

Further on you pass through **Edgecliff** with the Edgecliff Centre on the Right where the Railway Station is, and on the left Ascham School for Girls behind some shops. Go through the Ocean Street intersection and descend down into **Double Bay,** renowned for its high prices and coiffured nouveau class cafe society. Then up the hill still on the same road, now called New South Head Road, on the left you will pass the entrance to Redleaf Pool, a harbour swimming area, and then a little further on to the right is Cranbrook Anglican School for boys. As the road sweeps around to the left **Rose Bay** comes into view with the myriad of yachts, various restaurants on the water, a delightful walk around the bay, tennis courts and two golf clubs on the right - the pretentious *Royal Sydney Golf Club* and the *Woollahra Golf Club* whose course though shorter is just as good. Also Woollahra Oval is here, and is still home to the Eastern Suburbs Rugby Union teams.

Then on through the village centre with a variety of small shops and the occasional pub. Going up the winding hill, which in the City to Surf the runners call "Heartbreak Hill", you come upon the most stunning view of the harbour looking towards the east. Here is placed a girls Catholic private School - Sacred Heart Convent. Though there is stupidly placed here a 'no standing' sign, everyone stops and takes photographs. You also get the view another 300 yards along, which is probably safer. Then following the road which becomes Hopetoun Avenue to its end you will pass the

Watson's Bay lighthouse and eventually will come to a series of streets. I suggest you keep going as far as you can and you will come to Watson's Bay park, opposite the Watson's Bay Hotel which is a popular haunt of the late-teen to early 20 yuppies that are part and parcel of this whole area. It is their turf and their lifestyle. Big homes with amazing gardens, swimming pools, and very high fences adorn either side of any of the roads you care to take in this area generally called **Vaucluse**. A delightful park - Neilsen Park hosts a harbourside beach and there are others covered elsewhere. Have a beer at the Watson's Bay Pub or take a picnic lunch and have it in the park, or there is Doyle's Restaurant if you wish to impress. Further east of the road is **The Gap,** made famous not only because of its views but also by the number of suicides here. The area possesses spectacular views back to the city from the promontory which you can climb, (there is a very easy concrete pathway) and also out to sea. You get a magnificent view of the entrance to Sydney Harbour here, with the two imposing headlands providing the entrance. I have covered this drive in detail as it is indeed a most attractive route and very popular with tourists. For more detail on the suburbs see Attractions Section. (See Map pages 38-39). To get to Paddington, follow Oxford Street from Hyde Park.

By Ferry
Ferries travel from Circular Quay Wharf 4 to Double Bay, Rose Bay and Watsons Bay.

ATTRACTIONS
The first suburb on this trip is **Kings Cross**, probably one of the best-known Sydney areas. The Cross is sleazy, of that there is no doubt, with its strip joints, sex shops and ladies of the night. But, if you drive through during the day mid-week, it may seem like any other suburb. It is at night that it comes into its own. There are some excellent restaurants and night spots, and there are some places where you have to be brave to enter. It is not the type of place where you talk to strangers, and believe me, there are some strange people walking the streets. Nevertheless, there are people would not think they had seen Sydney if they hadn't been to the Cross. It is a haven for backpackers because of the number of cheap hostels, and it is certainly a central area, but I wouldn't think of staying there if I

was travelling with children.

Having said that, there are a couple of landmarks. The *El Alamein Fountain*, on the corner of Darlinghurst Road and Macleay Street, was built to commemorate the men of the Australian 9th Division who fought in North Africa during World War II. It is an unusually shaped ball of a fountain, and there are always hundreds of people in the park surrounding it.

A short walk away, although in a different suburb, is *Elizabeth Bay House*, at 7 Onslow Avenue, **Elizabeth Bay**, ph 358 2344. It was built for the Colonial Secretary, Alexander Macleay and his wife Eliza, and is presently furnished to the period, 1839-1845. In its day it was considered to be the finest house in the colony, and its views over the harbour would have been even more impressive then than they are now. It is a two-storey house with a grand winding staircase, and is maintained by the Historic Houses Trust. It is open Tues-Sun (Monday when a public holiday) 10am-4.30pm (except Christmas Day and Good Friday) and **admission is $5 adult, $3 child, $12 family.**

Paddington is another suburb that seems to be part of the city, but it is a charming part. It has many crooked streets lined with pretty terrace houses that are decorated with Paddington Lace, a distinctive wrought-iron trimming. The original village was established in the 1840s and housed the workers building the Victoria Barracks. Parts of the original little town can be seen in the area bounded by Shadforth, Prospect and Spring Streets.

Darlinghurst Road links Kings Cross with Paddington, or you can follow Oxford Street from the city.

Attractions in the area include numerous antique shops along Queen Street, and art galleries sprinkled along Oxford Street and the side streets such as Glenmore and Hargrave Streets. The Paddington Village Bazaar is held in the Uniting Church grounds every Saturday (see Shopping).

Victoria Barracks in Oxford Street, next to the Town Hall, ph 339 3543, is a Georgian-style building (1841-1848) and a living history of Australia's military. The Army Museum is open on the first Sunday of the month 1.30-4pm, and every Wednesday before the Changing of the Guard at 11am.

Centennial Park bordering Oxford Street and sweeping through to the Randwick Racecourse on one side and the Agricultural Showground on the other, was founded in 1888 to celebrate the centenary of the colony. The park is open daily sunrise-sunset, and there are facilities for hiring horses and bikes (see Sport). It is a delightful place to have a picnic with plenty of lakes and landscaped gardens.

Double Bay, one of the most up-market suburbs in Sydney, is reached in a car by following New South Head Road from Kings Cross; or by bus (324,325) from Elizabeth Street; or by train to Edgecliff and walk east down New South Head Road.

Known by Sydneysiders who can't afford to shop here as 'Double Pay', it is the most exclusive shopping area in Sydney, and all the well-known, top-class designers have outlets. The surrounding areas of Darling Point, Point Piper, Vaucluse, etc, are populated by people who can afford to shop here, and it is worth a visit just to watch the rich parting with their money.

As mentioned earlier New South Head Road continues through **Rose Bay** and on to **Vaucluse** where it is worth visiting *Vaucluse House*, which dates from 1803. It was the home of William Charles Wentworth, one of the intrepid trio who first crossed the Blue Mountains, and the father of the Australian Constitution. He, and his wife Sarah and their children, lived here from 1829 to 1853, and it is now furnished in that period. The house is set in 11ha with gardens, bushland and a Harbour beach frontage, and has out-buildings and stables. Free guided tours are available, and open hours are Tues-Sun 10am-4.30pm and Mondays if a public holiday. **Admission is $5 adult, $3 child, $12 family.**There are tearooms in the grounds, and they serve a la carte lunches, and Devonshire teas that you would die for. If you are not driving, Bus 325 from Circular Quay stops at the front gate.

New South Head road becomes Hopetoun Avenue as you pass through Vaucluse and this brings you to **Watson's Bay**. Apart from The Gap, Watson's Bay Hotel and Doyle's restaurant mentioned earlier it is an area replete with history. The actual headland is a military reserve.

Nearby is the anchor from the ill-fated *Dunbar*, a barque which was to carry passengers and goods on a regular basis between

Sydney and England, but was wrecked on the rocks of The Gap on its second voyage in August 1857. It was Sydney's worst shipping disaster, with 121 lives lost and only one survivor.

From **Watson's Bay** you can follow Old South Head Road to **Bondi Junction**, or turn off Old South Head Road left onto Military Road and head for **Bondi Beach** and the other beaches to the south. Bondi Junction is about 2km from the beach, and is the main bus/train link for public transport throughout this area. It is also quite a good shopping centre with a church stationed in its midst around which the centre has developed. Branches of David Jones and Grace Bros are here, linked by the Oxford Street pedestrian Mall, which has many specialty shops. Bus no 280 runs between Bondi Beach and Bondi Junction.

SOUTH

The southern suburbs are for the most part either industrial or residential, and if you arrived by air, you have already travelled through parts of them. The southern suburbs along the coast abut a myriad of beaches interspersed with sandstone cliffs. (see Beaches). The area from Bondi to Botany Bay is well known for its golf courses (more than 10) of which the famous ones are perhaps *The Australian, The Lakes and Bonnie Doon.* (see Sport)

The University of New South Wales faces Anzac Parade and takes up almost the whole suburb of Kensington. Well known for its excellence in various disciplines and for its high student enrolment (biggest in the country) the University looses out in the ascetical quality of its buildings which were thrown up in the 60s and 70s. It is built on the side of a hill on what was once a sandy swamp. There are a number of restaurants, take aways, bars and other services, and the Colleges provide accommodation during the holidays. Further south on the northern side of Botany Bay are the relatively new port facilities. This has effectively diverted most of the commercial shipping out of Sydney Harbour. However, there are a few places that are historically interesting on the shores of Botany Bay. The two main areas are **La Perouse**, on the north head of Botany Head, and **Kurnell** on the south head.

Bronte Beach

HOW TO GET THERE

By Train
To get to Kurnell, take the train to Cronulla, then local Bus 67 from the depot opposite the station, near Munroe Park. For the eastern suburbs between Botany Bay and Bondi Junction, the only means of public transport is Bus.

By Bus
Circular Quay to La Perouse Bus 394 leaves every 15 minutes. Bus no 398 runs an hourly service at 35 minutes past the hour. From Central Railway Station to La Perouse Bus 393 runs every 30 minutes. Other Buses travel the same route but terminate at Maroubra - Bus 395 from Central Railway Station and the 394 from Circular Quay.

By Car

Follow Anzac Parade all the way from Taylor Square in Oxford Street to La Perouse. To get to Kurnell from there, drive around the foreshores of the bay, crossing Endeavour Bridge and Captain Cook Bridge.

It is difficult to get to both places in one trip without a car.

ATTRACTIONS

La Perouse is named after Jean-Francois de Galaup, Comte de Laperouse, who was commissioned by Louis XVI in 1785, to set out on a voyage of discovery. The expedition consisted of two ships, *L'Astrolabe* and *La Boussole*. Two and a half years later, the two ships arrived in Botany Bay, a week after the arrival of the First Fleet. La Perouse and Captain Phillip apparently became good friends, and the Frenchman gave Phillip reports and letters to be sent back to his king. The French ships stayed in Botany Bay for a period of six weeks, then La Perouse set sail, never to be heard of again.

The whereabouts of the ships remained a mystery until the two wrecks were discovered on the reefs of Vanikoro, off the Solomon Islands, by Peter Dillon an Irish trader and adventurer.

The *La Perouse Museum* is housed in the Cable Station, inside a circle formed by the end of Anzac Parade. It contains many artifacts from the wrecks, as well as relics from their time in the Bay. The museum is open daily 10am-4.30pm, ph 661 2765, and **admission is $2 adult, $1 child.**

The *Cable Station* was designed and built between 1880 and 1881 to provide accommodation, offices and telegraph facilities for the officers of the Eastern Extension Australasia and China Telegraph Company. The company's submarine cable between La Perouse and Wakapuaka in New Zealand terminated at the station.

On the bay foreshore, where La Perouse landed, an obelisk commemorates his visit, and close by is the grave of Pere L.C. Receveur, a chaplain and naturalist with the expedition, who has the honour of being the first Frenchman to be buried on the Australian continent.

The *Macquarie Watchtower*, also in the circle formed by the road, was built between 1820 and 1822, to prevent smugglers entering Botany Bay.

A causeway from the tip of point leads to *Bare Island*, on which the fort was built in 1881, following Britain's decision to give self governing colonies the responsibility for their own defence. It only operated as a means of defence for 27 years, then it became a war veterans home, then a museum with exhibits associated with its early history.

Driving around **Botany Bay** and under the runway of the International Airport you travel over Taren Point Bridge and a few more kilometres further on you come to Captain Cook Drive, turning left and following the road to the end you come to Kurnell.

Kurnell has Captain Cook's Landing Place, an historic site of over 400ha. Cook landed at 3.00pm on April 28, 1770, and traditionally the first person to step ashore was his wife's young cousin, Isaac Smith. The spot where he scrambled onto dry land is marked with a small obelisk, and there is a larger one dedicated to the discovery nearby.

The site is also a monument to the Gwiyagal People, the Aboriginal tribe who inhabited the area at the time of European discovery.

A *museum and visitor centre* is one of the major features of the site, and it is open Mon-Fri 10.30am-4.30pm, Sat-Sun and public holidays (except Christmas Day and Good Friday) 10.30am-5pm. There are exhibits detailing Cook's life, exploits and achievements, including his notes and opinions on the country he had discovered.

There are also scenic walks, picnic and barbecue areas, and an historic walk, and the visitor centre has maps and leaflets on everything you can see and do.

The site is open between 7.30am-7pm, and an hour later during daylight saving. **Entry is $7.50 per car, $3 per motorbike, or $2 per person if you arrive by bus.**

The Sutherland Shire which incorporates this area extends over most of the southern area of Sydney. It is mainly a residential area interspersed with waterways such as the George's River and Port

Hacking. It is dotted with various shopping centres - the main one being Miranda Fair some 6 kilometres west of Kurnell.

WEST

The inner western suburbs were settled in the early days of the Colony and therefore have many buildings and homes from a bygone era.

HOW TO GET THERE

By Bus
Buses 412, 413, 438, 440, 461, 470, 480 and 483 travel south along George Street and pass the beginning of Glebe Point Road, Glebe, but the buses that actually drive down Glebe Point Road are 431, 433, and 434. Bus no 433 continues on to Balmain.

Bus 440 connects the city with Rozelle, passing through the suburbs of Camperdown, Annandale, Petersham and Leichhardt.

By Road
To get to **Glebe,** drive south along George Street, which becomes Broadway, then turn right at the traffic lights on the corner of Glebe Point Road. Incidentally, at that point Broadway becomes Parramatta Road and the Great Western Highway.

Or, if you are crossing the Harbour Bridge, take the Western Distributor, stay in the left lane, follow the sign to Western Suburbs, then take the first exit onto Bridge Road, which passes the Fish Markets and continues on to the heart of Glebe.

The best way to get to **Balmain** from the city is to drive south along George Street to Leichhardt, turn right at Norton Street, follow that street to its end, turn left, then right at the first traffic lights, and follow this street, which undergoes a few name changes before it becomes Darling Street and travels through the heart of Balmain.

If you are coming over the Harbour Bridge, take the Western Distributor, continue over Glebe Island Bridge, turn right into Victoria Road, then right into Darling Street, Balmain. This way by-passes **Camperdown, Annandale, Petersham** and **Leichhardt.**

By Ferry
Sydney Ferries travel between Circular Quay and three wharves in Balmain - Darling Street, Thames Street and Elliott Street.

ATTRACTIONS

The word 'glebe' means 'a gift to the church', and the suburb of **Glebe** was first settled in the late 1700s as a church-owned estate. The church in question was St John's Church, and it still stands on the corner of Glebe Point Road and St John's Road. Apparently by the 1820s the church had fallen on hard times, and the land was sold and subdivided. The high portions of Glebe, away from the insect-ridden Blackwattle Swamp (now known as Blackwattle Bay) were purchased by wealthy families, and houses such as Hereford House, Forest Lodge, Toxteth House and Lyndhurst were built. The land that was not so valuable became an area for worker's cottages, many of which have recently been restored.

By 1861, Glebe was Sydney's largest suburb and quite a stylish place to live, but by 1911 things had changed dramatically. The wealthier older families moved out, and the poor moved in, so by about 1930 there was nothing grand about giving your address as Glebe.

In a full turnaround, Glebe has become a trendy place to live again, and it has a small shopping centre with lots of art galleries and heritage shops. There are also many fine, cheap restaurants along Glebe Point Road, and a couple that are really up-market - The Abbey and Darling Mills.

The old historic homes are privately owned, so are not open to the public, except on special tours arranged occasionally by the Glebe Society, ph 660 3917.

If you are in Glebe on a Saturday or Sunday, you might like to visit the *Glebe Markets*, held in Glebe Public School, on the corner of Glebe Point Road and Derby Place. There are lots of stalls selling new clothes and jewellery, and others offering pre-loved treasures.

On Parramatta Road, opposite the start of Glebe Point Road, is Victoria Park, which has a wide expanse of lawns for picnics, and a public swimming pool, ph 660 4181.

The University of Sydney, on Parramatta Road, adjoins Victoria Park, and the Gothic-revival buildings of the main quadrangle blend well with the more modern architecture. Sydney University is Australia's oldest and grandest. The Great Hall has a Royal Window which illustrates the monarchy from the Normans to Queen Victoria.

The University's Fisher Library contains more than 400,000 volumes, and the Nicholson Museum has a quality collection of Egyptian, Etruscan, Greek and Roman art. Visitors are very welcome to explore the campus, and maps can be obtained from the Student Centre in the Main Quadrangle, the Chancellor's Committee Shop under the Clock tower in the Main Quadrangle, or from Media and PR, ground floor, John Woolley Building.

A better option, though, is to take a guided tour, which allows entry to some buildings that are not generally open to the public. The University of Sydney Guided Tours, ph 692 4002, **cost \$8 adult, \$1 child,** and last for a few hours. Lunches, morning and afternoon teas can be arranged in one of the University Union's rooms for a small additional cost. Bookings should be made at least one day before, as the guides are all volunteer workers. Proceeds from the tours go towards buying special equipment for the University.

After an afternoon spent in the halls of learning, why not grab a bite at one of the nearby eateries, and head for a show at either the Seymour Centre or the Footbridge Theatre, both of which are within walking distance.

Continuing along Parramatta road brings you to **Leichhardt**, which has a large Italian population, and consequently a large number of Italian restaurants are found in the main streets of Parramatta Road and Norton Street. Leichhardt Park, at the end of Mary Street, has several football ovals, acres of parkland, and an attractively sited public swimming complex, ph 810 0379, with views over Iron Cove.

The suburb of **Balmain** gets its name from Dr Balmain, who received the whole of the peninsula as a land grant. To give some idea of the size of his grant, his house was situated in Johnson Street in the suburb of Annandale. Balmain is a trendy area now, rivalling Paddington with its quaint terraces, art galleries and alternative life-style shops, but it wins hands down in the restaurant department. There are also many pubs that have outdoor beer gardens and live entertainment.

When driving to Balmain from Victoria Avenue, The *Dawn Fraser Swimming Pool*, named after Australia's swimming legend because this is where she began her swimming career, is in Elkington Park, ph 810 2183. The park adjoins Young Street, which runs off Darling Street to the left. Further along Darling Street, there is a set of traffic lights near the old town hall, and a left turn will take you into Rowntree Street and lead to the less outrageous waterfront suburb of **Birchgrove**.

Balmain Saturday Market is held in the grounds of St Andrew's Congregational Church, on the corner of Darling Street and Curtis Road, every Saturday 9am-4.30pm, ph 818 2674.

Darling Street continues to Darling Street Wharf, where there is a nice little park, Thornton Park. The ferries leave for Circular Quay from here.

Manly Ferry

MANLY

Manly is a suburb which has beaches both on the ocean and the Harbour, and attracts weekend visitors as well as holiday makers. On January 21, 1788, Captain Arthur Phillip recorded sighting a number of Aborigines in what is now Manly Cove, and stated that their appearance was much more 'manly' than those he had seen before. Hence the name.

HOW TO GET THERE

By Bus
Bus 144 runs to Manly from Chatswood Railway Station.

To travel by bus from Wynyard to Manly, it is necessary to take one of the many services that go through Neutral Bay Junction, and change there to the 144. There are a few direct peak hour services, but these are not for the relaxed tourist.

By Ferry
This is obviously the most pleasant way to visit Manly, and the trip from Circular Quay to Manly takes about 35 minutes. Ferries leave every 30 minutes. The ferry trip travels past the Heads, the entrance to the Harbour, and it can sometimes get a bit rough. Nothing to worry about, but the people sitting outside may get a little damp.

By Manly JetCat
This cuts the travelling time from the Quay by half, but it is much more expensive.

By Car
An old ad for visiting Manly said that it was "seven miles from Sydney and a thousand miles from care", but that doesn't sound as good when you convert it to the metric system. Suffice it to say that Manly is about 15km from the city centre. The best route to take is

over the Harbour Bridge, then follow the signs for Manly.

TOURIST INFORMATION

The Manly Visitors Information Bureau is right on the Ocean Beach, on South Steyne, ph 977 1088. It is open daily, 10am-4pm.

ACCOMMODATION

As mentioned above, Manly is a holiday destination for many people, and it is a great place to spend a couple of days or more, so here is a selection of accommodation, with prices for a double room per night, which should be used as a guide only.

HOTELS/MOTELS

4-Star

Manly Pacific Parkroyal, 55 North Steyne, ph 977 7666 - 145 rooms, licensed restaurant, cocktail lounge, swimming pool, spa, sauna - $220-260.

Radisson Kestrel, 8 South Steyne, ph 977 8866 - 85 rooms, licensed restaurant, swimming pool - $175-210.

All Seasons Welcome Hotel, 48 Sydney Road, ph 977 1977 - 80 rooms, licensed restaurant, cocktail lounge, swimming pool - $150.

3-Star

Manly Paradise Motel, 54 North Sydney, ph 977 5799 - 20 units, swimming pool - $75-105.

Manly Pines Motel, 2 Pine Street, ph 977 3445 - 16 units - $70-90.

Manly Beach Resort Motel, 6 Carlton Street, ph 977 4188 - 39 units, licensed restaurant - $60-78.

2-Star

A1 Pacific Motel, 19 Pacific Street, ph 977 1774 - 12 units - $50-69.

Steyne Hotel, 75 The Corso, ph 977 4977 - 36 rooms (some without private facilities), licensed restaurant - $60-68.

SERVICED APARTMENTS

5-Star

The Manly Waterfront Apartment Hotel, 1 Raglan Street, ph 976 1000 - 22 units, licensed restaurant, swimming pool - $195-270.

PRIVATE HOTEL

Manly Lodge, 22 Victoria Parade, ph 977 8655 - 33 rooms (some without private facilities), unlicensed restaurant, sauna - $60-75.

As with any holiday destination, there are plenty of flats, units and houses available for short-term rental. The Manly Visitors Information can help you out with these.

GETTING AROUND

It is possible to explore Manly on foot, but for places further afield, such as North Head, some help is needed. Manly Coach Tours, ph 938 4677, has a service, no 135, that departs from Stand 4, Manly Wharf Interchange for a *Scenic Explorer ride to North Head and the Quarantine Station*. **The fare is $3 adult, $1.75 child, a**nd you may leave the bus at any stop and pick up a later bus to continue the trip. The buses connect with the ferries from Sydney, and run every half hour on Saturdays, every hour on Sundays, and more frequently during the week.

EATING OUT

The Corso, a pedestrian mall that links the harbour to the ocean and runs through the centre of Manly, is liberally sprinkled with coffee shops, pubs serving counter lunches, and takeaway outlets. At the other end of the scale, the Manly Pacific Parkroyal, in North

Steyne, has an upmarket brasserie, and a bistro in its Charlton Bar.

Other **good restaurants** *you might like to try are:*

Le Kiosk, Shelly Beach, Marine Parade, ph 977 4122 - Licensed - mainly Seafood - **Expensive** - open Mon-Fri for lunch and dinner, Sat-Sun brunch, lunch and dinner - Amex, BC, DC, MC, V.

Faulty Bowers, 7 Marine Parade, ph 977 5451 - BYO (corkage $1.50 per head) - modern Australian - **Expensive** - open daily 8am-10.30am, noon-3.30pm - Amex, BC, DC, MC, V.

Brazil Cafe, 29 Belgrave Street, ph 977 3825 - BYO (no corkage) - wide variety of food - **Moderate** - open daily 9am-midnight - BC, MC, V.

Crusoe's Seafood Brasserie, Shop 210, Manly Wharf, ph 976 2400 - Licensed - specialise in Seafood but also has steak, chicken, pasta and salads - **Moderate** - open 7 days, Sun-Fri 8am-10.30pm, Fri-Sat until 11.30pm - BC, MC, V.

ENTERTAINMENT

There are a few pubs on The Corso - *Ivanhoe's*, *The Steyne* and *The Brighton*, which has bands and always draws a big crowd.

The Manly Pacific Parkroyal Hotel, on North Steyne, ph 977 7666, has a nightclub, *Dalley's*, which is open Wed-Sat 9pm-3am. It has live entertainment and the cover charge after 10pm is $5. In the Brasserie, also on the ground floor of the hotel, is Nell's Cocktail Bar.

OP's Nightclub, 22 Central Avenue, ph 976 2288, is open 7 nights from 6.30pm for dinner until 3am. The cover charge is $5 after 11pm. There is live entertainment every night and the dress rules for this venue are pretty strict. Mon is $2 drink night; Tues is cabaret one week, comedy the next; Wed is Ladies' Night with an all-male review; Thurs is locals night (because most people who live in Manly go out on a Thurs night) and features acts who have proved their popularity with the crowd; Fri-Sat have well-known performers from all over the country; and Sun has a DJ from 11pm.

The Old Manly Boatshed and *Pig and Whistle* - see Entertainment chapter.

There is no live theatre in Manly, but Manly Twin Cinemas is on East Esplanade, ph 977 0644.

Manly-Warringah Leagues Club is not in Manly, its address is 563 Pittwater Road, Brookvale, ph 939 6722. Belgrave Street in Manly becomes Pittwater Road at its intersection with Sydney Road.

SHOPPING

The Corso has several boutiques and specialty shops, souvenir stores, and some great cake shops which are always open.

The main shopping area, though, is on *Manly Wharf*. Completely renovated, Manly Wharf has changed from being a dreary, dirty, eyesore on the Harbour, to a thriving, squeaky-clean, modern complex with the grandiose name of the Manly Transport Interchange. It is the terminus for the ferries and buses, so I suppose the name is justified.

The Wharf has many boutiques and restaurants, and also amusement facilities, a ferris wheel, a restored historic carousel and McDonald's. It is open daily 9am-late, and for information phone 976 2555.

SPORT

The ocean and harbour beaches are there to be enjoyed, with no costs involved (except for some sun block-out), but if you yearn for other physical activities, here are some names and addresses.

Diving
Dive Centre Manly, 10 Belgrave Street, ph 977 4355, have diving courses, scuba hire and offer diving trips. They can arrange for experienced divers to go on shark dives at Manly Oceanarium.

Surfing
Aloha Surf, 44 Pittwater Road, ph 977 3363, hire anything from wetsuits to beach umbrellas, boogie boards to lessons by professional surfers.

Cycling
Manly Cycle Centre, 36 Pittwater Road, ph 977 1189, has bikes for hire - **$4 hourly, $15 daily, $45 weekly.**

Tennis
Manly Tennis Centre, cnr Belgrave & Raglan Streets, ph 977 3159, have courts for hire. For others, contact the Manly-Warringah Tennis Association Ltd, 68 Parks Road, Collaroy Plateau, ph 971 6886

Golf
Warringah Golf Club, Condamine Street, North Manly, ph 905 4028, 905 1326.

18-hole course, par 70, 5300m.

Green fees: $13 for 18 holes; $9 for 9 holes

Club hire: $14 for 18 holes, $10 for 9 holes, pull cart included.
Visitors are welcome after 10.30am on Mon, after 1.30pm Tues-Wed, and all day Thurs-Fri. Sometimes it is possible to get a game on the weekends, but it is imperative to book ahead. In fact, the club advises people to phone the club 48 hours before they want to play on any day, to check that there is a vacancy.

SIGHTSEEING

Manly Oceanarium is on West Esplanade, and is the round building you can see from the wharf, on the other side of the pool. It has a moving walkway beneath the water, enabling visitors to get really close to the marine creatures, and a seal pool that can be viewed from above and below. The three-level undercover complex also has a souvenir shop, and an audio-visual display.

The Oceanarium is open seven days, 10am-5pm, ph 949 2644, and **admission is $10 adults, $5 children, $27 family (2 adults + 3 children).**

Manly Waterworks, West Esplanade, ph 949 1088, are only open in summer (from October to Easter), on weekends and every day during school holidays. **An all day pass costs $14.95.**

Manly Art Gallery and Museum, West Esplanade, ph 949 1776, has a good collection of Australian art, ceramics and local history. Interesting local exhibits include paintings of Manly, swimming costumes and beach memorabilia. The gallery is open Tues-Fri 10am-4pm, Sat-Sun and public holidays noon-5pm.
Admission is $2 adults, children free.

The Quarantine Station, North Head, can only be visited by conducted tour because of the fragile environment. Public tours are held on Wed, Sat and Sun afternoon at 1pm and 3pm, and costs are **$6 adult, $4 child, $16 family (2 adults, 2 children).**

A small area of North Head, known as Spring Cove, was officially declared a Quarantine Station in 1832 by Governor Bourke, and for over 100 years, people were quarantined here on arrival to protect residents of Sydney from various epidemic diseases, such as smallpox and typhoid fever. The ranger-led walking tour lasts about two hours, and includes information on Aboriginal culture as well as early immigration to Australia, and explains the graffiti left by one-time residents. For further information, ph 977 6522.

The NSW National Parks and Wildlife Service, who has managed the Station since 1984, also organise **night tours,** which they call "Ghost Walks", on Saturdays for **$12 per person.** After the tour, visitors can enjoy real billy tea and damper topped with 'cocky's joy' (golden syrup - a sugary treacle which is yummy). Bookings are essential, ph 977 6522, or 977 6229.

Also on North Head is *The Royal Australian Artillery National Museum*, open Sat-Sun noon-4pm, ph 976 1138. The Royal Regiment of Australian Artillery is the oldest Corps in the Australian Army, and the museum is dedicated to the preservation of the history of Gunners in Australia which began in 1788 when Lieutenant Dawes was ordered by Governor Phillip to construct a redoubt on the eastern side of Sydney Cove, and position two 6 Pounder Guns.

The collection includes many guns used by the Australian Artillery both before and after Federation, and also ammunition, radars, search lights, uniforms and photographs. There is also a library, but it is not open to the public.

Tip

If you happen to be in Sydney on Boxing Day, North Head is a great place from which to view the start of the Sydney to Hobart Yacht Race. It is such a popular viewing spot that cars are not allowed into the area on that day, and you have to catch the Manly Coach Tour bus from Stand 4 ($3 return trip). It is a great morning out, and don't forget to take your Esky full of drinks and snacks, a hat, and some block-out.

Manly Scenic Walkway meanders around the Harbour foreshores from the Spit Bridge via Dobroyd Head to Manly, a distance of about 10km that takes the average walker about 3 hours to complete. The walk can be done in sections rather than the whole distance, or it can be a day's outing if you want to stop and have refreshments, or a swim, along the way.

Entry, or exit, points are: Spit Bridge, Clontarf Reserve, Cutler Road Lookout, Tania Park, Wellings Reserve and Manly Wharf. Probably the best way to walk it if you are staying in Manly, is to catch the Bus no 144 (Chatswood or St Leonards) and alight just before the Spit Bridge. Then you can walk back to Manly.

The Visitor Centre can supply you with a route map, and answer any questions you might have.

The Warringah Bicentennial Coastal Walk is being developed by the Warringah Shire Council, ph 982 0333. The idea is to have a series of headland pathways and lookouts which connect the ends of each beach to form a continuous coastline route. Presently, the section between Curl Curl and Mona Vale is completed, and detour to a roadside route will only occur if the coastal lagoons restrict access along the beaches. Unfortunately, north and south of this section are still roadside walks.

Several sections of the Coastal Walk have been made comfortably accessible to disabled people.

At the ends of each beach there is a Coastal Walkway logo, which will lead you onto the pathway, then markers along the way will stop you from getting lost. From Manly, perhaps it is best to catch a bus to the section you wish to walk, rather than walk to Dee Why. Details of the various sections, with the times for the walks in between, are:

Dee Why Head - 20 minutes - easy walking

Dee Why Escarpment - 30 minutes - hard walking; then 30 minutes walk to:

Long Reef Point - 20 minutes - easy walking; then 80 minutes walk to:

Narrabeen Head - 20 minutes - moderate walking

Turimetta Head - 35 minutes - moderate walking; then 50 minutes walk to:

Mona Vale Head - 10 minutes - moderate walking; then 80 minutes walk to:

Bilgola South Head - 20 minutes - hard walking; then 55 minutes walk to:

Bangalley Head - 50 minutes - hard walking.

From Bangalley Head there is a rough track leading to Barranjoey Head with its historic lighthouse and spectacular views of the peninsula.

Barrenjoey Head is managed by the National Parks and Wildlife Service. The narrow neck of land leading to the Head has Palm Beach on the ocean side, Barrenjoey Beach on the Pittwater side, and the Head reaches out into Broken Bay. On the other side of the entrance to Pittwater is West Head, in Ku-ring-gai Chase National Park.

KU-RING-GAI CHASE NATIONAL PARK

The second oldest National Park in Australia, Ku-ring-gai Chase covers 15,000ha of Hawkesbury sandstone bushland on the south side of Broken Bay, 24km north of the centre of Sydney.

The rugged landscape of the Park shows the dynamic changes which have formed the area over more than 220 million years. When dinosaurs were first making their appearance, Hawkesbury sandstone was being consolidated from sands deposited thousands of metres deep by giant rivers. Around 160 million years ago, dykes and diatremes of volcanic rock formed in the West Head area, especially near the present Garigal picnic area. Then between 2 and 12 million years ago, the gradual uplifting of the sandstone rock group formed the Hornsby Plateau. The continual ice-ages in the period from 10,000 to 1 million years ago, locked up the world's seas in polar ice-caps, and low sea-levels allowed streams to erode deeper into the landscape creating steep V-sided valleys. The sea-levels rose when the water was released from the ice-caps, flooding the valleys and creating the wide-bodied waterways of Pittwater and the Hawkesbury River.

The Park has hundreds of Aboriginal sites, the most common being rock engravings, cave art, axe grinding grooves and middens. (A midden is an accumulation of charcoal, shells and bones, usually found around caves along the river banks, where the Aborigines gathered to eat.) **The most accessible site for rock engravings is on the Basin Trail, off West Head Road. Ask at the information centres**.

The views from several of the lookouts in the Park are incredibly beautiful and, dare I say, breathtaking. And, if some of the countryside looks familiar to you it is because many episodes of "Skippy the Bush Kangaroo" were filmed in and around the park. If you look towards Broken Bay, I am sure Lion Island will remind you of our furry friend.

HOW TO GET THERE

By Car
There are several entrances to the Park:
on Kur-ring-gai Chase Road from the Pacific Highway at Mt Colah;
on Bobbin Head Road from Turramurra;
on Coal and Candle Drive, off Mona Vale Road at Terrey Hills;
on Mc Carrs Creek Road, a continuation of Pittwater Road from Church Point.
Admission to the Park is $7.50 per car.

Travelling by car is really the only way to see the entire Park, but if you only want to stay in one part, there are forms of transport that will get you there, but in all cases you are faced with quite a hike to get to any of the facilities. There is no entry fee for people who arrive by public transport, or who hike into the Park.

By Bus
Bus nos 155 and 157 travel from Wynyard to the McCarrs Creek Gate. Hornsby Bus Group Bus no 577 travels from Turramurra Station to Bobbin Head, ph 457 8888. Some buses on this service travel to the wharf at Bobbin Head, but most terminate at the Park Gate, and you have a long walk to where the action is.

By Ferry
If you are not into hiking, and haven't your own transport, this is the way to go.

Basin & Mackerel Beach Ferry Service, ph 918 2747, have an hourly service from Palm Beach and Mackerel Beach and the Basin, and the round trip takes 45 minutes. **The costs are $6 adult, $3 child for the return trip.** This service operates every day, even Christmas Day, because the people who live in the Basin and Mackerel Beach are land-locked, and this is their only form of transport to anywhere.

The ferry service also runs a daily cruise (Sept-May) from Palm Beach to Bobbin Head, leaving at 11am and returning at 3.30pm, with an hour for lunch at Bobbin Head (lunch is BYO food). **The costs for this are $18 adult, $9 child.**

CAMPING
The only camping area in the Park is at the Basin, and for information, ph 451 8124, Mon-Fri 9am-4pm. There is a Youth Hostel at Towlers Bay, via Church Point, ph 99 2196.

ACTIVITIES
As you enter the park, at any of the gates, make sure you pick up a copy of the Park map, or if you want to get one beforehand, contact the National Parks and Wildlife Service, 457 0322 (Mon-Fri), 457 9310 (Sat-Sun), or if you are in the city, drop into Cadman's Cottage.

Within the Park, *the Kalkari Visitor Centre* has loads of information, and a theatrette with videos on Aborigines and Australian animals, and displays on the Park's wildlife. The Chase Alive Volunteer Group provide guided tours around the Kalkari Discovery Track. Kalkari is open daily (except Christmas Day) 9am-5pm, ph 457 9853.

At Bobbin Head there is The Wildlife Shop (open daily except Christmas Day) which sells a wide variety of wildlife publications, posters, guidebooks, gifts and souvenirs.

Picnicking

Picnic facilities are found at Bobbin Head, Appletree Bay, West Head Lookout, Garigal Picnic Area, The Basin and Illawong Bay. If you are planning to have a barbecue, it is a good idea to take your own fuel, or better still, your own gas barbecue.

Kiosks can be found at Bobbin Head, Cottage Point, Appletree Bay (weekends only) and Akuna Bay.

Toilets are available at Bobbin Head, Appletree Bay, Kalkari, West Head Lookout, Garigal Picnic Area, The Basin, Illawong Bay and Akuna Bay.

If you are not in picnic mode, the takeaway outlet at Akuna Bay is also a coffee shop, ph 450 2653, that serves excellent light meals. Or if you feel like splurging, there is the Akuna Bay Restaurant, ph 450 2660, but phone ahead for this because it is not open every day. The same goes for the Cottage Point Inn ph 456 1008.

Boating

Boats can be hired at Bobbin Head, Cottage Point and Akuna Bay.

Bobbin Head Hire Boats, ph 457 9011, have 12 ft row-boats, licensed for 4 people - **$13 per day, $9 per half-day + $10 refundable deposit.** They also have 18 ft motor boats, licensed for 8 people - **$65 per day, $50 per half-day + $30 refundable deposit.** Also available are the traditional Halvorsens from 26 ft to 36 ft - enquire about the rates.

Cottage Point Boat Hire, ph 456 3024, have 14 ft aluminium runabouts with a 6HP outboard - **$20 for 1 hour, $30 for 2 hours, and $5 per hour after + $20 refundable deposit.**

Skipper A Clipper, d'Albora Marina, Akuna Bay, ph 450 1888, have some of the most luxurious charter boats in Sydney. They can provide you with a craft for two people, just to get away from it all, or you can party with eight of your friends on either a house boat, or a cruiser. You don't need a boat licence, only a short briefing, and you can be off cruising the beautiful Hawkesbury River. The boats come equipped with fuel, linen, gas, ice, towels, kitchen equipment, maps, blankets, doonas, first aid kit, radio cassette, ship-shore radio, dinghy, life jackets and pillows. Prices range from 3 nights midweek, May-Sept, on the Luxury 33' for **$650**, to 3 nights at the same time on the unequalled comfort of *The Diplomat* for **$1045.** For full information and rates, contact Skipper A Clipper on the phone number above.

Walking
It is possible to spend days exploring the park on its extensive network of tracks and trails. Wear your stout boots and a hat, grab a map and some water, and off you go.

WARATAH PARK
Bordering on Ku-ring-gai Chase National Park, in Namba Road, Duffy's Forest, is Waratah Park the home of "Skippy the Bush Kangaroo". The park is set in 12ha of native bushland, and features the ranger station from the TV series. Of course, you get to meet Skippy and her friends, and also koalas and emus, face to face, and at a distance you can see Tasmanian devils, and crocodiles. There is also a Bush Railway that has a 15-minute ride through the gum trees and rocky bushland of a typically Australian landscape.

The Bush Barbeque Bistro supplies everything you need to cook your own lunch, and the Snack Bar has light refreshments and quality souvenirs. Waratah Park is open daily 10am-5pm, ph 450 2377. To arrive by car, take the Mona Vale Road from Pymble, then turn left at Terrey Hills and follow the signs. By public transport, The Forest Coach Lines bus no 56 departs Chatswood Railway Station for Duffy's Forest, ph 450 1236 for timetables and fares.

Admission is $10.90 adult, $5.80 child, $29.50 family (2 adults, 2 children).

PARRAMATTA

The second oldest European settlement in Australia, Parramatta was founded by Captain Arthur Phillip on November 2, 1788, and became a city on October 27, 1938. The area had been discovered by Phillip in the previous April, when on an expedition to find land suitable for crops to feed the new settlement, which had been reduced to a diet of salt beef and bread.

Parramatta became the site of Australia's first orchard, vineyard, tannery, legal brewery, woollen mills, observatory, steam mill, market place and fair. It also was the terminating point of the first road, ferry and rail links out of Sydney. And, most importantly, it saw the beginning of Australia's wool industry.

'Parramatta' is an Aboriginal word meaning 'place where the eels lie down'. In keeping with this, Parramatta's Rugby League team is called *The Eels*.

HOW TO GET THERE

By Rail
There is a regular service between Sydney and Parramatta.

By Bus
There is no bus service between Sydney and Parramatta. Privately owned and operated bus services link Parramatta and neighbouring suburbs, eg Carlingford, North Rocks, Baulkham Hills, Castle Hill, Blacktown, St Marys. For information on which companies service which routes, contact the Association of Private Buses, ph 630 0511

By Road
From Sydney, George Street becomes Parramatta Road (Great Western Highway), and leads to the main street of Parramatta, Church Street.

From the northern suburbs there are two choices: by following Victoria Road from White Bay, after passing over the Glebe Island

Bridge and the Harbour Bridge; or by travelling to Lane Cove on the Pacific Highway, and turning into Epping Road, which travels to Epping Station. Continue over the railway bridge, then turn right onto Beecroft Road, then take the first left onto Carlingford Road. Travel to its end when it joins Pennant Hills Road, then turn left and follow the signs to Parramatta.

TOURIST INFORMATION

Parramatta Tourist Centre is in Prince Alfred Park, Market Street, Parramatta, ph 630 3703. It is open Mon-Fri 10am-4pm, Sat 9am-1pm, Sun and public holidays 10.30am-3pm. The staff are very friendly and have pamphlets and information on everything in Parramatta and surrounding areas. They can also provide maps for walking and self-drive tours, and will help plan your day's sightseeing.

Incidentally, the Centre is built on the site of the colony's first gaol, built in 1797.

ACCOMMODATION

There is so much to see and do in Parramatta that the city deserves more than a fleeting visit, so following is a selection of accommodation, with prices for a double room per night, which should be used as a guide only. Parramatta is in the Sydney 02 telephone area code.

4-Star

Parramatta Parkroyal, 30 Phillip Street, ph 689 3333 - 191 rooms, licensed restaurant, swimming pool - $215-230.

Gazebo Hotel/Motel, 350 Church Street, ph 630 4999 - 198 rooms, licensed restaurant, bistro, swimming pool, spa, sauna - $156-210.

Ramada Hotel Parramatta, 18-40 Anderson Street, ph 891 1277 - 188 rooms, licensed restaurant, heated swimming pool, spa, gym - $95-125.

3-Star

Parramatta City Motel, corner Great Western Highway & Marsden Street, ph 635 7266 - 44 units, licensed restaurant, swimming pool - $89.

The Waratah Inn (Hotel/Motel), 22 Great Western Highway, ph 893 9833 - 167 rooms, licensed restaurant, heated indoor pool, spa, sauna, gym - $95.

Out of Parramatta

Wesley Lodge Motel, 175 Hawkesbury Road, Westmead, ph 635 1233 - 57 units - 4-Star - $75-88.

Ermington Club Hotel/Motel, 1 River Road, Ermington, ph 638 0277 - 12 rooms, licensed bistro - 3-Star - $80.

Winston Hills Hotel, cnr Caroline Chisholm Drive & Junction Road, Winston Hills, ph 624 4500 - 6 rooms, licensed restaurant - 3-Star - $75.

Beecroft West Motor Inn, 643 Pennant Hills Road, Carlingford, ph 871 4022 - 24 units, licensed restaurant (closed Sun and public holidays), swimming pool - 4-Star - $95-105.

The Hills Lodge (Motel), cnr Windsor & Salisbury Roads, Castle Hill, ph 680 3800 - 69 units, licensed restaurant, swimming pool, tennis courts - 4-Star - $125-135.

EATING OUT

Parramatta has a good selection of restaurants, and the Visitor Centre has a complete list. Here are a few you might like to try.

River Canyon, cnr Phillip & Charles Streets, ph 689 2288 - Licensed - International cuisine, live music - **Expensive** - open Mon-Fri noon-3pm, Mon-Sat 6pm-midnight - Amex, BC, DC, MC, V.

Barnaby's, 66 Phillip Street, 633 3777 - Licensed - International cuisine - **Expensive** - open Mon-Fri & Sun noon-3pm,Mon-Sat 6pm-midnight - Amex, BC, DC, MC, V.

Courtneys Brasserie, 2 Horwood Place (off George Street), ph 635 3288 - Licensed/BYO - modern Australian cuisine - **Moderate** - open Mon-Fri 11am-midnight, Sat 5pm-midnight - Amex, BC, DC, MC, V.

River Palace, 2 Sorrell Street, ph 683 4488 - Licensed - Chinese cuisine - **Budget** - open daily for lunch and dinner - Amex, BC, DC, MC, V.

Fratelli, 54 Phillip Street, ph 893 8999 - Licensed/BYO - Italian cuisine - **Moderate** - open Mon-Fri noon-3pm, nightly for dinner - Amex, BC, DC, MC, V.

Black Stump, cnr Parkes & Anderson Streets, ph 633 1543 - Licensed - mainly steaks - **Moderate** - open daily for lunch and dinner - Amex, BC, DC, MC, V.

City Extra, 301 Church Street, ph 633 1188 - Licensed/BYO - modern, varied menu - **Budget** - never closes - Amex, BC, DC, MC, V.

ENTERTAINMENT

The main venue for cultural entertainment is *The Parramatta Riverside Theatres*. Built on the banks of the Parramatta River, there are three theatres which feature ballet, musicals, orchestral concerts, plays, films and workshops, and a fully licensed bar. For details of current programs phone 683 6166.

The Hills Centre in Carrington Street, Castle Hill, ph 899 2488, north of Parramatta, has a full calender of cultural performances.

Parramatta has ten cinemas in three locations -
the Village Centre in Westfield Shopping Centre, ph 633 3766;
The Roxy, 69 George Street, ph 635 8499;

the Greater Union complex in Macquarie Street, ph 633 2555.

Even if you aren't interested in going to the movies *The Roxy* is worth a visit. It is one of the few remaining Hollywood Spanish Baroque cinemas in Australia and is classified by the National Trust. It was originally one large theatre, but extensive restoration in 1976 altered it to three smaller theatres.

Several times a week there are free lunchtime concerts in Centenary Place, on the Church Street Mall, near Macquarie Street.

Licensed clubs in Parramatta include:
Parramatta Leagues, O'Connell Street, ph 683 1888;
Parramatta RSL, cnr Macquarie & Pitt Streets, ph 633 5177.

Night spots include:
Traders in the Parkroyal Parramatta, Phillip Street, ph 689 3333;
Parradise, 111 Argyle Street, ph 635 8000;
In Vogue, 10-12 Darcy Street, ph 891 1221.

SHOPPING

Westfield Shoppingtown Parramatta was the largest regional shopping centre in Australia before additions were made to Miranda Westfield in Sydney's south, and it is located in Church Street, near the railway station. The centre has Grace Bros, Target, Woolworths, Franklins, Norman Ross, Best and Less and Venture, as well as over 220 specialty stores, an International Food Court and a cinema complex, all under one roof. There is also parking for 12,000 cars, and sometimes it is still hard to find somewhere to leave the car.

Church Street, between Westfield and David Jones, which is on the riverside, has many specialty shops, and is a pedestrian mall between Darcy and George Streets. Other specialty shops can be found in the cross streets, Macquarie, George and Phillip.

Although I don't expect that you would be interested in buying a car, the other end of Church Street, from Parramatta Road is nicknamed Auto Alley because of the numerous car sales outlets.

SPORT

Parramatta Memorial Swimming Centre, in O'Connell Street, ph 630 3669, has four pools, a waterslide, and volley ball and barbecue facilities. There is also a heated swimming pool in Granville, at Enid Avenue, ph 637 1593.

There are two **public golf courses:**
Woodville Golf Course, 118 Rawson Road, Guildford, ph 632 3582;
Parramatta Golf Club, Park Parade, Parramatta, ph 635 6633. There are several excellent **private golf courses** where visitors are usually welcome.
Oatlands Golf Club Ltd, Bettington Road, Oatlands, ph 630 1269, is particularly scenic;
Muirfield Golf Club Ltd, Barclay Road, North Rocks, ph 871 1388, is a good course and has a nice club house.

Parramatta Council has ten *tennis courts*, and for information on locations and availability phone 689 9333.

For ten pin bowling, head for *Parramatta Super Bowl*, 20 Cowper Street, Harris Park, ph 633 5311.

If you are into *cycling*, the Visitor Centre has a map of Parramatta Valley Cycleway, which follows the river from Parramatta Park to Putney Point, 15km away. Of course, you don't have to travel the entire track if you don't want to. Included in the map are the road rules for cyclists, details of shared footpaths, etc, and a bike safety checklist. Unfortunately, there are no shops in Parramatta that hire out bikes, and those that can be hired in Parramatta Park cannot be taken out of the park.

Spectator Sports
The first recorded horse race in Australia was at Parramatta in 1810, and there were only two starters - "Parramatta" and "Belfast". "Parramatta" won. The interest in horse racing continues with over thirty meetings held every year at *Rosehill Racecourse*, James Ruse Drive, Rosehill. The $2 million Golden Slipper, the richest race for 2-year-old thoroughbreds in Australia, is the feature race of the track's Autumn Carnival (March-April).

Parramatta Stadium, in Parramatta Park, seats over 30,000, and is used for football games as well special events such as Carols by Candlelight. For current events, phone 683 5755.

Parramatta Speedway, Wentworth Street, Granville, ph 637 0411, is not far out of town for those who like the roar of motors and the smell of petrol. Meetings are held during the summer on Friday nights and public holidays.

Eastern Creek Raceway, The Horsley Drive, Eastern Creek, is a lot further out of town (take the Great Western Highway, and turn left at the traffic lights past Prospect Caravan Park) but it is Sydney's newest raceway. It has a large and changing program of races including: motor cycle grand prix, production bikes, super bikes, vintage bikes, touring cars, historic cars, sports sedans, production cars, club events, veteran cars, vintage cars and drag racing. It is impossible to list the dates for everything here, so the best idea is to phone 672 1000 and find out what is on when you are in town.

SIGHTSEEING

When Phillip returned to Parramatta in November 1788 to begin the new settlement, he selected a spot for the buildings and for the crops to be planted at what is now **Parramatta Park**. The first harvest of wheat, barley and maize was reaped in December 1789, and Phillip had a small house built for his own use nearby. The area was originally called Rose Hill, but on June 4, 1791, Phillip changed the name to Parramatta.

Parramatta Park is a great place for a picnic, and on the 3rd Sunday of each month from 1.30-4.30pm, steam trams are run to let youngsters appreciate this 'ancient' form of transport, **$2 adult, $1 child.**

The Tourist Centre has sign-posted an **Historic Houses Route**, which you can start at Parramatta Park, or at Lennox Bridge, which crosses the Parramatta River.

ATTRACTIONS

Old Government House was built in 1799, on the site of Phillip's original house, and Governor Macquarie had additions made in 1815. Later it was leased for some time by The King's

School, which is now situated in lush surroundings on Pennant Hills Road, North Parramatta. Ownership eventually passed to the National Trust of Australia (NSW), and the building was completely restored, and opened to the public. To the west of the building is an amphitheatre with grape vines and fruit trees that were planted in 1791. The house contains Australia's finest collection of pre-1855 colonial furniture, but not many, if any, of the pieces belonged to any of the succession of governors who resided there. Old Government House is open Tues-Thurs 10am-4pm, Sun 11am-4pm, ph 635 8149, and **admission is $4 adult, $2 child.**

As you enter the complex there is a gift shop, and there is also a coffee shop.

There is a *combined ticket* on offer that allows entry to Old Government House and Experiment Farm Cottage and **costs $5.50 adult, $2.50 child.**

West of the house is the **Governor's Bath House**, which was erected for Governor Brisbane in 1823, but has now been filled in. Originally, water was pumped from the river in leaden pipes to a central bath from which small cubicles radiated. Nearby is the site of Australia's first **Observatory**. It was erected by Governor Brisbane in 1822, but all that remains are the transit piers and an obelisk which was erected nearby in 1880.

The Gatehouse Gallery, on the corner of Pitt and Macquarie Streets, ph 891 6149, is the home of Parramatta Art Society, and is open to the public Tues-Fri 11am-3pm, Sun 10am-4pm. Admission is free and paintings by local artists are on sale.

The Tudor Gatehouse was erected in 1885 to replace a structure built by Governor Macquarie, and is open for inspection on Sundays 1.30-4.30 pm. **Admission is $1 adult, 50c child.**

Brislington, the oldest existing house in the inner city, is on the corner of Marsden and George Streets, in the grounds of Parramatta Hospital. It was built in 1821 by John Hodges, a former convict, as a pre-requisite of obtaining an inn licence from Governor Macquarie. The house was later occupied by the Brown family for 92 years (1857-1949). Brislington is now a medical and nursing museum, and is open to the public on Sundays and the last Thursday of each month, Feb-Nov, 10am-4pm, ph 635 0333. **Admission is $1 adult, 50c child,** and Devonshire teas are available.

The **Old Court House Tower** is the only part that remains of the original court house, built in 1896 and demolished in 1971. The old tower now forms part of the new Court House and Police Station, which is bounded by George, Marsden and Phillip Streets. The old court house was the second building on this site, the first being the Freemason's Arms, built by James Larra around 1800. In 1821, the hotel was sold to Andrew Nash who renamed it the Woolpack Inn, and it became a thriving success. Directly opposite, on the corner of George and Marsden Streets, is the present Woolpack Hotel, which opened for business in 1889.

St John's Cathedral is on the Church Street Mall, and although this church only dates back to 1855, the first church on the site was opened in 1803 and extended in 1820. Prior to 1803, church services, including weddings and christenings, were conducted in taverns or anywhere that people gathered, usually by a circuit minister. He apparently didn't visit very often because it is not unusual to find records that state that a couple were married and had a couple of kids christened all on the same day.

St John's Cemetery is a few blocks away on the corner of Argyle and O'Connell Streets. It is the oldest existing cemetery in Australia and has the oldest headstone, that of Henry Edward Dodd, who died in January, 1791. There are also many graves of the early settlers of the district.

The Town Hall is opposite St John's Cathedral on the site of the first market place established by Governor Macquarie. The Town Hall was erected in 1883, and while quite elegant on the outside, the inside leaves a lot to be desired.

Linden House is now in the grounds of the **Lancer Barracks** in Smith Street, but it was originally built in 1828 on a site in Macquarie Street. It has been described as a classical example of Australian architecture, and now houses a Regimental Museum. It is open Sundays and public holidays 11am-4pm, and **admission is $2 adult, 30c child.** The Barracks are still used by the Army.

Experiment Farm Cottage, 9 Ruse Street, is the site of the first land grant in Australia, that of 30 acres granted to James Ruse, who came to the colony on the First Fleet. The cottage, however, was not built by Ruse, but by a surgeon, John Harris, who owned adjoining land and bought out Ruse in 1793.

Ruse was the first settler to harvest wheat, although the seed given to him was from an earlier harvest in Parramatta Park by government labour. He married Elizabeth Perry, who was the first woman convict to receive her freedom in Australia.

The Cottage has been restored by the National Trust, and is furnished in the style of a mid-19th century gentleman's residence. It is open Tues-Thurs 10am-4pm, Sun and public holidays 11am-4pm, ph 635 5655 and **admission is $3.50 adult, $2 child.**

Elizabeth Farm, 70 Alice Street, ph 635 9488, was commenced in 1793 as a home for John and Elizabeth Macarthur, pioneers of merino wool production in Australia. It is the oldest existing house in Australia, and its design, with wide shady verandahs, became the prototype for the Australian homestead. It was used as a private dwelling up to 1969, and is now under the control of the Historic Houses Trust of NSW. It has been restored and free guided tours and audio visuals are available. The Farm is open Tues-Sun 10am-4.30pm, and **admission is $5 adult, $3 child, $12 family.** The farmhouse is set in an 1830s garden and there are tearooms that offer Devonshire teas and lunches.

Hambledon Cottage, in Hassell Street, was built in 1824 by John Macarthur for Penelope Lucas, the retired governess of his three daughters. (There is a rumour that the lady was also a very close 'friend' of John Macarthur.) For some reason, though, she was not the first person to reside in the house as Edward Macarthur, the eldest son, and Archdeacon Thomas Hobbes Scott lived there in 1825-1826. Miss Lucas moved in around 1826, and stayed until her death in 1836. Subsequently the Macarthur family offered the cottage to Governors Denison, Young and Robinson, as a holiday home. The Cottage is under the control of the Parramatta and District Historical Society, and is open to the public Wed-Thurs, Sat-Sun 11am-4pm. **Admission is $2.50 adult, $1.50 child.**

St Patrick's Catholic Church is at the other end of town, on the corner of Victoria Road and Marsden Street. The first Mass in Parramatta was celebrated by Father Dixon on May 22, 1803, but the first Catholic Church was built on this site in 1822. The present building is the fourth on this site, and was completed in 1936.

Lake Parramatta Reserve is in North Parramatta, and the Visitor Center has a map of two different routes from their office to the Lake. The Reserve covers about 65ha, and the Lake itself has an area of 9ha. It was formed by the damming of Hunt's Creek, and was part of Parramatta's water supply until 1909.

Along the drive on both sides of the Lake, and giving shade to the parking and picnic areas, are splendid specimens of Blackbutts, Grey Gums, Red Mahoganies, Bloodwoods, Turpentines, Rough-Barked Angophoras and Sydney Red Gums.

The Lake is very deep in some places, so boating is prohibited, and swimming is not encouraged. There are fireplaces, tables, toilets and a kiosk, ph 630 3104.

OUTLYING ATTRACTIONS

Koala Park

Situated north of Parramatta, in the suburb of West Pennant Hills, Koala Park was the first private koala sanctuary in New South Wales. Presently the park has lots of koalas on show all the time, but special photo sessions are held at 10.20am, 11.45am, 2pm and 3pm, when you can cuddle one of these not-so-cuddly creatures. Other animals you can meet face to face include kangaroos, emus and wombats, in fact all the native Australians are present.

Set in 4ha and fully landscaped with Australian plants, the park has an all-weather barbecue and picnic area, rest rooms, a souvenir shop and a kiosk for light refreshments. It is open every day (except Christmas Day) 9am-5pm, and **admission is $7 adult, $4 child 4-14 years.**

The preservation of the koala is the main theme of the park, and it also has Australia's first Koala Hospital for the treatment of sick and injured animals.

From Parramatta, drive north along Pennant Hills Road, then turn left into Castle Hill Road.

From Sydney, take the Pacific Highway north to Lane Cove, turn left onto Epping Road, which becomes Beecroft Road, turn left onto Pennant Hills Road, then right onto Castle Hill Road.

Alternatively, you can take the train from Sydney to Pennant Hills station, via Strathfield, then Bus no 655 to Koala Park.

Featherdale Wildlife Park

Situated in the suburb of Doonside, north-west of Parramatta, Featherdale has Australia's largest collection of Australian fauna. It is open every day (except Christmas Day) 9am-5pm, and the Koala Sanctuary opens 10-11.30am and 2.30-3.30pm. **Admission is $8 adults, $4 child 4-14 years,** and there is a kiosk, picnic facilities and a souvenir shop, ph 622 1644, or a recorded message line, 671 4984.

From Parramatta, follow the Great Western Highway to Prospect Caravan Park, then take the next on the right (Doonside Road) and follow the signs to Featherdale. From Sydney, the best way is via Parramatta. By public transport, take the train to Blacktown station, from either Parramatta or Sydney, then Bus no 725.

Australia's Wonderland

Australia's largest theme park, Wonderland is located on Wallgrove Road, Eastern Creek, west of Parramatta. If you are travelling with kids, this attraction is a must.

Set on over 200ha, **the park is as big as Disneyland,** and is divided into six exciting theme areas - *Hanna Barbera Land, International Village, Goldrush, Transylvania, The Beach (summer only) and The Australian Wildlife Park.*

Hanna Barbera Land has larger than life cartoon characters, who love having their photo taken, and live shows and performances at the Gum Tree Puppet Theatre.

International Village has the flavours of the world. You can browse through interesting shops, take wild rides such as "Bounty's Revenge", or dine or snack at the many outlets.

Goldrush has the mighty "Bush Beast", the largest, and most awesome wooden roller-coaster in the Southern Hemisphere; "Snowy River Rampage", where you can ride the whitewater rapids; and "Skyhawk", which proves that what goes up must come down.

The Beach has an array of swimming pools, cascades, aqua tubes, speed slides and free-fall slides, and is a great place to cool down in Sydney's summer.

The Australian Wildlife Park is over 4ha, and you can wander through many different Australian landscapes, and view a large range of native animals close-up in their natural open-range surroundings. Underground viewing domes allow you to get close to giant goannas and freshwater crocodiles, or if you are not that adventurous, you can cuddle a koala, or pat a kangaroo. There are also walk-through avaries, a nocturnal house, a wombat burrow, and a petting zoo.

Australia's Wonderland is open from mid-September to mid-July, every weekend, NSW official school holidays and public holidays 10am-5pm (on Saturdays, during daylight saving, the hours are extended till 9pm), ph 830 9100, or a 24 hour Info Line, 832 1777. There are no barbecue facilities, but, although there are plenty of places within the park where you can buy food, it is OK to take your own picnic lunch. **Admission is $26.95 adult, $18.95 child, which includes all rides and attractions, including the Wildlife Park, but excluding the carnival games.**

The Wildlife Park is open every day (except Christmas Day), 9am-5pm, and may be visited independently of Wonderland. **Admission is $8.50 adult, $6.50 child,** ph 957 4655. If you decide to have a special souvenir 'you and a koala' photo taken, the charge for this is $8. Alternatively, you can use your own camera.

To get to Wonderland by car, follow the F4 Motorway, take the Wallgrove Road exit, then follow the Wonderland signs.

By public transport, take the train to Rooty Hill station and connect with the Busways service direct to the park.

There is a *CityRail Wonderlink* all inclusive train, bus and admission pass available at railway stations, and for information on prices (which will vary with the distance travelled), ph CityRail on 13 15 00.

The Waterworks

Another attraction that appeals to children is The Waterworks, 10 Belmore Avenue, Mount Druitt, ph 625 4288. There is a swimming pool, complete with a little sandy beach, 6 tube slides, 1 giant slide, a whitewater rapids ride, go-karts, and small racing cars for tiny tots. The complex is open weekends and every day during the school holidays, 10am-5pm, and admission, which includes every attraction, is $14.95 per person, $50 per family (of 4 people). There is also a kiosk and barbecue facilities.

From Parramatta or Sydney, take the Great Western Highway to Mount Druitt, turn right onto Carlisle Avenue, then follow the signs to The Waterworks.

By public transport, take a train to Mt Druitt station and catch a bus, or walk, the rest of the way.

Sydney Crowd

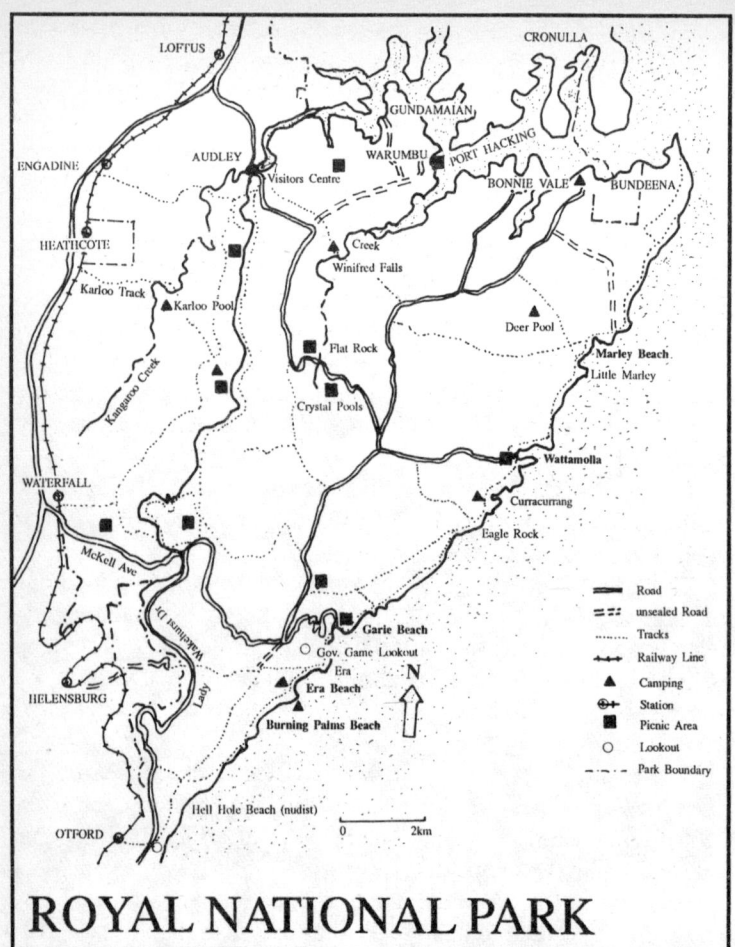

LOFTUS

CRONULLA

GUNDAMAIAN

ENGADINE

AUDLEY

WARUMBU

PORT HACKING

Visitors Centre

BONNIE VALE

BUNDEENA

HEATHCOTE

Creek

Winifred Falls

Karloo Track

Deer Pool

Karloo Pool

Marley Beach

Little Marley

Flat Rock

Crystal Pools

WATERFALL

Wattamolla

Curracurrang

McKell Ave

Eagle Rock

Garie Beach

Gov. Game Lookout

Era

Era Beach

HELENSBURG

Burning Palms Beach

Hell Hole Beach (nudist)

OTFORD

0   2km

	Road
	unsealed Road
	Tracks
	Railway Line
▲	Camping
	Station
■	Picnic Area
O	Lookout
	Park Boundary

ROYAL NATIONAL PARK

ROYAL NATIONAL PARK

Royal National Park was gazetted in 1879 as 'The National Park', and was the first public reserve in Australia to be so termed. In fact, the Park can lay claim to being the first in the world, because although Yellowstone Park in the USA was established in 1872, it was not officially gazetted as a national park until 1883. When Queen Elizabeth II first visited Australia in 1954, she bestowed the title 'Royal', but most Sydneysiders still refer to it as 'The National Park'.

The Park is situated south of Port Hacking, about 29km from the centre of Sydney, and covers 15,014ha of vegetation and landscape typical of the Sydney Basin sandstone.

The original inhabitants of the area were the Aboriginal people of the Dharawal tribe, who used the sandstone caves for shelter and managed to live adequately off the land and waterways. Not much is known of their lifestyle as all that remains of their culture are rock engravings, axe-grinding grooves, charcoal drawings and hand stencils.

The establishment of Royal National Park was caused by the then NSW Premier, Sir John Robertson, who saw a need for a recreation space for Sydney, many parts of which had become infested with vermin and disease.

Audley was the site of the first European settlement in the Park, and the idea seemed to be to make it as un-Australian as possible. The native mangroves and mudflats were replaced by grassed parkland and exotic trees, and added to the local fauna were deer, rabbits and foxes.

PARK FEATURES

The Park has been shaped from a sloping sandstone plateau, which rises from sea level at Jibbon Point in the north, to over 300m at Bulgo in the south.

The Park scenery is magnificent and varied. The waves from the open sea have produced majestic cliffs, broken every now and then by small creeks and beaches. Deep river valleys have been formed by streams flowing north to Port Hacking and east to the Pacific Ocean. The upper slopes have woodlands that merge with the heath vegetation on the plateaux. Gorges and valleys have forest and rainforest, the tidal channels of the rivers have mangrove, and the swamps are covered in sedges.

There are **numerous grassy areas** along the **Hacking River valley**, and from July to November the plateaux become a riot of colour from the wildflowers. There are **waterfalls** at *Wattamolla, Curracurrong, Uloola* and *National Falls*.

HOW TO GET THERE

By Rail
Trains on the Illawarra-Cronulla line stop at Loftus, Engadine, Heathcote, Waterfall and Otford, and from these stations there are walking tracks into the Park.

By Car
From Sydney, follow the signs to the **Airport**, then take General Homes Drive to either Bell Street or President Avenue at *Brighton-le-Sands*, turn right and at the end of the street turn left onto Princes Highway which will take you to the Audley entrance of the Park.

From Liverpool City, once crossing the bridge from Terminus Street you come to a major intersection, straight ahead is Newbridge Road, which leads to Sydney, but turn right here into Heathcote Road, and follow it all the way to the Princes Highway (between Engadine and Heathcote).
You can then do one of two things:
turn left and go back about 3km to enter the Park south of Sutherland (Audley entrance);
or turn right and head south to Waterfall and enter the Park there, about 1km north of the tollway.

From Wollongong, drive north along the Princes Highway. After reaching Bulli continue along Lawrence Hargraves Drive (don't go up the escarpment). Another way is to follow the Mt Ousley Road to the Princes Highway and turn right at Stanwell Tops to go to Stanwell Park. At the top of the Bluff, turn left along Lady Wakehurst Drive, then continue to the Otford entrance of the Park.

By Ferry
Cronulla National Park Ferry Cruises, ph 523 2990, have a service from the wharf near Cronulla railway station to Bundeena, and the trip takes 20-22 minutes. The first ferry from Cronulla leaves at 5.30am Mon-Fri, 8.30am Sat-Sun and public holidays. The last ferry leaves Bundeena daily at 7pm (summer), 6pm (winter).

NB   It should be noted that Bundeena is not within Royal National Park.

TOURIST INFORMATION

A *Visitor Centre and Wildlife Shop* is located at Audley and is open daily 9am-4pm (closed 1-2pm Mon-Fri), ph 542 0648. It has an exhibition on the history, geology and wildlife of the park, and advice on any aspect of a visit. The shop sells books, film, maps, posters, gifts and souvenirs.

PARK ENTRANCE FEE

There is no charge for traffic travelling through the Park from Sutherland to places south of the Park.

For cars that intend to stop within the park the following charges apply:
Cars - $7.50 per vehicle
Motor Bikes - $3 per bike
There is no charge for people who hike into the park for the day.

PARK REGULATIONS

All fauna, flora, Aboriginal sites and rock formations are protected. Wildfires can destroy lives and property, so be careful, especially during the bushfire danger period (normally October to March). Use only the fireplaces provided and observe Total Fire Bans.

Pets and Firearms are not permitted in national parks.
Vehicles, including motorbikes must keep to formed public roads.
Drive carefully.
Please use rubbish bins if provided; or take rubbish with you when
you leave the park.

CAMPING

Caravans and car camping are permitted at the camping ground at
Bonnie Vale, off Bundeena Road. It has toilet and shower blocks,
but no powered sites. In fact, there are only 44 sites in all, and
during school holidays and long weekends, ballots are held to allot
them. There are so many applicants that this seems to be the fairest
way. At other times there is not so much demand, and therefore
there is a good chance of securing a site.

For reservations, ph 542 0666.

Site fees are: $5 for first two people over 12 years of age, and
$1.50 for each extra person over 12 years of age.
Children under 12 are free.

There are lots of places for bush camping throughout the park, but
permits must first be obtained from the Visitor Centre. The permits
are free, but written on the back of them are the special conditions
that apply to camping in a national park, and this is the best way of
making sure that everyone is aware of them.

ACTIVITIES

Weekends see many organised picnics arranged by sporting clubs,
church groups, etc, and family picnics with the addition of aunts
and uncles, grandparents, etc, taking advantage of the wide expanse
of grasslands near the Audley causeway.

Picnicking

There are many picnic areas dotted throughout the park, but there
are only barbecue facilities at Audley, Warumbul, Wattamolla,
Garie, Red Cedar Flat and Karingal. Kiosks are found at Audley,
Wattamolla and Garie Beach.

Swimming

Safe salt water swimming is available at *Bonnie Vale, Jibbon, Wattamolla* and *Little Marley* beaches, and these are favourite spots for families.

Surfers head for *Garie, Era* and *Burning Palms* Beaches, which are patrolled by surf lifesavers on weekends and public holidays in summer.

Freshwater swimming is possible at *Blue Pools, Karloo Pool, Deer Pool, Curracurrang* and *Crystal Pools,* but care should be taken when swimming in rock pools. For one thing, the water is always freezing, so it is easy to get cramps, and for the other, it is not always easy to judge how deep a rock pool is, so it is best not to jump or dive into these pools. Spinal injury units of hospitals are always warning people about the dangers of diving into unknown waters.

Boating

The boatshed at Audley, ph 521 6467, has rowing boats, canoes and aquabikes for hire, and only these may be used in Kangaroo Creek, and in the Hacking River above the causeway. Private boats, etc, can be used downstream of the Audley causeway.

The boatshed is open Mon-Sat 9am-5pm, Sun and public holidays 9am-5.30pm. **The hiring fee for boats is $10 per hour, $18 per day; canoes are $2 cheaper; aquabikes cost $8 per half hour. A refundable deposit of $10 is required for each craft.**

Walking

The Park has over 150km of walking tracks that provide access to the wide range of scenery available, and the Visitor Centre has track pamphlets. Bungoona, Governor Game and Otford Lookouts offer chances to take spectacular photos, and National, Winifred and Curracurrong Falls are easily accessible.

Cycling

The best route for cyclists is Lady Carrington Drive, which is closed to motor vehicles, and is relatively flat. Ask at the Visitor Centre for directions.

If you are visiting the Royal National Park on a Sunday or Wednesday, you might like to check out **The Sydney Tramway Museum** in Pitt Street, Loftus, ph 542 3646. It is open Sun 10am-5pm, Wed 9.30am-3.30pm, but no one is admitted in the hour prior to closing.

Trams operated in Sydney for one hundred years to 1961, and a fleet of over 1500 vehicles provided the city with an efficient transport service. The Sydney Tramway Museum has an excellent collection of Sydney trams, and others from Brisbane, Ballarat, Melbourne and San Francisco, and also a selection of the buses which replaced them in Sydney. This fleet includes the last remaining double deck trolley bus.

Every open day, a number of the museum's trams operate along a kilometre of track, each return trip taking about 15 minutes, but the San Francisco PCC Streetcar only operates on the first Sunday of the month.

There is also a tramway waiting shed from Railway Square, the unique counterweight dummy from the Balmain line, and an extensive range of photographs and artifacts.

The museum has a shop with a range of books, post cards, video tapes and souvenirs, as well as snacks and drinks. There are also picnic facilities within the Museum grounds.

Admission is $8 adult, $4 child, and includes unlimited tram rides and use of facilities.

WOLLONGONG

Wollongong is situated on the coast of New South Wales, 80km from Sydney, and 238km from Canberra. It is the seventh largest city in Australia with a population of 174,770, and is the gateway to the Illawarra Leisure Coast. To its north, cosy mining villages dot the coastline against a dramatic backdrop of green escarpment. Here the Illawarra coastal plain is narrowest, at times reduced to naught as rocky sea cliffs reach right to the pounding waves.

In the seaside village of Thirroul, D.H. Lawrence wrote *Kangaroo*, and from Stanwell Park, aviator Lawrence Hargraves tested his box kites.

CLIMATE

Average temperatures: January max 26C (79F) — min 18C (64F); July max 17C (63F) — min 9C (48F). Average annual rainfall: 1275mm.

HOW TO GET THERE

By Rail
Electric trains run regularly between Central Railway Station and Wollongong, connecting with on-going services to Port Kembla.

By Bus
Wollongong Bus Service, ph (042) 297 131, have a service from/to Sydney Airport. *Pioneer* and *Greyhound* stop at the Wollongong Bus Terminal in Gipps Street at Harvey World Travel. Buses leave Sydney from underneath the Koala Motor Inn in Riley Street, Darlinghurst, which is the Pioneer/Greyhound Bus Terminal.

By Road
From Sydney, via the Princes Highway to Waterfall and then the

F6 (Toll $1.00), or continue along the highway if you prefer not to pay the toll. The highway and the tollway join above Bulli Pass about 18 km north of Wollongong. The views from here of the city especially on a clear night, are spectacular.

An alternative route is to take the highway and turn off to the left at the Stanwell Park signpost outside Helensburg about a kilometre after you have passed under the tollway. Head for Stanwell Park and follow the road for a spectacular drive along the coast.

Another interesting route is *via the National Park* to Stanwell Park. The turnoff to the left is just south of Sutherland. Through traffic does not have to pay the National Park entrance fee, though if you intend to stop on the way you should pay as you may get fined if you do not have a ticket. The cost $7.50 per vehicle.

TOURIST INFORMATION

The Tourism Wollongong Visitors Centre, 93 Crown Street (corner of Kembla Street), ph (042) 280 300, is open seven days a week, 9am-5pm Mon-Fri, 10am-4pm Sat, Sun, Public Holidays.

ACCOMMODATION

Illawarra's Leisure Coast boasts a comprehensive range of accommodation from caravan parks on many of the beaches and lakesides, to an international style resort hotel, a leisure village, quality motels, hotels, holiday units and superb convention facilities.

Here is a selection with prices for a double room per night, which should be used as a guide only. The telephone area code is 042.

Northbeach Park Royal, 2 Cliff Road, ph 263 555 — 203 rooms, licensed restaurant, swimming pool, spa, sauna, gym, tennis, bicycling — $170-290.

City Pacific International, 112 Burelli Street, ph 297 444 — 65 rooms, licensed restaurant, swimming pool — $50-130.

Golden Pacific North Beach Motel, 16 Pleasant Avenue, North Wollongong, ph 263 000 — 18 units — $70-95.

Metro Motor Inn, cnr Crown Street & Mt Keira Road, ph 288 088 — 36 units, unlicensed restaurant, swimming pool, spa — $63.

Beach Park Motor Inn, 10 Pleasant Avenue, North Wollongong, ph 261 577 — 15 units, bbq — $60-70.

Piccadilly Motor Inn, 341 Crown Street, ph 264 555 — 37 units, unlicensed restaurant — $60-65.

Boat Harbour Motel, 7 Wilson Street, ph 289 166 — 44 units, licensed restaurant (closed Sun and public holidays) — $78-85.

Downtown Motel, 76 Crown Street, ph 298 344 — 31 units, licensed restaurant (closed Sun) — $55-78.

SERVICED APARTMENTS

Belmore Deluxe Apartments, 39 Smith Street, ph 246 500 — 34 units, licensed restaurant (closed Sun) — $105-140.

GETTING AROUND

Car Hire

Auto Rentals, ph 297 766; Avis, ph 284 111; Budget, ph 273 000; Thrifty, ph 289 544.

Local Transport

There are local bus services both government and privately owned. The major local service is John J. Hill, ph 294 911 to get the schedule for the route you are interested in. But most people use a car, or a bike. The train that runs to Bomaderry in the south from Sydney is sometimes used to go two or three stations in Wollongong. The main rail link north of the city centre to Sydney has a regular service stopping at Nth Wollongong, Fairy Meadow, Towradgi, and other main suburbs north. Services south are infrequent.

Church Services
All major denominations are represented in the city and they can be contacted by checking their listing in the local phone book in your hotel. Weekend services are held throughout the city, at St Michael's Anglican Cathedral, Market St; St Andrew's Presbyterian on Kembla Street; and St Francis Xavier's Cathedral has masses daily 7.00am Mon-Sun alternating with another at 5.40pm - Tues/Thurs or noon Wed/Fri with extra masses on Sunday.

EATING OUT

Wollongong's cosmopolitan community offers you a wide choice of superb restaurants, snack bars and coffee lounges. The following is a list of recommended restaurants, rated
Expensive (main course $15+),
Moderate (main course $10-$15)
Budget (main course under $10).
Some names and addresses:

Akubra Restaurant (in Tattersall's Hotel), 333 Crown Street, ph 291 885, Licensed - a la carte & bistro - **Moderate** - open Thurs-Sat 6-11pm - No credit cards accepted.

Anchorage, (in Boat Harbour Motel), cnr Campbell & Wilson Streets, ph 289 166, licensed - a la carte, international, ocean view - **Expensive** - open Mon-Sat 7.30-9.30am, 12-3pm, 6-10pm - Amex, BC, DC, MC, V.

The Beach House Seafood Restaurant, 16 Cliff Road, ph 285-410, licensed - seafood mainly, ocean views - **Expensive** - open Mon-Sun 10.30am-midnight - Amex, BC, DC, MC, V.

Burelli's (in City Pacific Hotel), 112 Burelli Street, ph 297 444, licensed - Blackboard Menu Smorgasbord other than main course - **Budget** - open 12-2pm Mon-Fri, Mon-Sun 5.30-9pm - Amex, BC, DC, MC, V.

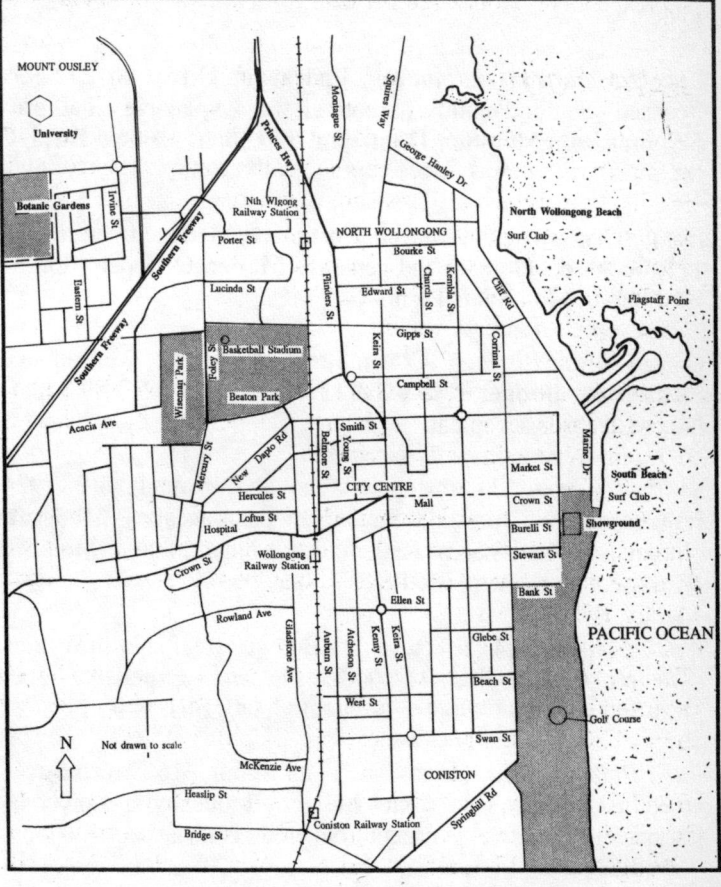

Crown Street Chinese, 150 Crown Street, ph 297 818, licensed - Chinese & Malay - **Budget** - open Mon-Sat 11.30-2.30pm, Mon-Sun 5-10pm - No credit cards accepted.

Fuji Yama, 35 Flinders St, ph 262 609, licensed - specialise in Japanese barbecue - **Budget** - open Mon-Sat 6-10pm - BC, MC, V. Do not go in your best clothes as they throw the food at you, no joke!

The Harbourfront Restaurant, Endeavour Drive, ph 272 999, licensed - Seafood mainly, harbour views - **Expensive** - (half price 5-7pm) - open Mon-Sun 11am-3pm, 5.-9.30pm - Amex, BC, DC, MC, V.

Heidi's German Restaurant, cnr Corrimal & Market Streets, ph 271 110, licensed - German and general - **Moderate** - open Mon-Fri 12-2.30pm, Mon-Sat 6-11pm - BC, MC, V.

Oxford Tavern Bistro, 47 Crown Street, ph 283 892, licensed - a la carte steak - **Budget** - Mon-Sun 11.30am-2.30pm, 5.30-9.30pm - No credit cards accepted.

Southern Crepes, 11 Crown Street (opp. Showground), ph 284 924, BYO (Corkage $1/person) - Savoury crepes, pancakes - **Moderate** - open Mon-Sun noon-11.30pm, Ice Cream Parlour Mon-Sun 10am-11.30pm - BC, MC, V.

Windjammers, 2-14 Cliff Road (cnr Bourke Street), North Wollongong, ph 263 555 - licensed - buffet, a la carte - **Expensive** - open Mon-Sun 6.30am-10.30pm - Amex, BC, DC, MC, V.

Plant Room, for vegetarians The Plant Room, 316 Crown Street, ph 273 030, is the place to eat - **Budget** - frequented by university students wishing to experiment - No credit cards accepted.

During business hours a good place to eat is the *Food Court,* lower level of the Gateway on the Mall shopping complex, cnr Crown & Keira Streets. They have tables in the centre and you can choose from Chinese, Italian, Austrian, Mexican, crepes, chicken, etc.

McDonald's have outlets on the Princes Highway, Figtree, Cowper Street, Warrawong and Princes Highway, Fairy Meadow.

Pizza Hut are at Crown Gateway, Wollongong, ph 272 277; cnr Princes Highway & McGrath Street, Fairy Meadow, ph 280 122; cnr King Street & Kemblawarra Place, Warrawong, ph 752 144; and cnr Shellharbour Road & Woolworths Avenue, Warilla, ph 964 433. You can try them for home delivery.

Kentucky Fried Chicken can be found at cnr Princes Highway & McGrath Street, Fairy Meadow; 74 Princes Highway, Unanderra; cnr Kemblawarra Road & King Street, Warrawong; 136 Princes Highway, Dapto; and Holm Place, Shellharbour Square.

Recommended Club Restaurants:
Wollongong Ex-Services Club, 82 Church Street, ph 288 522;
The Fraternity Club (Italian ambiente), 11 Bourke Street, Fairy Meadow, ph 833 333;
Illawarra Master Builders Club, 61 Church Street, ph 296 466.
All are budget priced meals with generally very good quality service and food.

ENTERTAINMENT

Pubs and Bars
A lot of good bands play on Thursday nights especially at

The Oxford Tavern - No cover charge unless the band is well known, and then it will be $5.00 maximum. Ages 18-30.

Hal's Tavern - same as above.

Illawarra Tavern is close to the university and on the main road into the city from the north. Has a large verandah which is popular in summer and Bands play most nights.

Champion Hotel at Tarodgie has a very large entertainment area called *Waves* which can fit 2,000-3,000. Big Bands from Sydney and international acts play here at prices 1/3 the cost in Sydney.

North Wollongong Hotel, mainly university students - has a band most nights.

North Beach Park Royal has *Splashes* which is well known and popular among the 18-30 age group. Many good bands play here and also operates as a disco. Dress requirement: pants, shirt with collar and shoes. Contained within the same complex is the *Beach Bistro* which is little more up-market.

University Bar - enjoyable non-threatening place frequented by all ages.

Post Office Tavern - just a drinking hole. Occasionally they have bands, otherwise the piped music is very loud.

Clubs

Shellharbour Workers is a big club that attracts many international acts and always has good bands.

Dapto Leagues always has good bands also, though it is not as big as Shellharbour Workers.

Entry is by membership or being signed in by a member or belonging to an RSL or other Leagues Club. If you are a visitor from out of town or reasonably well dressed you should have no trouble with entry. Dress in the clubs is normally shirt with a collar, trousers and shoes. On the other hand, the pubs are more relaxed.

Hours vary but normally after work until midnight during the week and until 2.00am Friday and Saturday nights.

There are other clubs, where there are discos or live-music for those who want to boogie the night away.

The clubs in Wollongong itself are:
Collegians RLFC, 3 Charlotte Street, ph 297 711.
Illawarra Master Builders, 61 Church Street, ph 296 466.
Illawarra Leagues Club, (Steelers), 87 Church Street, ph 294 611.
The Wollongong Club, 41 Smith Street, ph 284 244.
Wollongong Ex-Services, 32 Church Street, ph 288 522.

Movie Theatres

For movie goers, Wollongong has two cinema complexes in the centre of town -

Regent Theatre, 197 Keira Street, ph 289 238. This is an older theatre, not as popular as it used to be.

Town Cinemas, Burelli Street, ph 284 888. There are 3 cinemas in the complex owned by Greater Union.

Hoyts have a cinema complex in the Warrawong Shopping Centre on Cowper Street. It has 6 theatres.

Performing Arts

Illawarra Performing Arts Centre, Burelli Street, ph 263 366, has live theatre and musical presentations both from local community groups and schools, and also acts from out of town. The Wollongong Symphony Orchestra performs there regularly.

The BHP Youth Orchestra is based in Gleniffer Brae an old manor house which also has the *Wollongong Conservatorium.* Concerts are held throughout the year, and in the spring and summer months some are outdoors. Tours of the old home and grounds can be arranged. For information and bookings ph 213 533.

Theatres

The Bridge Street Theatre, 24 Bridge Street, Coniston, ph 296 144 has regular live shows.

The Hope Theatre at the University of Wollongong, (enter from Northfields Avenue some 500 metres west of the roundabout) have professional shows - Australian Chamber Orchestra, Sydney Symphony Orchestra, together with productions from the creative arts students at the university. Ph 213 584 for bookings and ph 214 214 for information and bookings on shows that are on or coming up.

The Roo Theatre, Kiama, is a small theatre group that put on shows regularly. Contact Tourism Wollongong for more details.

SHOPPING

Crown Street is the main and major shopping centre of Wollongong. Part of the street is now a mall with David Jones, Grace Bros and many stores in this area. There are other shopping centres in the various suburbs of the city.

Westfield Shoppingtown, Princes Highway, Figtree, has 80 specialty shops, ph 298 422. *Westfield Shoppingtown* on Cowper Street has 130 shops, ph 761 566. *Shellharbour Square Shopping Centre,* Lakes Entrance Road, has about 100 shops, ph 968 266, and is open 7 days. However, there are shopping centres of various sizes besides the large ones listed above that dot the metropolitan area with many corner stores open at all hours. If you are after fashionable and more expensive goods, generally speaking it is best to head for Crown Street Mall. The large suburban shopping centres cater mainly for supermarket and household goods, though there are other specialty shops that may have what you want.

SPORT

Cycling
There are many routes where you can cycle, and a bike is a boon in this compartively spread out city. *One cycleway* starts from North Wollongong Beach and goes through parkland along the coast through a number of suburbs, Fairy Meadow and Towradgi to Corrimal. You can hire bikes at the North Wollongong start of the cycleway, in Stuart Park. Otherwise you can try at any of the cycle shops in the city.

Golf
There are quite a few golf courses in the area. Here are a few:

Wollongong Golf Club, off Corrimal Street and on the coast, ph 296 911, 18 holes, par 70 course, 5791 metres. Visitors welcome.
   Green Fees: $15
   Club hire : $6 a set.
   Buggy Hire: $2

Shellharbour Golf Club, Dunmore road, Shellharbour, ph 965 835, 18 holes, par 70 course, 2756 metres. Visitors Welcome.
   Green Fees: $10
   Club Hire : $5
   Buggy Hire: $2

Russell Vales Golf Course, Princes Highway, Russell Vale, ph 835 322, 18 holes, par 54 course, 2756 metres, Visitors welcome.
   Green Fees: $11; $6 for 9 holes
   Club Hire : $11; $6 for 9 holes
   Buggy Hire: $1.50

Port Kembla Golf Course, Golf Place, Primbee, ph 741 159, 18 holes, par 72 course, 6103 metres, Visitor Welcome.
   Green Fees: $15; $9 after 4pm.
   Club Hire : $10
   Buggy Hire: included in club hire.

Kembla Grange Golf Course, Princes Highway, Kembla Grange, ph 611 647, 18 holes, par 72 course, 6309 metres, Visitors welcome.
   Green Fees: $15; $12 for 9 holes
   Club Hire : $8 ; $6 for 9 holes
   Buggy Hire: included in club hire.

Horse Riding

There are a number of horseriding schools and places where you can hire horses.

These ones are out of the city area but within half an hour's drive. *Otford Farm Trail rides,* ph 941 296; *Darkes Forest Riding School,* ph 943 441.

One closer in is *Dunmore House,* Dunmore, ph 378 603.

Scuba Diving

There are quite a few schools in the area. Enquire at:

Illawarra Aqua Centre, 235 Windang Road, Windang (at the entrance to Lake Illawarra), ph 964 215.

Pro Dive Shellharbour, Shop 2, 17 Addison Street, Shellharbour, ph 963 644.

Skating

There are no ice skating rinks in the area, however, there are three roller skating rinks. Two are north of the city centre:

Blandfordia Pty Ltd., 50 Beach Road, Woonona, ph 852 942.

Thirroul Roller Skating, 264 Lawrence Hargraves Drive,
ph 682 082.
The other is *Dapto Interskate,* 102 Kanahooka Road, Dapto,
ph 616 333.

Ten-pin bowling

There are four centres
Northern Ten Pin Bowl have two locations -
103 Princes Highway, Corrimal, ph 836 222; and 1 Molloy Street,
Bulli, ph 836 645.
Warrawong Bowl, King Street, ph 740 678, is the closest to the
city. *Shellharbour Bowl,* Sunset Ave, Warilla, ph 969 922, is south
of the city centre.

Tennis

As with any australian locale the place abounds with courts for hire.
Here are some contacts:
Ace Tennis, O'Briens Road, Figtree, ph 286 398.
City of Wollongong Tennis Club, Foleys Road, Gwynneville,
ph 293 766. *Wollongong District Tennis Association,* Beaton Park,
Wollongong, ph 286 570.

Yacht/Boat Hire

Wollongong surrounds *Lake Illawarra* which is a very popular spot
for sail boats, although many people head further south to areas
around *Nowra,* some 100km further down the south coast of NSW.
If you wish to hire a boat of any kind, we suggest you contact
Tourism Wollongong, as they may have some current names. It may
be worthwhile to also contact the **Maritime Services Board** for
information on conditions and licensing requirements, ph 008 422
718 (price of a local call).

You could try the *Illawarra Yacht Club* , Northcliffe Drive,
Warrawong, ph 746 622.

SPECTATOR SPORT

Football

Four codes are played during the winter months and part of Autumn and Spring - *Rugby League, Rugby, Soccer (Futbol for Europeans) and Australian Football.*

Rugby League
Rugby League is the big game in the district and their are a myriad of clubs relating to this code. The city team that plays in the Winfield Premiership is called the *Illawarra Steelers,* so named after the major industry in the area - steel. The primary sponsor is BHP, the district's major employer, and a reason for the city's existence. **Steelers Club,** 3 Burelli Street, ph 272 255. Their ground is the Showground on Harbour Street, next to the ocean, a 10 minute walk from the Crown Street shopping centre.

Rugby Union
Rugby Union is an amateur code and has gained in popularity with the success of the national team. One of the main teams in the district is the *Vikings,* and their ground and club is located cnr Swan Street and Corrimal Street, ph 299 666. Others are the University and the Technical College in North Wollongong, called *Tech,* Foleys Road, ph 298 596.

Australian Football
Australian Football has a small but dedicated following. They have a club at Pioneer Road, Towradgi, ph 834 555.

Soccer
Soccer is very big in the area, with many local clubs and grounds dedicated to the game. The major team is called the *Wollongong Wolves.* They play in the National Soccer Competition. The main club is the Wollongong City Soccer Club, Carters Lane, Fairy Meadow, just north of the city centre, ph 263 988.

Basketball
Wollongong is represented by the *Illawarra Hawks* who play in the National Basketball League. They play at Beaton Park off Foley Street, ph 280 299. They have a very strong local following.

Netball
This is another sport that has come to prominence in the last couple of years. The Illawarra District Netball Association runs regular competitions and is based at Fairy Meadow, Figtree and Berkley, ph 716 571.

Cricket
This is the national summer sport and is played everywhere. They do not have a club as such, but if you want to watch a game just ask at any pub or phone Tourism Wollongong and they will suggest a ground. You could contact the *Illawarra Cricket Assocation*, ph 283 339.

Horse Racing
There are regular meetings at Kembla Grange which is between the Southern Freeway and the Princes Highway south of Unanderra. It is a picturesque setting and can be easily seen from the road. Turn off at Northcliffe Drive if heading south by car down the expressway. *Illawarra Turf Club*, ph 617 211 for more information.

Greyhound Racing
Dapto Showground, Princes Highway. Regular meetings are held here.

Bulli Trotting Track opposite Point Street on the Princes Highway also have regular meetings as they do with the pacing, ph 671 467. You could try the NSW Greyhound Breeders, Owners and Trainers Association, ph 672 221 for more information.

Pacing (Harness Racing)
Regular meetings are held at *Albion Park Showground* off Flinders Street. Contact Tourism Wollongong for more information. Also there are some meetings at *Bulli Trotting Track*, Princes Highway, ph 674 224.

BEACHES

Listed below are the beaches stretching from Stanwell Park to Kiama.

The attributes listed are
Dressing Shed, which normally will include a shower and toilets.
Patrolled, which is normally on weekends and school holidays in summer. Beaches are not patrolled in winter.
Pool, Rock pool suitable for children.
Surfing suitable for *board and body surfers*.

Normally all the beaches back onto a park or a reserve, and there are clear directions from the Highway as to how to get to the beach. The only exception to this is when the Highway goes inland around Lake Illawarra, but if you head along Northcliffe Drive and then south along King Street, which becomes Windang Drive, you will continue to keep in touch with the ocean.

The beaches in this area tend not to be topless unlike Sydney. North Wollongong and Thirroul especially are family beaches. Remember that if a beach has been closed (you will see the signs stationed on the beach) do not surf. There is a reason for its closure and it is done to protect you.

Included is the distance from Wollongong city centre.

Stanwell Park Beach, 14km north, Surf Club, Dressing Shed, patrolled, surfers and board.

Coledale Beach, 12km north, surfers and board, Pool 300 metres south.

Austinmer Beach, 9.5km north, Surf Club, Dressing Shed, patrolled, surfers and board, pool.

Thirroul Beach, 8km north, Surf Club, Dressing Shed, patrolled, surfers and board, pool in the park off the beach.

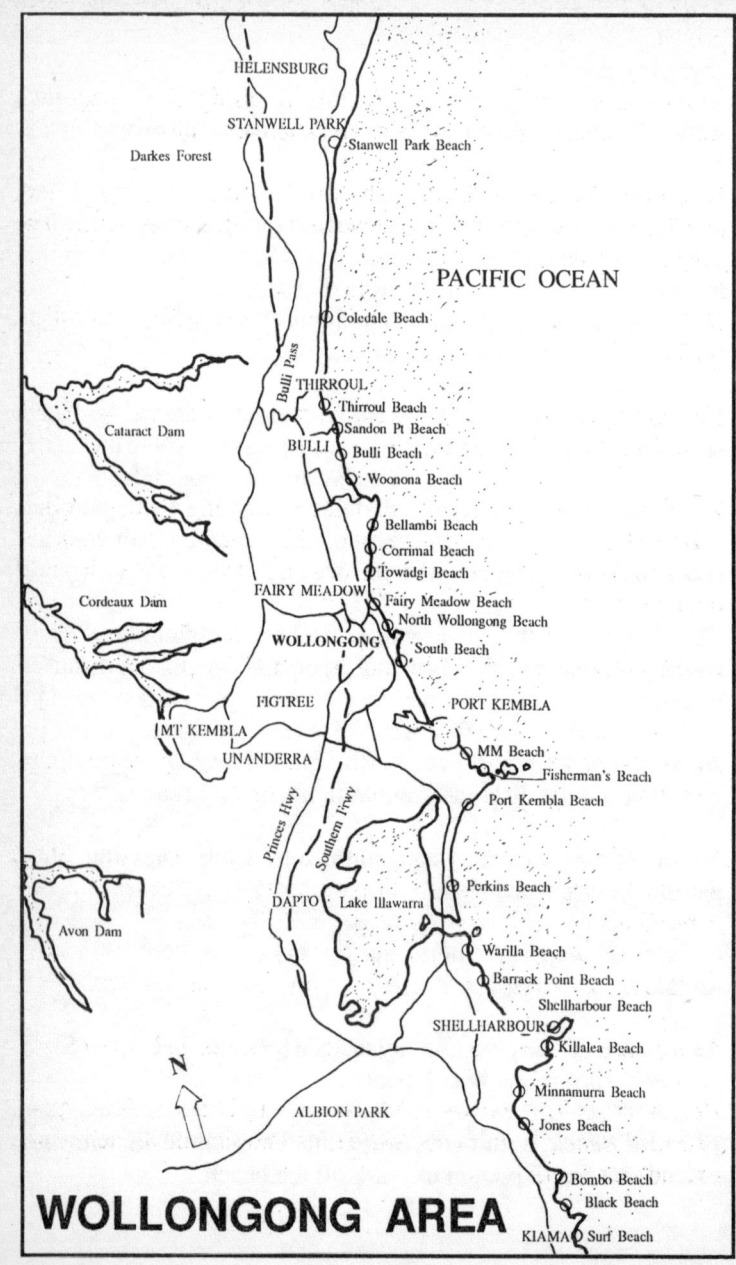

WOLLONGONG AREA

Sandon Pt Beach, Bulli, 7km north, Surf Club, Dressing Shed, patrolled, surfers and board, pool.

Bulli Beach, 6.5km north, Surf Club, Dressing Shed, patrolled, surfers and board, pool at Collins Rock at the south end.

Woonona Beach, 5.5km north, Surf Club, Dressing Shed, patrolled, surfers and board, stretches 2km to Bellambi Beach. The centre is not patrolled.

Bellambi Beach, 3.5km north, Surf Club, Dressing Shed, patrolled, surfers and board, pool.

Corrimal Beach, 2.5km north, Surf Club, Dressing Shed, patrolled, surfers and board.

Towadgi Beach, 2.2km north, Surf Club, Dressing Shed, patrolled, surfers and board, pool on north side. This beach is continuous and is only patrolled near the surf club, as is Fairy Meadow beach which it adjoins.

Fairy Meadow Beach, 1.5km north, Surf Club, patrolled, surfers and board.

North Wollongong, 0.5km north, Surf Club, Dressing Shed, patrolled, surfers and board, pool.

South Beach, opposite city centre, Surf Club, Dressing Shed, patrolled, surfers and board. A particularly long beach - 2.5km approximately.

M M Beach, 6km south, board, but only in certain swells.

Fishermans Beach, no surf, protected by Big Island.

Port Kemble Beach, 6km south, Surf Club, Dressing Shed, pool, patrolled - surfers, north end only, runs into Perkins Beach which extends for 5km, board.

Perkins Beach - south end, 11km south, Surf Club, Dressing Shed, patrolled, surfers and board.

Warilla Beach, 12km south, Surf Club, surfers and board.

Barrack Point Beach, 13km south, Surf Club, Dressing Shed, patrolled, surfers and board.

Shell Harbour, 13.5km south, pool.

Shellharbour Beach, 14km south, board.

Killalea Beach (Dunmore), 15km south, surfers and board.

Minnamurra Beach, 16km south, surfers and board. Both these beaches back on to a State Recreation Reserve.

Jones Beach, 16.5km south, surfers and board.

Bombo Beach, 18km south, surfers and board.

Black Beach, Kiama Harbour, 20km south, surfers, pool.

Surf Beach, Kiama, 21km south, Dressing Shed, surfers and board.

SIGHTSEEING

Most historic buildings can be visited on a *walking tour* commencing at Flagstaff Hill (parking available). The sights visited are: Wollongong Head Lighthouse; Breakwater Lighthouse; Belmore Basin; Drill Hall; Throsby's stockman's hut monument; Market Square; Illawarra Historical Museum; Congregational Church; Wollongong Courthouse; St Michael's Provisional Cathedral; Wollongong Uniting Church; The Town Hall; Wollongong East Post Office; Tourist Information office; St Francis Xavier's Provisional Cathedral; and Andrew Lysaght Park. A map is available from Tourism Wollongong.

Mount Kembla Historic Village, 7km (4 miles) from Wollongong was the site of the 1902 mining disaster, but it is full of art and craft centres today.

Wollongong Botanic Garden, in Keiraville, opposite the university, is a pleasant spot for picnics and quiet walks, and offers many areas of interest — Sir Joseph Banks Plant Houses, where plants from the wet tropics, deserts and temperate regions are displayed. The Garden is open daily 8am-6.45pm in summer, and 8am-4.45pm in winter.

The Wollongong City Art Gallery, 85 Burelli Street, ph 287 791, has a fine collection of modern and traditional paintings, with changing exhibitions. It is open Mon-Fri 10am-5pm, Sat-Sun noon-4pm.

Magnificent views of the coastline can be obtained from *Mount Kembla Lookout*, *Sublime Point* and *Bulli Lookout*, all of which are only about 15 to 20 minutes' drive from the centre of town. The Golden Fleece Restaurant and the Panorama House Restaurant at Bulli Tops both have great views of the coast.

Kelly's Falls, 2km off the Princes Highway at Stanwell Tops, has a picnic area and easy walking tracks to the falls. Flannel flowers are abundant in spring and early summer. Nearby is *Symbio Koala Gardens,* which has native and exotic animals, free barbecues, swimming and wading pools and lunchtime demonstrations of things from milking a cow to handling reptiles. The gardens are open daily from 9.30am, and they advertise that feeding time is 'all the time'. To get to these attractions, take the old Princes Highway from Wollongong, not the F6 Freeway.

While you are in the area, drive to *Bald Hill Lookout*, where there is a memorial to Lawrence Hargraves, and if the wind is favourable you will see many brightly coloured hang-gliders floating by.

Stanwell Park is in the valley below, and you can call in and browse through *Articles Art Gallery,* ph 942 491, and have a Devonshire tea on the outdoor terrace. The bluff (Bald Hill Lookout) overlooking Stanwell Park from the north is world famous spot now for *hang-gliders*. They come from everywhere to leap off the bluff over the sea, and sail through the air for hours landing in the park below, or on the beach if they happen to overshoot.

South of Wollongong is *Lake Illawarra*, renowned for fishing and prawning, and often ablaze with colourful sailing boats and sail boards. The lake is actually a lagoon covering an area of 35 sq km, with its entrance at the foreshore suburb of Windang.

The Illawarra Escarpment State Recreation Area has many fine walking trails through the rainforest, ph 294 756 for details.

Australia's largest steel mill is located around the foreshores of *Port Kembla Harbour*. The harbour sees millions of tons of coal exported each year from the surrounding mines, as well as steel from the steelworks.

Wollongong has two *bicycle tracks*. The one to the north starts at North Beach and goes to Corrimal (see Cycling). The southern one starts near the Windang bridge and skirts the shores of Lake Illawarra.

FESTIVALS

The Festival of Wollongong is held each year in November.

OUTLYING ATTRACTIONS

Shellharbour

The town of *Shellharbour* is around twenty minutes' drive south from Wollongong on the coastal road. There are caravan and camping areas, modern motels, licensed clubs, an attractive corner pub, golf, bowls, great restaurants and beautiful beaches.

The name Shellharbour comes from the many Aboriginal shell middens found here and at nearby Bass Point. The location is listed on the Heritage Commission Register, and is regarded as one of the two most important archaeological sites on the NSW coast.

Bass Point is a popular diving area, as part of its waters form a marine reserve. There is an airport at nearby **Albion Park,** and joy flights are offered. Nearby is the turnoff to *Jamberoo Recreation Park,* where you can play mini golf, go bobsledding, grass ski, or take the chairlift to the mountain top. There is also a maze, a licensed family restaurant, children's play area and a barbecue hut. For more information phone 360 114.

Kiama

Kiama is 36km (22 miles) south of Wollongong, and the *Kiama Visitors Centre* is at Blowhole Point. *The Blowhole* is the main attraction, but nowadays it only seems to 'blow' in nasty weather. In any case, it is floodlit until 9.30pm.

The best way to explore Kiama is on foot, strolling around the foreshore area. First, visit the burial site of one of the members of the First Fleet, and then walk around the showground that over-looks Storm Bay's jagged rocks, to the town's popular Surf Beach. *Some of the town's attractions are:*

The Terraces, a row of historic timber cottages, are now gift and specialty stores, and a good place to pick up a bargain. Most of the stores are open daily 10am-5pm.

The Family History Centre, Railway Parade, ph 331 122, has comprehensive microform and data inventory to help people to trace their family trees. The Centre is open daily 9.30am-4.30pm.

The Quarry Leisure Centre, Havilah Place, ph 321 877, has a 25m heated swimming pool, a wading pool, sauna, spa, aerobics, and facilities for indoor sports.

Minnamurra Falls

The Falls are 15km (9 miles) west of Kiama, in a dense subtropical rainforest, and plunge some 50m (164 ft) into a deep gorge. There is a delightful walk from the parking area through the rainforest to the Falls, and the round trip takes about an hour.

Barren Grounds Nature Reserve

The Reserve is 25km (16 miles) west of Kiama on the Jamberoo Mountain Road, and affords magnificent views from the lookout. There is a unique hanging swamp and bird observatory, and picnic and barbecue facilities.

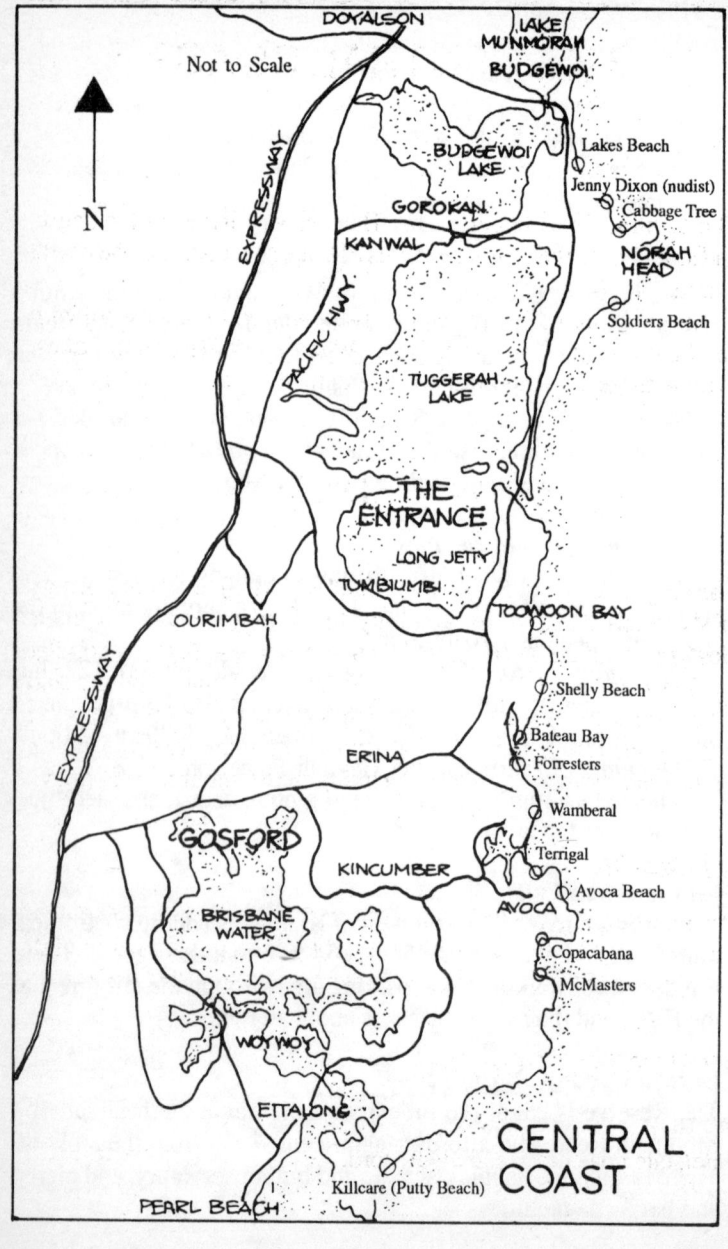

THE CENTRAL COAST

The Central Coast begins at the Hawkesbury River in the south, and stretches to the southern shores of Lake Macquarie in the north, and historic St Albans in the west.

The area is roughly divided into two — the City of Gosford with Brisbane Waters, and the Shire of Wyong with Tuggerah Lakes. Within these two districts there are many seaside and holiday centres.

GOSFORD CITY

The City of Gosford is 88km north of Sydney. The natural beauty of the district and close proximity to the major cities has made Gosford an attractive living and recreation area, with many popular surfing beaches and the Brisbane Waters for fishing, sailing and other recreational pursuits. Although for many years, it has been a holiday and retirement area, many young families are now settling in the district as an alternative to living in the suburbs of Sydney.

CLIMATE

Average temperatures: summer max 25C (77F) — min 18C (64F); winter max 17C (63F) — min 10F (50F). Average annual rainfall is 1300mm (51 ins), average ocean temperature is 20C (68F).

HOW TO GET THERE

By Bus
Interstate coachlines call at Gosford.

By Rail
There is a good electric train service from/to Sydney, and the State Rail Authority has mini-fares, family fares and combined rail/coach fares.

By Road
From Sydney via the Pacific Highway all the way to Gosford, or the F3 expressway from either Wahroonga (north of Sydney) or Normanhurst (west of Sydney) to the Gosford turn-off, then the Pacific Highway.

TOURIST INFORMATION

The Gosford Tourist Association has three offices:
    200 Mann Street, Gosford, ph (043) 252 835, open Mon-Fri 9am-5pm, Sat-Sun 9am-3pm.
    Rotary Park, Terrigal Drive, Terrigal, ph (043) 846 577, open Mon-Fri 9am-5pm, Sat-Sun 10am-4pm.
    Cnr West & Bullion Streets, Umina, ph (043) 432 200, open Mon-Fri 9am-3pm, Sat-Sun 11am-1pm.
    The Association has compiled some very good self-drive tours of the area, which encompass all the attractions. Visitors are well advised to pick up their brochures.

ACCOMMODATION

Accommodation is not a problem in the area, although it is wise to book in advance during the summer holiday period. Here is a selection with prices for a double room per night, which should be used as a guide only. The telephone area code is 043.

Gosford

Willows Motor Inn, 512 Pacific Highway (opposite Reptile Park), ph 284 666 — 50 units, licensed restaurant, swimming pool, spa, bbq - $82-84.

Gosford Motor Inn, 23 Pacific Highway, ph 231 333 — 36 units, bbq, swimming pool — $67-73.

Bermuda Motor Inn, cnr Henry Parry Drive & Pacific Highway, North Gosford, ph 244 366 — 17 units, pool, bbq — $60-70.

Rambler Motor Inn, 73 Pacific Highway, West Gosford, ph 246 577 — 55 units, unlicensed restaurant, swimming pool, spa, bbq — $53-76.

Woy Woy

Glades Country Club Motor Inn, 15 Dunban Road, ph 417 374 — 22 units, licensed bistro, swimming pool, bbq — $62-80.

Ettalong

Ettalong Beach Tourist Resort, 189 Ocean View Road, ph 411 999 — 32 units, licensed restaurant — $57-70.

Avoca

Avoca Beach Motor Inn, 360 Avoca Drive, ph 822 322 — 36 units, licensed restaurant, swimming pool, tennis court — $90-100.

Terrigal

Holiday Inn Crowne Plaza, The Esplanade, ph 849 111 — 177 units, licensed restaurants, swimming pool, spa, sauna, gym, tennis — $170-250.

Cobb & Co Motor Inn, 154 Terrigal Drive, ph 841 166 — 40 units, licensed restaurant, swimming pool, spa, sauna, gym, bbq — $105-210.

Clan Motor Lodge, 1 Ocean View Drive, ph 841 566 — 25 units, unlicensed restaurant, bbq — $75-95.

Wamberal

Apollo Country Resort, 871 The Entrance Road, ph 852 099 — 43 rooms (private facilities), licensed restaurant, swimming pool, spa, bbq, tennis — $85-120.

Kincumber

Kincumber Hotel/Motel, Avoca Drive, ph 692 166 — 4 units, bistro — BLtB $70.

EATING OUT

There are Pizza Huts at Gosford and Woy Woy, and Homestead Chicken are on the Pacific Highway, West Gosford, ph 241 053. Branches of McDonald's are found in all the major towns.

The following is a list of recommended restaurants rated:
Expensive (main course $15+),
Moderate (main course $10-$15),
Budget (main course under $10).

Gosford
The Admiral's Quarters and the *Terrace Restaurant*, both in the Central Coast Leagues Club, ph 233 131;
The Admiral's Quarters - Licensed - seafood smorgasbord (Fri) a la carte (Sat) - **Moderate** - open Fri-Sat 6.30-10.30pm.

Terrace Restaurant - Licensed - wide selection of food - **Moderate** - open Mon-Fri noon-2pm, nightly 6.30-11pm.

The Karrabee Floating Restaurant, Dane Drive Gosford, ph 242 733 - Licensed - open menu - **Moderate** - open daily noon-3.30pm, 6pm-midnight.

The Willows, 512 Pacific Highway, North Gosford, ph 284 666 - Seafood - **Expensive** - open Mon-Fri noon-2pm, nightly 6pm-midnight.

Woy Woy
The Everglades Country Club, Dunban Road, ph 411 383 - Licensed - Malaysian/Chinese - **Moderate** - open Thurs-Sun 6-11pm.

Terrigal
Holiday Inn Crowne Plaza Terrigal on Sea, has lounges and restaurants galore. *La Mer* gourmet restaurant, *Norfolk Brasserie* carvery, and *Florida Ocean Terrace* bistro, are open daily, are Licensed, and would have to fit into the **Expensive** category.

Jardines, 150 Terrigal Drive, ph 841 621 - Licensed - seafood - **Expensive** - open daily noon-2pm, 6pm-midnight.

Peppertree Restaurant, 1 Ocean View Drive (in the Clan Motor Lodge), ph 841 566 - Licensed - international cuisine - **Budget** - open Mon-Sat 6.30-11pm.

Sabu by the Sea, cnr Church and Campbell Crescent, ph 846 122 - Licensed - Sri Lankan and northern Indian - **Moderate** - open Thurs-Sun noon-2pm (budget lunch $9.90), nightly 6-10.30pm.

The Skillion Cafe Restaurant, Skillion Arcade, 52 The Esplanade, ph 843 091 - BYO (Corkage $2 per bottle) - varied menu - **Budget** - Thurs-Sun 11.30am-2.30pm, Wed-Mon 6-11pm.

Ettalong

The *Beef and Barramundi* Restaurant, Sea Sands Motel, 189 Ocean View Drive, ph 413 566 - Licensed - seafood/steaks - **Moderate** - open nightly 6pm-midnight.

Wamberal

Lantern Palace, 871 The Entrance Road, ph 845 646 - Licensed/BYO (Corkage $2 per person) - Chinese cuisine - **Moderate** - open daily noon-2.30pm, 5-10.30pm.

ENTERTAINMENT

The Holiday Inn Crowne Plaza Terrigal on Sea has the *Key Largo Night Club* open Thurs-Sat, with state of the art light and sound and sophisticated art deco surrounds.

Central Coast Leagues Club, Dane Drive, Gosford, ph 233 131, has live shows, and their Club Troppo is popular with the young folk.

Erina Leagues Club, Ilya Avenue, Erina, ph 652 233, has plenty for everyone.

There are cinemas at Gosford, 7 Watt Street, ph 241 489; Avoca, 69 Avoca Drive, ph 822 156; and Kincumber, Avoca Drive, ph 691 011

SHOPPING

Gosford has three shopping centres:

Stockland Gosford, Mann Street, ph 244 299;

Gateway Centre, 237 Mann Street, ph 251 333;

Marketown Place Gosford, cnr Henry Parry Drive and William Street, ph 247 311.

Stockland Gosford is the biggest of the three, but they have all felt the impact of the more modern *Central Coast Fair*, Erina, ph 651 266, which is bigger, and attracts a large clientele from all over the Central Coast. It has Grace Bros and a branch of all the regulars found in the Sydney shopping centres, e.g. Sussan, Katies, Lowes Menswear, Mathers Shoes, etc.

SPORT

Golf

The following clubs welcome visitors, but there are a lot of midweek competitions held in the Central Coast, so it is always a good idea to phone ahead and book a time.

Gosford Golf Club, Racecourse Road, Gosford, ph 250 361.
18 hole course - Par 71 - 5800m

 Green Fees: $13

 Club Hire: $7

 Buggy Hire: $2

Mon, Thurs and Fri are best for visitors, although you can often get a game after noon on Tues and Wed, and after 3pm on Sat and Sun.

Terrigal Memorial County Club, 64 Dover Road, Wamberal, ph 842 755. 9 hole course - Par 66 (18 holes) - 5022m (18 holes)

 Green Fees: $7 for 9, $10 for 18

 Club Hire: $8

 Buggy Hire: $2

Tuggerah Lakes Golf Club, Shelly Beach Road, Shelly Beach, ph 32 1103. 18 hole course - Par 72 - 6083m
   Green Fees: $15
   Club Hire: $15 including pull buggy
   Buggy Hire: motorised buggy $20 for 18 holes, $12 for 9
Visitors can usually get a game after 1.30 during the week, but it it is still best to phone ahead.

Tennis
There are many courts for hire in the district, and here are two associations that can either let you have one of their courts, or can put you on the right track for a court near your lodgings.

Gosford District Tennis Association, Vaughan Park Courts, Racecourse Road, Gosford, ph 252 921.

Empire Bay Sports & Recreation Association, 52 Kendall Road, Empire Bay, ph 694 623.

Lawn Bowls
There are bowling clubs galore dotted all over the Central Coast, and all welcome visitors. The Tourist Association will be able to advise you of the club closest to where you are staying.

Ten Pin Bowling
Central Coast Ten Pin Bowling Association, The Entrance Road, Forresters Beach, ph 845 615.

Gosford City Bowl, Brooks Avenue, Wyoming, ph 283 701.

Roller Skating
Frogys Roller Disco, 70 Mann Street, Gosford, ph 243 484.

For all other sporting facilities, contact the Tourist Association.

SPECTATOR SPORTS

Horse Racing
Gosford Race Club has twenty meetings a year at the course on

Racecourse Road, Gosford West. They are always held on a Thursday, and for current race dates, ph 25 0461.

Football
Rugby League, Rugby Union, Australian Football and *Soccer* are all played on weekends in Winter, and the Tourist Association will have details of venues and times.

SIGHTSEEING

The town site of Gosford was first referred to as the Township at Point Frederick, then in February 1839, when the plan was sent to Governor Gipps for approval, as the Township of Brisbane Water. The plan was returned by the Governor in April marked as the Plan of Gosford, with no explanation to indicate the reason for its name. It was later discovered that the Governor had served with the Earl of Gosford in Canada, and had taken the opportunity to honour his friend.

Originally, timber cutting was the main economic product of the district, then from the 1880s, citrus orchards began to dominate the local farms in the Narara, Lisarow, Wyoming, Holgate and Ourimbah areas. These farms were close to the railway, but later as roads developed, farming spread on to Somersby plateau. By 1928-29, the district supplied 34% of the state's citrus crop.

The 1880s also saw the Gosford area become a tourist venue, with the completion of the railway in 1887, and visitors came for the fishing, and for hunting trips.

In recent times Gosford's development has been influenced by other factors, such as the metropolitan expansion of Sydney, improvements to the roads, and changes in lifestyles.

The majority of people visit the area now for the surf, sun and sand, but there are quite a few attractions worth visiting.

Old Sydney Town, Pacific Highway, Somersby (west of Gosford) is the largest heritage park in New South Wales, and is a faithful re-creation of Sydney as it was 200 years ago. There is live street theatre, and demonstrations of different crafts take visitors back to the 18th and 19th centuries.

The park has many eateries, from fine restaurants to damper and billy tea places, or you can take your own food and make use of the barbecue facilities. Old Sydney Town is open Wed-Sun and all NSW school and public holidays, 10am-5pm, ph 401 104, and **admission is $13.90 adult, $7.50 child, $38 family (2 adults and 2 children).**

Henry Kendall Cottage & Historical Museum, 68 Wells Street, East Gosford, was built for the famous poet in 1836 by Peter Fagan. It is now an historical museum with displays of various items from the past. Open Wed, Sat & Sun, and public and school holidays, 10am-4pm, ph 252 270.

The Australian Reptile Park, Pacific Highway, North Gosford, was the first major tourist attraction on the Central Coast, and is a popular science exhibit. The park supplies venoms to countries all over the world for antivenenes and other research. There are picnic and barbecue facilities, and the park is open daily 9am-5pm, ph 284 311.

The Starship Cruise & Ferry Service has two venues for cruises. The *Lady Kendall* departs from Gosford Wharf, Wed, Sat & Sun to cruise on the Brisbane Waters, and the *Trinity Queen* leaves from The Entrance Wharf for cruising Tuggerah Lakes and Wyong River, Sun-Thurs 10.30am and 1.30pm. Both vessels operate daily during school holidays, ph 231 655.

The Fragrant Garden, Portsmouth Road, Erina, ph 677 546, has a very large collection of fragrant plants, crafts and pot-pourri in an olde-worlde garden. There is a mud-brick gallery, waterfall and a herb roof, and souvenirs are for sale.

The Ferneries, Oak Road, Matcham, ph 677 370, is set in 20ha (50 acres) of rainforest walks and picnic areas. There are kangaroos, emus and peacocks, and paddle boats and a playground for children. A large variety of ferns and palms are for sale, and there are picnic and barbecue facilities, open daily.

Central Park Family Fun Centre, The Entrance Road, Forresters Beach, ph 842 770, has something for everyone — ten-pin bowling, five giant waterslides, a mini golf centre, senior and junior Grand Prix cars, BMX track, maze, mini bikes, Sunday markets. Open daily 9am-5pm, Sat and holidays 9am-10pm.

FESTIVALS

Gosford's Australian Springtime Flora Festival is held in September.

OUTLYING ATTRACTIONS

BEACHES
The coastal beaches in the Gosford area are *Killcare, McMasters, Copacabana, Avoca, Terrigal, Wamberal and Forresters*. They each have their own attractions, and all are patrolled on weekends from October to April, with daily patrols during the school holiday periods.

Apart from *McMasters* and *Forresters*, they have dressing sheds, and a choice of takeaway food outlets close to the beachfront.

If you are a mad surfer, choose any of the above beaches, except *Terrigal*, which is protected by the headland, and is a great beach for families with small children.

The crystal clear waters right along the Central Coast offer some of the **best diving in Australia,** and there are fascinating wrecks off Terrigal in reasonably shallow water.

There are *numerous schools* that teach diving, and after 5 days tuition, which **costs around $300**, you are awarded a C card. The Tourist Information Centres have a list of schools, but if you are past that stage, fishing and diving charters can be arranged through
Central Coast Fishing & Dive Charters, The Scenic Road, McMasters Beach, ph 851 355, or
Terrigal Diving School in the Haven Seafood building on the beach at Terrigal, ph 841 219.
Erina Sail N Ski, 2/251 The Entrance Road, Erina, ph 65 2355, has sailboards, waveskis, waterskis and wetsuits for hire, and

sailboard lessons are available at Terrigal Lake. They are open seven days.

The Blue Bead Arabian Stud, is located at Razina Park in Picketts Valley Road, 5 minutes from Terrigal and Avoca Beaches. They offer riding on mountains trails for the experienced, and instruction for beginners and improvers. Bookings are essential, and the stud is open seven days, ph 822 346.

TUGGERAH LAKES

The administrative centre of the Tuggerah Lakes district is **Wyong**, 22km north of Gosford on the banks of the Wyong River. The Lake system extends from Killarney Vale in the south to the township of Lake Munmorah in the north, and consists of three lakes — Tuggerah, Budgewoi and Munmorah. The biggest lake is Tuggerah Lake, and it has the only opening from the ocean, appropriately enough, at The Entrance. There are no sharks in the lakes.

One of the most popular holiday places in New South Wales, Tuggerah Lakes has grown like Topsy. Once it was strictly a fisherman's paradise with basic fishing shacks. Now there are first class motels, hotels, restaurants and sporting facilities.

HOW TO GET THERE

By Rail
There is a regular electric rail service from Sydney to Wyong, and local buses from the station to the other areas.

By Road
From Sydney, via the Pacific Highway, or the F3 from Wahroonga or Normanhurst to the various destination turnoffs.

TOURIST INFORMATION

The Tuggerah Lakes Tourist Association has offices at: Marine Parade, The Entrance, ph 329 282, 331 966;

Wallarah Point Park, cnr Wallarah Road, Gorokan, ph 924 666.

ACCOMMODATION

As with any holiday centre, there is a great deal of accommodation to choose from in the Tuggerah Lakes district. Here is a selection with prices for a double room per night, which should be used as a guide only. The telephone area code is 043.

Wyong

Central Coast Motel, cnr Pacific Highway & Cutler Drive, ph 532 911 — 18 units, swimming pool — $50-65.

The Entrance

El Lago Resort, 41 The Entrance Road, ph 323 955 — 39 units, licensed restaurant, swimming pool, spa, sauna, tennis — $92-102.

Ocean Front, 102 Ocean Parade, ph 325 911 — 31 units, licensed restaurant, bbq — $75-130.

Sapphire Palms Motel, 180 The Entrance Road, ph 325 799 — 20 units, swimming pool, spa, bbq — $48-85.

Tienda Motel, 309A The Entrance Road, ph 323 933 — 30 units, swimming pool, spa — $55-75.

Lake Front Motel, cnr Coogee Avenue & Main Road, ph 324 518 — 13 units, swimming pool, bbq — $44-74.

Long Jetty

The Coachman Motor Inn, 33 Gordon Road, ph 323 692 — 7 units, unlicensed restaurant, swimming pool, bbq — BLtB $45-125.

Palm Gardens Resort, 44 Kitchener Road, ph 331 000 — 15 suites, swimming pool, spa, sauna, bbq — $60-150.

Buccaneer Motel, 398 The Entrance Road, ph 343 100 — 17 units, swimming pool, bbq — $45-100.

The Entrance Motel, 212 The Entrance Road, ph 322 226 — 14 units, swimming pool, bbq - $45-70.

Bateau Bay

Palm Court Motel, 61 Bateau Bay Road, ph 323 755 — 10 units, unlicensed restaurant, swimming pool — $50-95.

Bateau Bay Hotel/Motel, The Entrance Road, ph 328 022 — 6 units, licensed restaurant — BLtB $60.

Toowoon Bay

Kim's Toowoon Bay, Charlton Avenue, ph 321 566 - 34 bungalows, (most doubles but 4 for families), licensed restaurant, cocktail bar, spa in each bungalow (deluxe bungalows have private pool) - Full board $170-340.

Budgewoi

Hibiscus Motel, 2 Diamond Head Drive, ph 909 100 — 13 units, bbq — $55-70.

Noraville

Sea'N' Sun Motel, 115 Budgewoi Road, ph 964 474 — 13 units, spa, mini golf, bbq — $45-75.

Toukley

Toukley Motor Inn, 236 Main Road, ph 965 666 — 13 units, swimming pool — $45-70.

Twin Lakes Motor Inn, 57 Main Road, ph 964 622 — 11 units, swimming pool, bbq — $43-80.

EATING OUT

The district has several licensed RSL and bowling clubs, and these usually offer reasonably priced meals. There are also many takeaway and fast food outlets, both in the towns and on the beachfronts.

Here are some restaurants you might like to try rated:
Expensive (main course $15+),
Moderate (main course $10),
Budget (main course under $10).

Lobster Pot Inn, 261 The Entrance Road, The Entrance, ph 327 463 — Licensed - seafood and a la carte - **Expensive** - open daily noon-2pm, 6.30-11.30pm.

El Largo, 41 The Entrance Road, The Entrance (in the motel), ph 323 955 - Licensed - international cuisine - **Expensive** - open daily noon-2pm, 6-11pm.

Sounam Thai, 27 The Entrance Road, The Entrance, ph 328 806 - Licensed/BYO (Corkage $3 per bottle) - Thai cuisine - **Moderate** - open daily noon-11pm.

Aunty Mary's Steak & Ale, 27 Fairview Avenue, The Entrance, ph 326 868 — Licensed - seafood entrees, cook your own steak, children's menu — **Moderate** - open from 6pm Tues-Sun and public holidays and daily during school holidays.

Aquarius Argonauts, The Entrance Road, Long Jetty, ph 331 477 — Licensed/BYO (Corkage $1 per bottle) - Greek and French cuisine - **Moderate** - open nightly 5.30-11pm.

The Bay Cafe, 141-143 Bay Road, Toowoon Bay (next to the post office), ph 327 135 — BYO - seafood - **Expensive** - open Mon-Sat 6-11pm.

Hey Hey It's Satay and Steamboats, 2986 Main Road, Toukley, ph 971 664 - BYO (no corkage) - Malaysian/Chinese - **Moderate** - open Tues-Sun 6-10.30pm.

Foxy's Bistro, 207 Main Road, Toukley, ph 963 535 - Licensed - steakhouse - **Budget** - open nightly 6-10pm.

Lighthouse Restaurant, 9 Mitchell Street, Norah Head,
ph 964 4507 — Licensed - steak/seafood - **Expensive** - open
Wed-Sun 11.30am-2pm, 6-10.30pm.

ENTERTAINMENT

Tuggerah Lakes Memorial Club, 6 Gallipoli Street, Long Jetty, ph
323 399, appeals to all ages. It has a bistro (open daily), a dining
room (open Tues-Sat), and a nightclub, **Club Frenzy,** (open Fri,
8.30pm-2am, Sat 8.30pm-1am, no cover charge). The prices are
very reasonable.

The Entrance Hotel, The Entrance Road, The Entrance,
ph 322 001, has a bistro (open daily), and a great beer garden for
the whole family.

There are **cinemas** at The Entrance, and *Youtheatre at the Entrance*
is at 40 Stella Street, Long Jetty, ph 326 029.

SHOPPING

The people who live in this neck of the woods head off to Central
Coast Fair, Erina, for their shopping days, but there are small
centres in the area which provide the necessities of life, and have
K Marts, banks, and the usual small shops -
  Bay Village, Bateau Bay, ph 322 255
  Lakehaven, Lakehaven Drive, Kanwal, ph 927 800

SPORT

Golf
The following clubs welcome visitors, but it is still wise to book
ahead to make sure of a game.
Toukley Golf Club, Key Street, Toukley, ph 96 5811. 18 hole course
- Par 72 - 6171m
  Green Fees: $12
  Club Hire: $6
  Buggy Hire: $2

It is relatively easy to get a game on Mon and Thurs, and after 1.30pm on other days.

Wyong Golf Club, Pacific Highway, Wyong, ph 521 361. 18 hole course - Par 72 - 6063m
Green Fees: $12
Club Hire: $10
Buggy Hire: $2.50 for a pull buggy
$20 for a motorised buggy.

Tennis
The following associations can put you on the right track.
Wyong District Tennis Club Ltd, cnr Rose and Ithome Streets, Wyong, ph 532 311.

Toukley District Tennis Association, Ray Street, Toukley, ph 965 033

Lawn Bowls
The Tourist Association offices will be able to advise you of the club nearest to where you are staying. There is no doubt that you will be made welcome in whichever club it is.

Ten Pin Bowling
Astro Lanes, 470 The Entrance Road, Bateau Bay, ph 329 999.

Roller Skating
El Coasta, 389 The Entrance Road, Long Jetty, ph 323 370.

SPECTATOR SPORT

Horse Racing
The Wyong Race Club Ltd, ph 521 083, has meetings of turf, harness and greyhound racing. The greyhound races are held every Saturday afternoon, with the first race beginning at 1pm. The horse races are held on Thursdays (first race 12.30pm), but not every week, and the harness racing on Mondays (first race 12.30pm), but again not every week. You can contact the club on the above number, and they will be happy to tell you of forthcoming meetings.

Football

All four codes are played on weekends in Winter, and the Tourist Association will have information on the venues.

SIGHTSEEING

The Forest of Tranquility, Ourimbah Creek Road, Ourimbah, is the home of Willy Wombat's rainforest walk, the best walk in a rainforest in the Sydney environs. There are gas barbecues, a children's playground, and picnic area, and rainforest plants are for sale. Open Wed-Sun and all public holidays, ph 621 855.

Crackneck Lookout, in Hilltop Avenue, Bateau Bay, offers sweeping views of the coastline to Norah Head and Bungary Point, over the three lakes and the three power stations.

Bateau Bay Golf Range is the largest golf range on the Central Coast, and venue of Australian Golf Schools. Practice facilities include grass tees, target greens, bunker and distance markers. Open 7 days, ph 323 277.

Long Jetty Catamaran Hire, cnr Tuggerah Parade and Pacific Street, Long Jetty, ph 329 362, hires out catamarans, sailboards, canoes and pedal boats. They also have lessons in water skiing, and sell fishing tackle and bait.

The Aqua Slide, adjacent to the Lakeside Plaza carpark in Taylor Street, The Entrance, ph 343 563, has The Space Spiral, Outer Orbit and Cosmic Crusher rides, and the good news is, the pool is heated.

Each afternoon at 3.30pm, near the children's playground in the **Memorial Park,** The Entrance, everybody gathers to **feed the pelicans.** The attraction is sponsored by The Entrance Cinema and El Lago Resort, and the menu is supplied by Clifford's Fish Shop.

The pelican has been adopted as the symbol of the tourist industry on the Central Coast, and the daily feeding ensures that this symbol doesn't disappear. There is no doubt that they are fascinating creatures, with wing spans up to 2m, and those incredible beaks, but there are many locals who are not exactly enamoured of them.

To start with, they eat fish and are not well mannered enough to limit themselves to the afternoon meals supplied by humans, but tend to fish for themselves in the lakes. And, they are much better at it than those people sitting in boats and on the shore with hooks and lines. Then they have lice, which they shed in the water to bite anyone who dares to swim in the area. It is not that the pelicans do this on purpose, but try telling that to a kiddy who is suffering from itchy bites. Of course, the pelicans came before people starting feeding them, but not in such large numbers.

At Dunleith Caravan Park, North Entrance, ph 322 172, there is a Shell Museum, with an extensive display of shells and early photographs of the area, along with models of aquatic animals.

Norah Head Lighthouse, circa 1903, is open for visitors only by arrangement with the Visitor Centres. At Cabbage Tree Bay, the tiny settlement where the road to the light house commences, the are steps leading down to a lovely little rock pool, which is very popular with children. You can also drive down the steep road before the steps, but parking is usually a problem. There is a surfing beach alongside, but it is not patrolled, and there is a dangerous riptide.

Edward Hargraves Homestead, in Elizabeth Drive, Noraville, is not open for inspection, but can be viewed from the road. Edward Hargraves discovered gold near Bathurst in 1851, causing the first gold rush in Australia.

Toukley **has a good-sized shopping centre,** and the Toukley & District Senior Citizens Club in Hargraves Street, has loads of entertainment and things to do, ph 965 075. Toukley RSL is also a very busy club, and visitors are always welcome, as they are at Toukley Bowling Club.

Warnervale Airfield, near the expressway (follow the road through Toukley, crossing the Pacific Highway) offers joy-flights every Sunday, and other days by appointment, ph 925 174.

Smokey Mountain and Brizzley Flats Steam Railroad, in Mountain Road, Warnervale, ph 927 644, offers a different day out for all the family with steam train rides through the surrounding picturesque valleys. It operates on Sundays and public holidays from Boxing Day until the last Sunday in October, except Good Friday and days of total fire ban. For further information, ph 927 644, or contact one of the Visitors Centres.

BEACHES

The coastal beaches in the Tuggerah Lakes area are:
Bateau Bay; Shelly Beach; Toowoon Bay;
The Entrance; North Entrance; Soldiers Point;
Cabbage Tree Bay; Jenny Dixon; The Lakes Beach.

Jenny Dixon Beach and Cabbage Tree Bay are not patrolled, and Jenny Dixon has some nude bathers.

There is a great rock pool for kiddies at *Cabbage Tree Bay* with dressing sheds close by, and although the adjacent beach looks attractive, it has a very strong undertow, and is only recommended for strong swimmers.

Many board riders gather around the point between Soldiers and Cabbage Tree, and they often report that they have seen sharks.

The other beaches are patrolled every weekend and all through the school holidays, and have dressing sheds and handy food outlets.

From the Lakes Beach surf club, miles of sand and surf stretch northwards, but it should be remembered that the site of the surf club was chosen because it is the safest part of that beach for swimming.

Board riders are found all along the coast, and they argue amongst themselves as to which is the best stretch of surf.

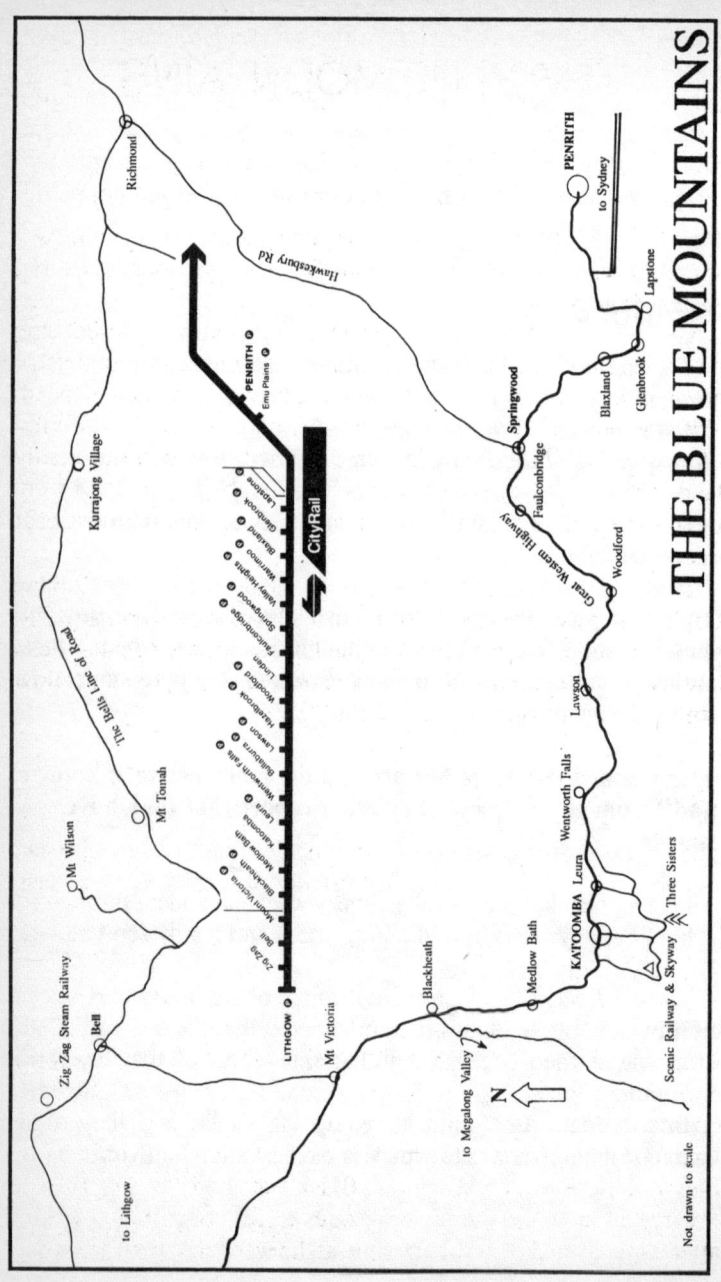

THE BLUE MOUNTAINS

THE BLUE MOUNTAINS

The City of the Blue Mountains, comprising 26 towns and villages, stretches from Penrith, 53km from Sydney, to Mount Victoria, 122km from Sydney.

The Blue Mountains derive their name from the ever-present blue haze caused by the sun's rays striking the minuscule droplets of eucalyptus oil which evaporate from the leaves of the dense forest.

It was not until twenty-five years after the arrival of the First Fleet that the Blue Mountains were crossed in search of grazing land. The intrepid explorers who performed the feat in 1813 were Blaxland, Wentworth and Lawson, and three mountain towns bear their names.

In the 1920s and 30s, the Blue Mountains was the Holiday Capital of New South Wales, then it declined in popularity, as people travelled further afield. In the last few years there has been a revival, and the Blue Mountains is once again a popular tourist centre. The population of the area is 70,800.

CLIMATE

The area has distinct seasons and is cooler than Sydney all year. Occasionally snow falls in winter, usually July, but it does not last.

HOW TO GET THERE

By Rail
Electric trains depart from Central Station in Sydney roughly every hour from 4.02am to 11.09pm every day with stops at Lapstone, Glenbrook, Blaxland, Warrimoo, Valley Heights, Springwood, Faulconbridge, Woodford, Hazelbrook, Lawson, Wentworth Falls, Leura, Katoomba, Medlow Bath, Blackheath and Mt Victoria.

CityRail have special off-peak fares to Katoomba — any train after 9am on weekdays, or any time at the weekend, with same day return, for $10.60. For further information ph (02) 13 15 00.

By Bus

AAT Kings, ph (008) 334 009, Newmans, ph (02) 567 5788, and Australian Pacific Tours, ph (02) 693 2222, have daily tours departing from Sydney Day Tour Terminal, Circular Quay West at 9am, returning 5.30pm.

Fantastic Aussie Tours, ph Sydney (02) 281 7100 or Katoomba (047) 821 866 have three hour tours which connect with trains from Sydney at Katoomba Railway Station. Tour times are 10.30am, 11.30am and 2pm.

They also have full day tours of Jenolan Caves departing from Katoomba Station at 10.30am, connecting with the 8.22am train from Sydney, and on weekends and public holidays they operate an Explorer Bus which picks up and drops off in Katoomba and Leura at the main attractions and restaurants. It meets most trains from Sydney, and connects with trains returning to Sydney.

By Road

From Sydney, via Parramatta Road to Concord then the F4 Freeway. The toll at Silverwater is $1.50. It can be avoided by going via Parramatta Road and then joining the F4 at Woodville Road, Parramatta. The F4 after the Nepean River rejoins the Great Western Highway for the climb up the mountains.

TOURIST INFORMATION

Blue Mountains Tourism Authority, Echo Point Road, Katoomba, ph (047) 820 756.
Glenbrook Visitor Information Centre, Great Western Highway, Glenbrook, ph (047) 396 266. Open Mon-Fri 8.30am-5pm, Sat-Sun 8.30am-4pm.

Supplementary information centres are:
Full of Surprises, 130 The Mall, Leura, ph (047) 841 768;
Cottage Ware, Main Street, Katoomba, ph (047) 824 009;
Blackheath Taxi Services, 342 Great Western Highway, Blackheath, ph (047) 878 366;
Mt Victoria Newsagency and General Store, Great Western Hwy, Mt Victoria, ph (047) 871 231.

ACCOMMODATION

Here is a selection of accommodation, with prices for a double room per night, which should be used as a guide only. Many of the hotels include Bed and Breakfast in their prices. Ask about this when contacting them. The telephone area code is 047.

Katoomba

Alpine Motor Inn, cnr Great Western Highway & Orient Street, ph 822 011 — 20 units, unlicensed restaurant, swimming pool, sauna -$80-125.

Lilianfels Blue Mountains, Lilianfels Avenue, ph 801 200 - 86 rooms, licensed restaurants, indoor swimming pool, sauna, spa, gym, tennis - $235-285.

Mountain Heritage Country House Retreat,(motel), cnr Lovel & Apex Streets, ph 822 155 - 40 units, licensed restaurant, swimming pool — $135-205.

Katoomba Town Centre Motel, 224 Katoomba Street, ph 821 266 — 13 units, spa — $80-100.

Echo Point Motor Inn, Echo Point Road, ph 822 088 — 36 units, licensed restaurant — $54-75.

3 Sisters Motel, 348 Katoomba Street, ph 822 911 — 20 units, unlicensed restaurant — $47-80.

The Cecil Guest House, 108 Katoomba Street, ph 821 411 — 25 rooms, unlicensed restaurant, bbq, spa — DBB $80-$120. They offer Murder in the Mountains weekends that are a lot of fun. Contact The Cecil direct for information and brochures (PO Box 97, Katoomba).

The above is certainly not exhaustive but should give you some idea of the standard in the area.

Leura

Fairmont Resort, 1 Sublime Point Road, ph 825 222 — 210 rooms, licensed restaurant, swimming pool, spa, sauna, gym, tennis, squash — $233-328.

Resort Hotel Leura, Fitzroy Street, ph 841 331 — 71 rooms, licensed restaurant, swimming pool, spa, sauna, gym, tennis, squash, — $140-155.

Leura House, 7 Britain Street, ph 842 035 - 14 units, unlicensed restaurant - $132.

Medlow Bath

Hydro-Majestic Hotel, Great Western Highway, ph 881 002 — 55 rooms, licensed restaurant, pool, tennis — $128. Unbelievable view from the restaurant.

The Blue Mountains Guest House, 40 Portland Road, ph 881 064 - 8 rooms, unlicensed restaurant, tennis — $65.

Mt Victoria

Mount Victoria Motor Inn, Station Street, ph 871 320 — 12 units — $70-100.

The Victoria & Albert Guest House, cnr Station Street & Harley Avenue, ph 871 241 — 30 rooms, unlicensed restaurant, swimming pool, spa, sauna, bbq — $80-160.

Jenolan Caves
(180km from Sydney)

Jenolan Caves Motel, ph (063) 593 304 — 28 units — $99-105.

Jenolan Caves House (Hotel Section) — 72 rooms (some with private facilities), unlicensed restaurant — $70-105.

Blackheath

Blackheath Motor Inn, 281 Great Western Highway, ph 878 788 — 18 units, spa — $74-120.

High Mountains Motor Inn, 193 Great Western Hwy, ph 878 216 — 21 units, unlicensed restaurant, swimming pool — $55-85.

HOW TO GET AROUND

Bus

Pearce Omnibus, ph 511 077, have services connecting Penrith and Faulconbridge; Springwood and Winmalee; Blaxland and Mt Riverview.

Katoomba Woodford Bus Company, ph 824 214, operate services between Katoomba, Leura and Wentworth Falls; Bullaburra and Lawson; Hazelbrook and Woodford; Katoomba Falls, Scenic Railway and Skyway. (No service on public holidays)

Katoomba Leura Bus Service, ph 823 333, links Leura, Katoomba, Echo Point, North Katoomba, Blackheath, Medlow Bath and Mt Victoria. (No service Saturday afternoon, Sunday or public holidays)

The Blue Mountains Explorer Bus operates every Sat-Sun and Public Holidays and meets the train at Katoomba Station on the hour from 9.30am to 4.45. It takes a tour to 17 places of interest returning to the rail station. The area it covers is within Leura and Katoomba. You can alight and then get the next bus from there. Cost $14 adults, $7 child, $35 family.

Car Hire

Cales Rentals, 136 Bathurst Road, Katoomba, ph 822 917;
Avis Blue Mountains, 1 Sublime Point Road, Leura, ph 823 466.

Taxi

Blackheath Taxi and Tourist Services, ph 828 366; *Springwood District Taxis,* ph 511 444; *Blue Mountain Taxi Cabs,* ph 591 387; *Katoomba Radio Cabs,* ph 821 311; *Hazelbrook Taxi Service,* ph 591 387.

EATING OUT

If you would like a superb meal in a HOTEL, try:
Grand View Hotel Dining Rooms, Great Western Highway, Wentworth Falls, ph 571 001 - Licensed - a la carte & bistro, known for the roasts and the beer and wines - **Moderate** - open Mon-Sun noon-3pm, 6-9.30pm - Amex, BC, MC, V.

The Resort Hotel Leura's Jasmine Restaurant, Fitzroy Street, Leura, ph 841 331 - Licensed/BYO, corkage $3 per person - a la carte - **Expensive** - open Tues-Sat 6.30-10pm - Amex, BC, DC, MC, V.

Fairmont Resort Jamieson Restaurant, 1 Sublime Point Road, Leura, ph 825 222 - Licensed - buffet, a la carte - **Expensive** - open noon-3.30pm, 6.30-10pm - bookings essential - Amex, BC, DC, MC, V. Also has another restaurant, *The Terrace,* that is Buffet only.

The Hydro Majestic Hotel, Great Western Highway, Medlow Bath, ph 881 002 - Licensed - a la carte & bistro - open noon-2.30pm, 6.30-8pm - **Moderate** - Amex, BC, MC, V.

The Imperial Hotel, Great Western Highway , Mt Victoria, ph 871 233 - Licensed - bistro - open Sun-Thurs 6-8pm, *Leadlight Restaurant* open Fri-Sat 6-9pm - **Expensive** - Amex, BC, MC, V.

GUEST HOUSES that serve great meals:

Katoomba
Felton Woods Manor, The Manor Restaurant, cnr. Lurline and Merriwa Streets, ph 822 055 - Licensed - international a la carte - open Mon-Sat 7-9.30pm - **Moderate** - Amex, BC, DC, MC, V.

The Clarendon Theatre Restaurant, cnr Waratah and Lurline Streets, ph 821 322 - Licensed - international - open Fri-Sat, seated 7.30pm - **Moderate** - $42 show and meal included - Amex, BC, DC, MC, V. They have class acts.

The Jamieson Restaurant, cnr Apex & Lovel Streets, ph 822 155 - Licensed - international a la carte - open Mon-Sun 6.30-11pm - **Expensive** - Amex, BC, DC, MC, V.

The Cecil Guest House, 108 Katoomba Street, ph 821 411 - BYO, no corkage fee - open Mon-Sun 8.15-9am, 6.30pm one sitting, book by 4.30pm - **Moderate** - Amex, BC, MC, V.

St Mounts Restaurant, 194 Great Western Highway, Blackheath, ph 878 195 - Licensed/BYO, corkage $8 per bottle - French Provincial - open Sat-Sun 12.30-3pm, Wed-Sun 6.30-10pm - **Expensive** - Amex, BC, MC, V.

Mt Victoria
The Manor House, Montgomery Street, ph 871 369 - international, blackboard menu - open Sat-Sun & Public Holidays, 7-10pm - **Moderate** - Amex, BC, DC, MC, V.

The Heritage Restaurant, 19 Station Street, ph 871 241 - Licensed/BYO, no corkage - French/Australian Provincial - open Mon-Sun 6.30-10pm - **Expensive** - Amex, BC, DC, MC, V.

For a touch of nostalgia make sure you visit the National Trust classified *Paragon Cafe* at 65 Katoomba Street, Katoomba, ph 822 928. It is fully licensed and is the home of the famous Paragon Chocolates.

ENTERTAINMENT

The entertainment revolves around 'events' that are staged in the towns throughout the mountains - Art and Craft shows, Pottery and Garden Shows, Music Festivals, etc. Check with the Tourism Authority at either Glenbrook or Echo Point, Katoomba, for details of these, and for theatre and cinema performances in Leura and Katoomba.

Katoomba RSL, cnr Lurline & Merriwa Streets, ph 82 2624, has live entertainment on the weekends.

SHOPPING

The mountains abounds in plant nurseries, orchards (especially along the Bell Line of Road), small art galleries, craft and antique shops.

SPORT

Many people go to the mountains to bush walk (see Sightseeing), but there are facilities for other sports, including lawn bowls, golf, horse riding, tennis, squash and swimming. Check details at the Tourist Centre.

SIGHTSEEING

Lower Blue Mountains

Lapstone-Blaxland
Lapstone *Zig-Zag Walking Track* begins behind the RAAF base at Glenbrook, and follows the original railway cuttings with views of the arches of Knapsack Viaduct.

Glenbrook Native Plant Reserve, Great Western Highway, is open Wed, Sat, Sun noon-4pm, has Blue Mountains flora, an information centre, and sells books, plants and seeds.

Blue Mountains National Park, Glenbrook Area, has bushwalking, picnicking, camping. Information and advice plus publications are available from the Visitors Information Centre, Bruce Road, Glenbrook, ph 392 950.

Lennox Bridge, Mitchell's Pass Road, Glenbrook, was built in 1833 and is the oldest bridge on Australia's mainland. The bridge is well sign-posted from the Great Western Highway.

Wascoe Siding, Grahame Street, Blaxland, has a miniature railway and picnic area, and is open on the first Sunday of each month, except January.

Springwood
Two extremely *good bush walks* originate in Springwood:
The first an easy 90 minute walk to Birdwood Gully starts from Bednall Road.
The second to Sassafras Gully, is rated medium, and access is either from Holmdale Street, Sassafras Gully Road or Bee Farm Road.

The Local History Centre and a Community Art Gallery are in Braemar, an early Federation home which is classified by the National Trust, as are the Frazer Memorial Presbyterian Church and Springwood Railway Station.

In the cemetery is the grave of Sir Henry Parkes, regarded by many as the Father of Federation.

Faulconbridge
Norman Lindsay Gallery and Museum, Chapman Parade, ph 511 067, is the home of this famous Australian artist and writer. There are displays of his paintings, etchings, ship models and family mementoes, and a special Magic Pudding room. The house is set in delightful gardens with dozens of statues, some of which are also "delightful". There is a shop and a good coffee shop. Open Fri-Sun and public holidays 11am-5pm.

Central Blue Mountains

Bull's Camp, Great Western Highway, Linden, was used as a camp for convicts working on the road across the Blue Mountains. It is now a good picnic spot.

Collier Galleries "Selwood", 41 Railway Parade, Hazelbrook, ph 586 759, is a mid-Victorian house which has been classified by the National Trust. It is open Thurs-Mon 9am-5pm, and has a fine collection of paintings and pottery.

There are *two interesting bushwalks* **emanating from Lawson:**
one begins at South Lawson Park, Honour Avenue, and goes to
Adelina, Junction, Federal and Cataract Falls — 90 minutes, easy;

the other starts in North Lawson Park, Bernards Drive, and walks
along Dantes Glen and Lucy's Glen to Frederica Falls — 180
minutes, easy.

Wentworth Falls
Yester Grange, Yester Road, ph 571 110, is a 19th century house
with a collection of 19th century water colours, Victoriana and
ceramics. The house is set in bush and parkland and Devonshire
teas and light lunches are available. Open Wed-Fri 10am-4pm,
Sat-Sun and public holidays 10am-5pm.

Wentworth Falls Lake, Sinclair Crescent, is a pleasant picnic spot
with a playground and tame ducks. Row boats are available for hire.

There are *several walks* **with good views in this area -**
   * From Falls Road to Fletcher's Lookout, Undercliff Walk, to
Den Fenella — easy walk with views and wildflowers, 90 minutes.
   * To Princes Rock with views of Wentworth Falls and Jamison
Valley, 20 minutes.
   * To the top of the Falls, 30 minutes.
   * To Undercliff Walk, Den Fenella, Overcliff Walk to Valley of
the Waters with panoramic views, 150 minutes.

Upper Blue Mountains

Leura
Sublime Point, at the end of Sublime Point Road, has great views
of the Three Sisters and the Jamison Valley.

The Everglades Gardens, cnr Fitzroy Street & Denison Road, is
classified by the National Trust as one of the Great Gardens of
Australia. There are unique sandstone terraces, magnificent mature
trees and native flora, and a grotto pool, open daily from 9am.

Leuralla, an historic art deco mansion, has a collection of 19th century Australian art, and a Memorial Museum to Dr H.V. Evatt, first President of the United Nations Organisation. There is also a toy and railway museum.

Gordons Falls Reserve is a pleasant picnic area with playground and toilets, and from it there is a walk to Pool of Siloam and Lyrebird Dell.

Leura Cascades on Cliff Drive is another picnic area, and there are number of bushwalks that start from this point, with the Round Walk taking about 40 minutes.

Katoomba
The best way to see the attractions of Katoomba is to follow Cliff Drive. From the Railway Station, take Lurline and Merriwa Streets to the Drive around the Jamison and Megalong Valleys. Along the drive there are many lookouts, all signposted, the most famous of which is undoubtedly **Echo Point**, from where there are the best views of **The Three Sisters, Mennhi, Wimlah** and **Gunnedoo**. These rock formations are very important in Aboriginal legend, and are floodlit at night. From the point you can also see the **Ruined Castle** and **Mount Solitary**, and it is possible to pick out many animal shapes on the mountains on the other side of the valley.

From *Echo Point the Giant Stairway* of almost 1000 steps leads to the floor of the Jamison Valley and the Federal Pass; and the Prince Henry Cliff Walk leads left towards Leura or right towards the Scenic Railway Complex. The Point has picnic facilities, a restaurant and a takeaway food outlet.

Katoomba Falls Reserve is another picnic spot because the cascades, and several walking tracks begin behind the kiosk.

The Scenic Railway and Skyway on Cliff Drive, ph 822 699, offer a ride down to the Jamison Valley, which is not for the faint-hearted, or a ride over the valley in the Skyway. The complex also has the cafeteria-style Revolving Restaurant, a fun parlour and a souvenir shop, and is open daily 9am-5pm.

Cahill's Lookout is also on Cliff Drive and is another picnic spot, this time with view of escarpment and valley, and of Boar's Head Rock. The Drive ends at the Great Western Highway, at Katoomba Holiday Caravan Park.

Explorers' Tree, on the highway 2km west of Katoomba, commemorates the crossing of the Blue Mountains by Blaxland, Wentworth and Lawson. From behind the tree a Katoomba to Jenolan Caves walk begins, which takes 2-3 days. More information is available from the tourist information centres.

Blackheath

Evans Lookout, Evans Lookout Road, offers superb views of the Grose Valley.

Govett's Leap, Govett's Leap Road, also has views of Grose Valley and of Bridal Veil Falls, the longest single drop fall in the Blue Mountains. National Parks & Wildlife Service Heritage Centre, Govett's Leap Road, ph 878 877 has an exhibition on natural features of the Blue Mountains, and nearby Fairfax Heritage Track is suitable for disabled people.

Blue Mounts Rhododendron Garden, Bacchante Street, is set in native bushland. It is open 9am-5pm and admission is by a donation. There are easy walking tracks and picnic facilities.

From Anvil Rock and Wind-eroded Cave, Hat Hill Road, Blackheath, you can get good views of the Grose Valley.

Mount Victoria

A visit to the village of Mt Victoria is like taking a step back in time, with buildings of sandstone and iron lace, and others of colonial weatherboard, housing antiques, crafts and tearooms. Attractions include the Post Office, Toll House and Railway Station, the Scenic Drive and Mount York where explorers Blaxland, Lawson and Wentworth realised they'd crossed 'The Impenetrable Barrier'. Victoria Falls, Mount Piddington and Pulpit Rock Reserve are also worth a visit.

The Mounts Area

Rich volcanic soils and high rainfall produce the lush vegetation for which the Mounts are renowned. A beautiful area with famous gardens, lookouts and walks.

Cathedral of Ferns, Mount Wilson, off the Bell Road is a beautiful rainforest with nearby picnic area. Mount Wilson is really quite something. A delightful village with large homes of the once famous and wealthy graced with huge lawns and protected by large trees. It is a beautiful place in which to have a weekend break.

Mount Tomah Botanic Garden, ph 672 154, was a Bicentennial project of the Royal Botanic Gardens, Sydney. It features cool-climate planting with sections representing specific geographic areas of the world. There are panoramic views, a visitor centre, picnic areas and a restaurant. The garden is open daily (except Christmas Day and Good Friday) 10am-4pm (Mar-Sept) 10am-5pm (Oct-Feb). Admission is $5 per car or motorbike, $2 per cyclist or pedestrian.

FESTIVALS

Lawson Festival — March;
Wentworth Falls Autumn Festival — April;
Yulefest — June/July;
Springtime in the Blue Mountains — September thru November;
Leura Gardens Festival — October;
Leura Village Fair — October;
Blackheath Rhododendron Festival — November;
Glenbrook Festival — November.

For dates and attractions for these festivals it is best to contact the Blue Mountains Tourism Authority, PO Box 8, Glenbrook, 2773, ph (047) 39 6266.

OUTLYING ATTRACTIONS

Hartley
Hartley Historic Site, Hartley, ph (063) 552 117, is open Thurs-Tues 10am-1pm, 2-5pm, and includes the old Courthouse, churches and inns, and an information centre. Hartley is about 35km west of Katoomba.

Hartley's Lyndoch Orchards, Great Western Highway, Little Hartley, were the first family orchards in the historic Hartley Valley. The orchards are open daily 9am-6pm, and jams, apple juice and cider are for sale.

Zig-Zag Railway
Situated about 7km east of Lithgow, the Railway is an engineering feat. It is a system of tunnels, cuttings and stone viaducts built 1866-69 to overcome the steep descent from the Blue Mountains to the Western Plains beyond. Open Sat 11am-4pm, Sun, public and school holidays 10am-4pm, ph (063) 514 826. There are picnic areas, and rides are available on an old world steam train.

Jenolan Caves
Probably the best-known limestone caves in NSW, the caves were discovered in the 1830s when the victim of a bushranger tracked his attacker to his hideout in the caves. The entrance to the caves is in a narrow gorge reached through the Grand Arch, about 24m high. The view from Carlotta Arch which overlooks the Blue Lake, is superb. Many of the caves are open for inspection, and guided tours are available.

Caves House, right at the caves complex, is a charming hotel, with a restaurant, bar and accommodation. There are several bush walks in the area, and daily tours are run from Sydney and Katoomba.

Penrith
Situated on the Nepean River, less than an hour's drive from Sydney, Penrith is one of the most rapidly growing regions in Australia.

The biggest tourist attraction is *Panthers,* the world's largest licensed club, set in 81ha (200 acres), where bona fide visitors are most welcome. The club has two cable water ski lakes, a miniature car racing track, swimming pool with water slides, tennis complex and a lake with canoes, windsurfers and paddle boats. It also has a motel, six restaurants, the biggest variety of poker machines in the state, cocktail bars and a Cabaret Room.

Other major attractions Penrith offers are the *Nepean Belle Paddle Wheel Showboat, the Museum of Fire, Warragamba Dam and African Lion Safari.*

For information on these, contact the *Tourist Information Centre* at 250 High Street, ph 327 671, and get a copy of their magazine "The Nepean Experience".

They will also be able to tell you what is on at the Q Theatre and the Joan Sutherland Performing Arts Centre.

LIST OF MAPS

INDEX